GESTALT THERAPY
THE SECOND GENERATION

◆

A Living Legacy
to Fritz and Laura Perls

Second Edition Revised

Edited by
Bud Feder
and
Ruth Ronall

**Contemporary
Case Studies**

To order additional copies of this book, contact:

THE GESTALT INSTITUTE PRESS
433 METAIRIE ROAD
SUITE 113
METAIRIE / NEW ORLEANS, LOUISIANA 70005 USA

Phones: 1.800.786.1065 or 504.828.2267

Website: www.gestaltinstitutepress.com / www.teachworth.com

Email: ateachw@aol.com

ACKNOWLEDGEMENTS AND DEDICATION

I gratefully acknowledge the cooperation, assistance and patience of our contributing therapists. They were not only willing to expose their intimate work to the public view, but also were very supportive throughout this task, which proved to be much more difficult and time-consuming than anticipated. I want to express my particular appreciation to each client whose commitment to growth provided the inspiration through their individual case study.

Finally I dedicate the re-issuing of the second edition of this book to my longtime friend and colleague Ruth Ronall who died in 2007. We spent many a year together co-leading workshops and writing, including co-editing the first edition of this volume.

I hope that the innovative approaches used by the gestalt therapists in these case studies will be of value to you and your practice.

Bud Feder
Aug 1, 2011

CONTENTS

Part I: Individual Therapy

Chapter 1: For Emily: Whenever I May Find Her   5
Jon Frew

We begin the book with this case history because it is an exemplary presentation of Gestalt Therapy in action. Frew's main focus is on confluence and contact. Note the patience and sensitivity and respect with which he treats Emily (Editors).

Chapter 2: Bill: Finding Roots in the Hidden Ground of Loss   23
John Mitchell

A classic usage of Gestalt Therapy principles and therapist-client encounters. Mitchell provides numerous examples of interruptions of contact and his ways of handling them therapeutically (Editors).

Chapter 3: The Broken Doll: A Survivor's Journey Into Life   45
Ruth Wolfert

A description of a long-term multi-layered therapy with a client whose awareness deepens dramatically as the therapy progresses (Editors).

Chapter 4: The Integration of Self Psychology/Intersubjectivity Theory into the Practice of Gestalt Therapy   85
Stephen G. Zahm, Ph.D. and Elaine K. Breshgold, Ph.D.

Following a presentation by Zahm of his long-term therapy with an initially "frozen" client, he and Breshgold provide a theoretical incorporation of self psychology/intersubjectivity principles into his Gestalt approach (Editors).

This is an original contribution to Gestalt Therapy theory and practice and might alert therapists to the possibility that a client's diet may affect her or his mood or behavior. Although brief, the report is rich in ideas as well as lively descriptions of the author's work and person (Editors).

Ronall presents the beginning phase of therapy with a woman in her sixties who had recently lost her husband and who was stuck in obsessive efforts to fill the void. A paradoxical intervention leads to a dramatic shift in her behavior, appearance and thinking. The narrative is accompanied by explanations in Gestalt terms of the author's thinking (Editors).

This unique contribution provides us with an insight into the mind of a Gestalt Therapist who is also an unashamed medical practitioner. McFarlane describes two difficult cases requiring her to combine psychological and medical acumen. She ends with a challenge to all of us: biologically- and psychologically-oriented alike (Editors).

Part II: Work with couples, children and their families, groups, and organizations

Carroll tells us about a case of a child she treated according to the Oaklander Model using clay and projective materials. She describes individual sessions in which she employs play, as well as sessions with the child, mother, stepfather and distant natural father, enabling all these members of the family to better understand and accept each other (Editors).

Ruth Lampert

Lampert's chapter will be of special interest to family therapists who routinely see the family as a whole. By contrast she begins her therapy with the grandmother and gradually and with great sensitivity includes all the relevant members of the family, ending up with a multigenerational group. In addition she weaves into the narrative Gestalt Therapy principles as well as her personal reactions (Editors).

Anne Teachworth

You will find Teachworth's chapter rewarding reading since she presents with clarity and detail a novel approach to couples therapy, using the concept of parental introjection as the basis for her understanding and treatment of the couple's conflict. She describes how through experiments she helps each client become more aware of her/his parental introjects, thereby allowing them to gradually make undistorted contact with each other and her (Editors).

Bud Feder

In this study Feder describes a situation in which he and his co-therapist, a very good friend, undertook to help a couple resolve their severe conflict. They encourage the expression of feelings with the therapist couple participating, thereby modeling openness and enhancing contact. To everyone's sorrow, the case ended with the couple separating. An interesting question is posed by Feder — should he consider this case a success or failure (Editors)?

Jay Earley

Earley focuses on the therapeutic experience of an individual in a Gestalt Therapy interactive group. Along the way he provides the reader with his rationale for this method — which is a departure from customary Gestalt Group Therapy — as well as describing experiments which support this mode (Editors).

After giving us a brief history of marathon groups, Aylward tells us the complete story of a marathon in which he was a coleader. In addition to describing colorfully development of the group-as-a-whole and work with individuals, he explicates the rationale for the leaders' actions as well as providing guidelines for prospective marathon group therapists (Editors).

We are pleased to present Klepner's timely chapter on group therapy with men who are under the cloud of threats of HIV/AIDS. Into his description of the group process and individuals' development are numerous examples of his use of Gestalt principles. Throughout the chapter the reader is struck by Klepner's courage and creativity in facing and addressing catastrophic situations and desperate people — never giving up (Editors).

Houston's contribution challenges the reader to accompany her on her travels as consultant to two Gestalt training communities. We watch her "speak and think gestalt Therapy" with the members of the communities and she shares her ideas about the different outcomes of her consultation — outcomes which are dependent on the degree of openness to her approach. Her description of the different fates of these organizations is written in an elegant and erudite style — a pleasure (Editors).

FOREWORD

Malcolm Parlett

❖❖❖

Case studies have always had a central place in the literature of psycho-analysis, but not in Gestalt therapy. Of course, we have traditions that the analysis do not have — for instance, live demonstrations, and discussions of the techniques and assumptions that these reveal. The workshop format, so embedded in Gestalt life, encourages openness in showing each other how we work and the possibility of learning about the art or craft of Gestalt therapy from the example of the other practitioners. Occasionally, demonstrations have been videotaped or transcribed, thereby acquiring some durable status. There have also been one or two attempts to describe a particular case at a conference, with panelists who then discuss it. But ideas of shifting the focus away from the immediate to the reported, from single instances to patterns over time — as required in case study writing — have never found favor. So there are remarkably a few instances where Gestalt therapy as it is frequently practiced — i.e. over months or years — has been thoroughly documented.

Some Gestalt therapy training courses, but undoubtedly not all, require the writing of a clinical case study as a requirement to graduate from the course. This has been a welcome development, and my own experience of helping students write these, and my examining of others' efforts, has convinced me that it is a valuable undertaking — very difficult to do well but worthwhile, as a source of immense learning.

Overall, however, Gestalt therapists rarely put pen to paper (or fingers to a keyboard) to write about those with whom they work, whether they work with individual patients/clients, or couples, or families, or groups. As an editor of a journal, I know the infrequency of case studies being submitted for publication. The British Gestalt Journal has received only four in the course of its life (of which at the time of writing only one has been published) compared to dozens of articles on the theory and general practice of Gestalt therapy. Among those who espouse our Gestalt approach — which extols the uniqueness of each person's life and which is suspicious of generalization — writers opt for the general rather than for the specific, or they write about incidents of therapy, not about the overall impact on a person's development.

Thinking about it more, the scarcity of case histories in our field is both extraordinary and disquieting. Here we are, a professional specialist group, who do not appear to document what we do, except in a general and theoretical sort of way, shorn of the particulars. In failing to produce "public" accounts of what happens in a course of therapy, we are cutting ourselves off from critical examination by others in our field (a factor which I am sure has a lot to do with people's reluctance to write case studies). But we are also denying our students and trainees a significant source of material from which they can learn about Gestalt therapy — for instance, how the therapeutic relationship is worked through; what applications and directions of the therapy (if any, and there usually are some) are envisioned by the therapist at different stages; and not least about the practical questions that arise for all therapist (e.g. about timings, missed appointments, vacations, etc.) and which rarely get attention as topics for general papers.

From another point of view, of course, the few number of cases studies in the Gestalt literature is not surprising. After all, Gestalt therapy, soon after its inception, entered a phase in its life when "talking about," let alone "writing about," was renounced. Under the hot sun of the Sixties, with Fritz Perls in his Esalen phase, the kind of reflection that goes with writing case studies dried up; indeed serious writing of any kind about Gestalt therapy subsided to a trickle. What was on offer were transcripts of short encounters lasting minutes. Only in recent years has the climate definitely changed. The rains have arrived and, with the new fertility, much is now being written.

Given the new growth in the literature of Gestalt therapy, it has been only a matter of time before someone recognized the need for a book of case studies. As a professional community, let us be grateful to Bud Feder and Ruth Ronall for planting the seeds of the project, for nurturing the creative process through difficult times, and now for harvesting this first crop.

Before lyrically subsiding into collective self-congratulation or lapsing into retrospective recriminations over the years of drought, we also need to acknowledge the difficulties of writing about cases, given the nature of Gestalt therapy, and how it is different from other approaches such as psychoanalysis.

The fact that the analytic tradition relies heavily upon writing about cases has something to do with the models of reality and kinds of knowing which are valued by analysts. Freud was a would-be scientist, one cast in the Newtonian paradigm. Thus, he was interested in explanation, in reducing complex human phenomena to a set of laws and principles that was universally valid. Freud's was a world where the medical profession-inspired analyst regarded people as separate bundles of personal characteristics, symptoms, and historical residues, like the "properties" that describe material objects. Despite interest in human experience, Freud was no phenomenologist. His interest in phenomena was getting underneath them, relating them to a sub-stratum of theory. The analyst formulates a theory of the patient. The formulation is an intrinsic part of the treatment. Skill in theory-applying, in interpreting, is the critical therapeutic skill, and a well written case history, applying the theory, is probably the royal route to receiving the praise of fellow analysts.

Contrast this with Gestalt therapists. Ours is essentially a postmodern world view (and has been since long before postmodernism was labelled). We acknowledge relativity, chaos, complexity, and the thousands of strands of connection which exist between people in complex fields of constantly evolving interaction, where the fact of the observer's status in the picture cannot be overlooked. We recognise the dangers of objectification, of diagnoses which effectively "fix" a realty into a defined shape that persists, and the impossibility of leaving out the role, thoughts, feelings, and personal life and predilections of the therapist herself or himself. We know the effects of field shifts — for instance, how the "same" intervention made with two different persons, or even with the same person at different times, inevitably has disparate results and often a different meaning altogether. Above all, we know that a good many of the actual feelings and experiences of therapy cannot be put in words at all; and when they are articulated that the words are as much a function of the describer as the described. We know that we need sometimes not so much a technical language but almost the talent of poetry to capture what is happening in any convincing way. In addition, in the world of Gestalt therapy, unlike psychoanalysis, it is not clear that writing case studies is a way of demonstrating professional prowess to one's peers.

So we have no great tradition of how to write in detailed ways about the actual work we do, and this partly relates to our history, partly to our models of reality, and partly to the fact that writing case studies is extremely taxing. We might as writer-practitioners include a vignette — there are plenty of those in the literature — but the organization of a whole set of vignettes into a coherent overall pattern, is something rarely accomplished. It can seem forbiddingly difficult to capture the essence of what has happened, or the flavor of the significant exchanges, or the coming together of many different currents in a person's life that suddenly enable a new kind of choice to be made. We need skill in writing. We need sensitivity in how to convert the flow of dialogue and the mysteries of unfolding relationship into a linear description. We need to be able to give the reader a sense of the "laminated field," the realties and sub-realities, the various frames of therapeutic discourse, the contextual complexities of the ground which support and make meaningful the figure of our interventions and therapeutic choices. Ideally, too, we require an ability to capture the magic of moments, the atmospheric as well as the down to earth features of our work, if the true nature of it is to come to life to a reader.

Challenging though it is to do, case study writers almost are obliged like the writer of fiction — to find the genre, the style, the voice in which to write. There needs to be some match between the "case" (which in Gestalt therapy has to include the whole therapy and the therapist in its scope) and the way in which it is written. If one adds in the reader of the case study, whom the writer needs to contact via the writing, the field of case study writing becomes complex indeed.

There is an invitation for the skilled writer of the case study to combine technical excellence with a substantial measure of pure artistry. As with Gestalt practice in general, lucidity and groundedness need to be balanced by the imaginal and experimental, left brain with the right brain. The fundamentally aesthetic basis of the approach is revealed — or should be — as central. Gestalt practitioners learn and apply process skills; they deal in nonstandard ways with diverse fields; they are continuously recreating their ways of practice for situations never encountered before. Their versatility and ability to make adjustments moment by moment and week by week are not desirable extras. They constitute the very stuff of what they do. Like chefs, standup comedians, sailors of yachts, or potters — they attend to momentary shifts; they are necessarily involved in attentive monitoring and creative adjustment. The Gestalt therapist is innovatively and perpetually engaged in the search for formedness — even if sometimes the only form that seems possible in a chaotic period is to end on time or agree to meet again.

The case study is perhaps not a natural medium for an approach where so little can be pre-assumed, where so much has to be invented on the spot, and where so many happenings depend on knowing the context of all that has gone before. Time will tell what kinds of account can be written, what it is possible to capture and convey, as the writing of case studies becomes more common.

Among the present collection are some very good attempts. I shall not say which ones I think are best. What is important is that there is an interesting variety, a selection of approaches to the task, and that this history-making collection has begun a process. Different accounts will appeal to different readers. Some you will enjoy in particular, others may leave you with questions. The experience of reading them will stimulate your own thinking about your practice — your beliefs, preferences, style of working. Each of us has a stance — where we stand in terms of Gestalt Therapy theory and practice — often which can be traced to what we imbibed (or have consciously discarded) from our teachers. Each of us is a specialist in certain kinds of interchange and each of us has a particular points of emphasis. Awareness of what these are will be restimulated by reading the present book.

Each of the writers, contributing to the whole of the collection, is also contributing to establishing a new tradition. What I want to acknowledge most is that the contributors, as well as the Editors, deserve our thanks for taking the risk of writing what they do — and for making it easier for others to follow, perhaps to emulate, perhaps to try and do better. Their efforts are those of pioneers, and I salute them.

Bristol, England
July 1996

◊

INTRODUCTION

"There are as many Gestalt therapies as there are Gestalt therapists ..."
—*Laura Perls*

*"These are the two legs upon which Gestalt therapy walks:
how and now ..."*
—*Fritz Perls*

◆◀◆

Case studies have been important contributions to the development of
most schools of psychotherapy. Gestalt Therapy is one of the exceptions. In
its literature we find very few case histories, and most of these of individual
therapy. This paucity of material prompted us to undertake this collection
of original descriptions of the work of Gestalt therapists from the U.S.,
England and Canada. Because we believe that. Gestalt Therapy values and
supports the development of personal style in a therapist's life, we invited
contributions from therapists who, we knew, were working in different
ways and we took great care, when editing, not to blur these differences.
We believe we have selected case studies which are valuable for teaching
and learning. We trust you will find our collection interesting, useful and
in some cases, provocative. At times we ourselves have not agreed with an
author's approach, yet we felt it was important to include that chapter since
we want to provide the reader with a broad spectrum of developments in
Gestalt Therapy. Also, we made sure to include examples of therapeutic
modalities other than individual therapy.

Part I consists of studies of Gestalt Therapy with individual adults.
The reader will notice how the therapists differ in approach and focus, yet

remain within the framework of Gestalt Therapy. Take, for instance, the different ways in which different therapists treat confluence in women.

Part II contains examples of work with couples, children and their families, and groups, as well as a case of organizational consultation. Again note the differences in style, for example in the two cases of couple therapy: in one study, a single therapist focusing on introjects; in the other, co-therapists using and exploring the feelings, experiences and present relationships of all four persons in the room.

It took us three years to collect and edit the chapters in this book. We consider it time well-spent and as the reader may have guessed by now, we greatly enjoyed the work and hope you will enjoy the results. We are aware, however, that we have by no means exhausted the field and we see this collection as inspiration for others to publish case studies.

—Bud Feder

—Ruth Ronall

August, 1996

◊

GESTALT THERAPY
THE SECOND GENERATION

◆◄┃►◆

A Living Legacy
to Fritz and Laura Perls

Second Edition Revised

Edited by
Bud Feder
and
Ruth Ronall

**Contemporary
Case Studies**

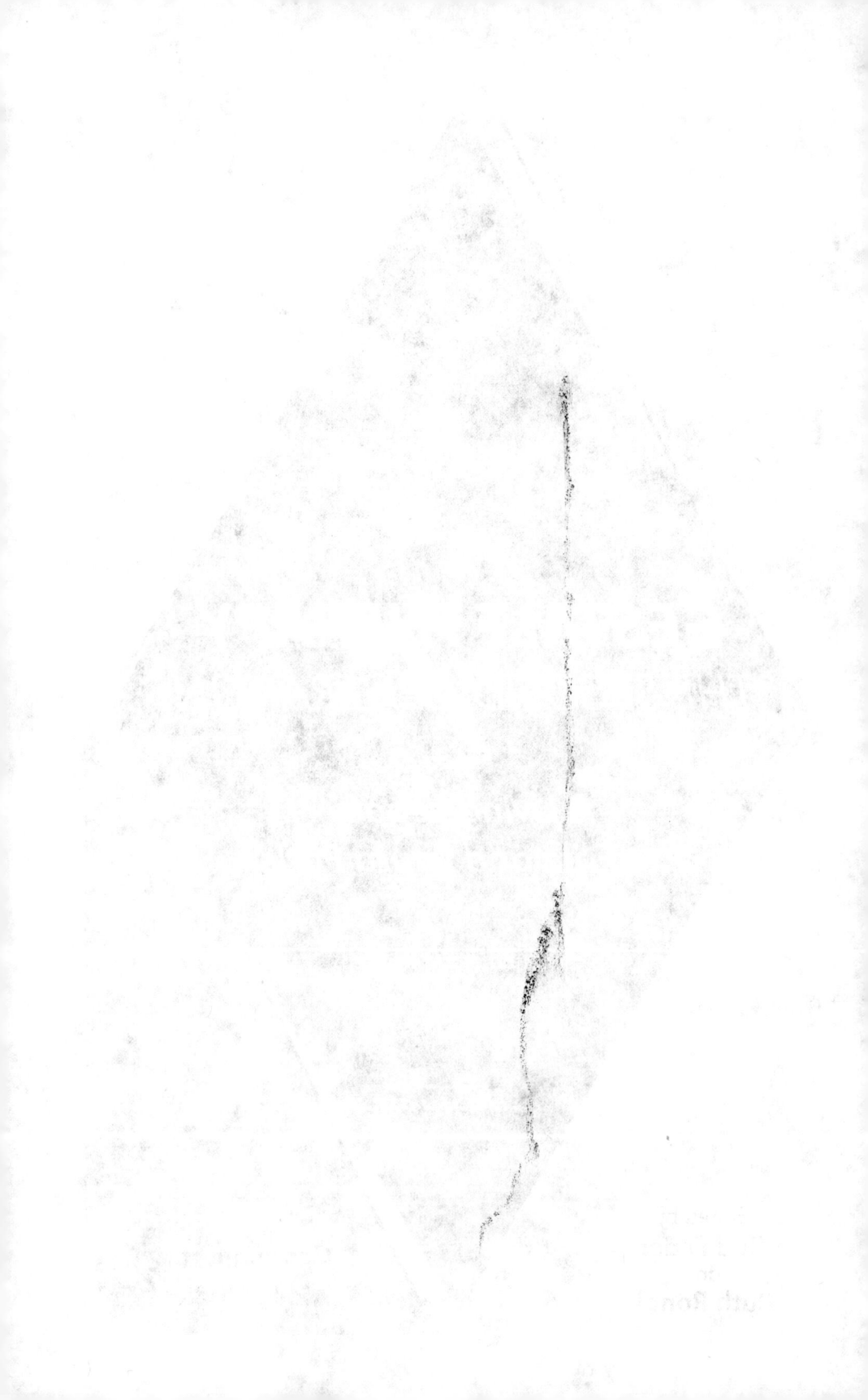

Part I

Individual therapy

1

FOR EMILY: WHENEVER I MAY FIND HER

Jon Frew[1]

❖❖

This will be a story about a woman I will call Emily and the course of a therapy which, at the time of writing, has lasted three years.

I believe you will identify in some ways with Emily. We all have our characteristic ways of missing opportunities for contact with others. Inevitably compromises are reached, bargains struck, solutions achieved in all of our lives which interfere with the process called "free functioning" in Gestalt therapy theory. We settle for less in our relationships with those who love us the most. Often these solutions, creatively discovered at an early age when contact with others is not supported, reify into tenacious patterns which can be observed by the Gestalt therapist. There are names for these patterns, terms which were defined by Fritz Perls and Laura Perls over fifty years ago and the one which most captures the story of Emily is "confluence."

This chapter will begin with a brief description of the theory of contact and confluence in Gestalt therapy. The next section of this chapter will detail selected pieces of Emily's childhood experiences. I will then outline the key events which prompted Emily to begin therapy with me and the status of her family and relationship situation at that time. The therapy itself will be chronicled with a particular emphasis on a series of sessions which took place in the past nine months. My intent in discussing these sessions will be to contrast the outcomes of a number of different types of interventions I

---

1   The author acknowledges that the title of this chapter was adopted from the title of a Paul Simon song published in 1966.

employed in my work with Emily. Finally I will summarize the work to date with Emily and comment on some recent developments which will shape our contact in the future.

A most salient feature of Gestalt therapy is, simply put, the process we call "contacting." Contact is the experience of differences and it is more. Contact is an ongoing process, which occurs between individuals and their environment. In each contact episode, the individual is compelled to finish that episode in the most growth-producing manner, given the current conditions of the organism-environment field (Perls, Hefferline, and Goodman, 1951, p. 229). Contact that occurs between individuals is referred to as interpersonal contact. Through contact we engage aspects of our environment, experience the resolution of needs and tensions, mature and change and come to understand ourselves and others more sharply. The hallmark of contact is excitement. One of the dimensions of contact is defined in Gestalt therapy by the polarities of confluence and isolation (Jacobs, 1989, p. 32).

Confluence is a condition of no-contact. "We are in confluence with everything we are fundamentally, unproblematically or irremediably dependent on: where there is no need or possibility of a change" (Perls et al., 1951, p. 451). We will see that Emily frequents the polarities of confluence and isolation and that a pattern of confluence "set in" very early in her life as a creative adjustment because she was irremediably and problematically dependent on her mother with no possibility of a change. That pattern of diminished contact framed by isolation and confluence pervades all of Emily's close relationships and inevitably manifested itself in the therapy relationship limiting our opportunities for contact.

In confluence the individual clings to unawareness prohibiting the occurrence of anything new or different. In confluence, contact cannot be made because contact involves the appreciation of differences the person has become unable to know. "We pathologically keep the field undifferentiated, giving up our knowledge of the difference of ourselves and the environment … like children, we are unable to play our part in changing our circumstances …" (Latner, 1986, p. 85). Decisions and behavior become automatically ordered by the prime directive of the confluent interpersonal system — no difference, no contact, no change. The child learns to understand her own feelings by closely monitoring the feelings of others. There is no solace outside the system. In a time of desperation, Emily once said to me "Only my mother or daughter could help me now because only they are feeling exactly what I am feeling."

Moments of confluence can be a positive part of the contacting process. You can feel "as one" with the ocean, with a piece of music or with another person while lovemaking. Confluence in this context is a fleeting experience, a relief from the weight of being separate. Confluence in the context of this chapter refers to a disturbance of contact … an inveterate state of fusion with another in which differentiation and separation are experienced as terrifying and intolerable while the isolation inherent in confluence is experienced as inevitable and unavoidable, and tolerable.

How does a Gestalt therapist approach a therapy with someone so absorbed in confluent relationships?

> The antidotes to confluence are contact, differentiation and articulation. The individual must begin to experience choices, needs, and feelings, which are his own and do not have to coincide with those of other people. He must learn that he can face the terror of separation from these people and still remain alive. (Polster & Polster, 1973, p. 95)

Emily grew up in a small rural community. She had two older sisters, one twenty years older and the other twelve years older. The vast majority of her childhood memories involve only herself and her mother and father, as both sisters were out of the household by the time that Emily was six years old. The primary family system in which the groundwork was laid for the patterns to be discussed in this chapter consisted of Emily, her mother and her father. Emily's mother was forty years old when Emily was born and her father was in his late forties.

Emily's father worked at a nearby manufacturing facility while her mother was at home tending to a small family-owned general store which was open seven days a week and occupied the front part of the family home. Emily has distinct memories of the bells that would ring when a customer would enter the store and of the frequent interruptions in her contact with her mother who would drop whatever she was doing to run to the front of the house, into the store, to wait on the customer. When Emily was older, she was expected to take care of the customers if mom and dad could not.

Emily's mother and father were alcoholics. Their capacity to respond to the needs of their customers and vendors became increasingly impaired as their drinking problems progressed. Emily reported two clear sets of experiences related to the operation of the store. In the first, she would be attempting to wait on a customer or assist a vendor and would feel overwhelmed by the demands of the situation. There were questions she could not answer or calculations she could not make. Competency and adequacy are ongoing issues for her. In the second, her mother would be in the store dealing with the public in such an impaired state that Emily felt intense humiliation and embarrassment. She has never felt proud of her mother and to this day her mother can embarrass her by something she says or does in public.

Developmentally Emily's figure-formation process (defined as the individual's awareness of emerging sensations and needs and how the person addresses those needs through contact with the environment) was derailed before the train left the station. The only caregiver physically available to respond to her needs was her mother, who consistently neglected them or abruptly cut them off. When dad was home, mom took care of his needs first and foremost. At other times, there was the store and always there were mom's needs which were not being met by her husband. A child whose needs are consistently neglected or who is abandoned in "mid-need" creatively adjusts to the situation.

Emily remembers being alone much of the time. Her father paid little attention to her. Emily remembers how mom would "startle" when dad came home from work or called for her and how mom would immediately run to her father. Emily remembers her mother and father drinking excessively around the kitchen table. She was not welcome there and would retreat to her room. Emily remembers a closed and locked bedroom door with strange and frightening sounds coming from behind the door. Emily remembers a look of disgust and repulsion on her mother's face when she came out of the bedroom. Emily remembers her mother coming into her room during the day or at night, uninvited, the smell of alcohol on her breath, wanting to cuddle or talk to her. At those times Emily would feel a mixture of being invaded, disgusted and overwhelmed and, at the same time, grateful for the touch and attention of her mother. It was at moments like these that the seeds of confluence were being planted. At those times Emily would hug her mother hard being aware of a gnawing fear that someday her mom would die and of a growing sense that her mother depended on her "exclusively for her emotional sustenance.

Emily began therapy with me three years ago. Two events prompted her to seek me out. Emily had been seeing a female psychiatrist on and off for over ten years. The psychiatrist's psychoanalytic stance replicated for Emily a very familiar relationship in which the neutrality her therapist maintained fostered confluence (there was no boundary for Emily to bump against) and isolation. When Emily called me, she had just received a final bill from her psychiatrist's receptionist with a typed note stating that the psychiatrist had retired (no closure is another hallmark of confluence). At about the same time, Emily's second husband had left her to attempt to reignite his relationship with his ex-wife.

Emily was quite shaken by the sudden and unexpected loss of her therapist and her husband. I soon learned, however, that her primary lines of defense consisted of the confluence rooted in her relationships with her mother and her daughter and those lines of defense were still intact.

It became evident very quickly that Emily's sense of self (which is defined in Gestalt therapy as the moment to moment series of contacts with the present and immediate situation) was fixed and rigid and that Emily did not experience a sense of self as separate from her mother and daughter. A diagram I put in my notes at that time to describe Emily's sense of self looked like this:

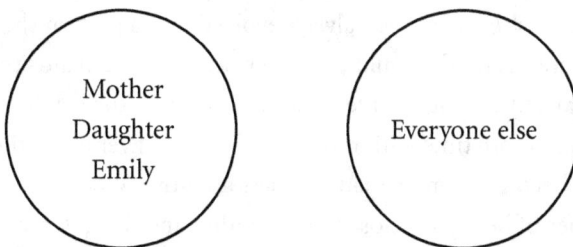

Emily was alive and well to the extent that her mom and daughter were alive and well. When Emily began therapy with me she was experiencing a moderate level of anxiety related to the loss of her therapist and husband. The losses were serious but not "life-threatening."

When I began to see Emily she was thirty-six years old. Her father and oldest sister were deceased. Her second husband had just moved out. She was living with her seven year old daughter from her previous marriage. She was employed as a school bus driver, a job which allowed her to be near home most of the day and gave her summers free. Her mother lived in the home next to the one occupied by Emily. She told me that before her father died he told her that it was her job to take care of her mother. Emily described a relationship with her mother which was devoid of boundaries. Emily spent as much time in her mother's house as her own. Doors were never locked and Emily, mom and daughter floated back and forth between houses to visit, "to check" on each other, to share meals, to clean and do housework as if it were one house. Indeed it was this arrangement that ultimately drove her second husband away. He criticized Emily constantly about her relationship with her mother. He resembled Emily's father by being very demanding of her attention and critical of her shortcomings as Emily's father had been of Emily's mother. Emily was inclined to discuss and complain about her relationship with her husband in our initial sessions. On one hand, she experienced intense discomfort (and at times disgust) When he got too close to her physically and sexually. On the other hand, when he withdrew from her to be with another woman, she panicked and wanted him back.

Throughout her adult life, Emily would latch onto men out of some vague sense of loneliness or following the introject that "she should be married." Her relationships with men always evolved into a pattern she observed between her parents. Emily would come to resent their demands that she attend to their needs. Being unable to say a direct "no," she would make excuses or spend more time with mom and daughter Eventually the men in her life would become more demanding, less attentive to her and very critical, accusing her of being too close to her mother and daughter and of being frigid and uptight sexually.

She acknowledged early in her therapy that she didn't really like men. She had introjected (swallowed whole) her mother's attitude that men were to be tolerated and served in return for financial security. She had an abundance of her own experiences with self-centered men whose attitudes and demands disgusted her as she had observed her father evoke disgust in her mother. Emily's distaste for men was supported by the fact that she did not like her father and had no warm, positive memories of him. When I met Emily, her reliance on her husband was financial and practical but not emotional. Although Emily was experiencing a moderate level of anxiety about her husband's activities with his ex-wife, she was ambivalent about his departure. She would tell me later in our therapy that the ideal spatial position for him would be in a trailer behind her house — not too close (and demanding) and not too far away. Their relationship, indeed any relationship Emily had ever had with men, was not classically confluent. To Emily men were strange and different entities who ultimately "only wanted one thing" and were not shy about expressing that need.

After our initial sessions, Emily admitted that it was her relationship with her mother that troubled her the most. It was imperative for her to keep her mother alive and she stated that for as long as she could remember, she was terrified that her mother would die. Emily had almost no life of her own with the exception of the time she spent at work. When she was away from her mother, she would feel mildly anxious and guilty. To remedy those feelings, she would check on her mom many times during the day and evening and almost always took her mother on any trip she would make, unless she caved in to her husband's criticism and left mom behind. Then she would experience guilt toward her mother and resentment and rage toward her husband. As her daughter got older she would send her next door to "be with grandma" which would be a solution to the dilemma of meeting her husband's need to be alone with her and Emily's need to take care of mom.

As we discussed her relationship with her mother in these initial sessions, Emily acknowledged an occasional desire to be away from the house without her mother coming along. Typically the desire would be replaced by a projected sense of how lonely and empty her mother would feel in that house "all by herself." I would say, "How do you know she feels that way?"

The response in confluence is a matter of fact, "I just know." This felt sense of her mother's inability to cope with being alone always led her (unless her husband intervened) to bring her mother along wherever she was going. Her mother never asked to go anywhere because in a confluent system there is no direct expression of need. As the therapy progressed, Emily stated that she occasionally experienced resentment about being saddled with mom. Often that resentment was deflected toward her sister who lived cross-town and spend very little time with mom.

After laying some groundwork for me in regard to her fear that something would happen to alter the confluence with her mother, Emily moved back to discussing her relationship with her husband — a topic which evoked much less anxiety. My notes indicate that the majority of our therapy time in the first six months was devoted to her husband.

By this time he had moved back in. As Emily experienced him, he would alternately invade her with his demands and then withdraw from her either satisfied or frustrated, hurling insults as he retreated. We explored her resistance to setting limits with him and expressing her needs to him. She would tell me that saying "no" made her feel mean and hurtful and she was indebted to him for all that he had done for her. To evade this dilemma she would make excuses — "I'm too tired" or "I don't feel well." As far as her needs were concerned, as time passed the only need she could identify was for him to stay away from her or for him to take care of himself. In this she was expressing the desire to reside at the isolation end of the isolation confluence polarity referred to earlier.

Eventually Emily's husband moved out permanently. To this day he continues to call almost daily and to come into her home uninvited. He still criticizes Emily for her relationships with her mother and daughter and for not taking care of his needs. The physical separation has assisted Emily in setting limits with him which in Gestalt therapy is the process of saying what you want or don't want at any moment, the process of contact. In the past Emily would only set a limit when she had stored sufficient resentment to say "no" with a reservoir of anger. Now she can say "no" calmly and without guilt. Therapy has enabled her to be more contactful.

At that point our focus shifted to her relationship with her mother. Emily had endured the separation with her husband. Any notion that she could survive (or that her mother could survive) even a relatively brief separation from her mother was met with strong objection. One year into Emily's therapy with me, she related an incident that had occurred the day before. Mom had gotten lost. Emily always knew where mom was and that day, she was not home and had no appointment that Emily was aware of. Emily's mild alarm quickly became abject panic after several phone calls failed to track mom down. Within minutes Emily's anxiety had intensified to terror and she became convinced that her mother was dead.

It turned out that mom struck out on her own that day to get her hair done at a different beauty parlor from the one she usually visited. Such spontaneity and independent thinking disrupts the confluent system. In this instance the disruption was so great that Emily touched the terror of losing her mother and was shaky from the experience the next day as she related these events to me. I asked her if she considered calling me that day. She looked puzzled and said, "What could you have done?" As I quizzed her further, she stated that the only person who could have helped her in those moments of terror was her daughter because "only her daughter would be feeling exactly what she was feeling."

When Emily lost her mother that day she made contact with that terror of being totally alone. Only the thought of being with her daughter gave her any relief. There is no contact available within a relationship in which there are no perceived differences; she took some comfort in the assumed shared experience with her daughter. No one outside the confluent system could provide comfort because they did not feel what she felt.

The experience called "contact" in Gestalt therapy is very difficult to describe. As our therapy progressed, it became clear to me that Emily was contact-starved. She had settled for the elusive security of denying differences with those she loved the most. She dreaded the day when her mother and daughter would be gone and there would be no one like her. She had a reoccurring dream of being an old lady alone in an old house, boarded up on the outside, dark and cold on the inside. No one can get in and Emily has no reason to go out.

Gestalt therapy theory does not approach impaired contact abilities from a historical perspective. Rather, interrupted contact in the present moment becomes the basis of a functional diagnosis which assists patient and therapist understand how contact is short-circuited before a connection can be made.

In the case of Emily, however, a historical perspective provides a useful view of the origin of Emily's confluent relationship with her mother. As I mentioned before, Emily spent the vast majority of her childhood alone in her room starving for contact with her mother and waiting for the next day when her father and the alcohol would be out of the way and her mother would return to her. Her isolation was enforced by her disgust, embarrassment and sense of being invaded when her mother was in her drunken state. Her confluence with her mother was cemented by her urge to "hang on" when her mother was available to her. After her father died and her mother quit drinking, Emily finally had a permanently clear path. She latched on to her mother and "hung on for dear life." Emily clung to her mother like a life raft. She had no confidence in her ability to swim. She had no reason to believe that other boats would come by if she let go of her mother.

As I am writing this chapter I am in the process of teaching my four year old daughter how to swim. Through that process I have learned that my daughter will not learn how to swim until she learns that she can let go of me and grab onto me, release and touch, release and touch. I stand close by and support her contact with the water by being available to her whenever she wants to be held up while she is learning how to hold herself up. Contact is like that ... an endless rhythm of release and touch. For Emily her life has alternated between staying out of the water (the isolation polarity) and holding on to her mother (who is holding on to her) to be in the water (the confluence polarity).

Emily's terror of being without her mother is her anticipation of a life "out of the water" and a life without touch. The task of therapy was evident. Emily must learn how to swim in the stormy seas of non-confluent relationships. The pond in which she had begun that learning process was our relationship. Our lessons became more focused.

As I became increasingly aware of the need to create more contact opportunities in our relationship, I realized that a type of "creeping confluence" had beset our therapy sessions. "Indeed someone can be involved in a confluence contract without having been consulted or having even 'negotiated' its terms" (Polster & Polster, 1973, p. 93). And I was.

I mentioned earlier that Emily's relationship with men could never be classically confluent because to Emily men were inherently strange and different entities. That barrier did not prevent the evolution of a therapy relationship that was almost devoid of conflict, comfortable and easy for Emily and for me. Over a relatively short period of time Emily became "fundamentally, unproblematically, and irremediably dependent" on me and on our weekly meetings. In our talking about her husband and her mother, "there was no possibility for a change." This creeping confluence is not surprising in light of Emily's dominant contact style which prevailed in her relationship with her previous therapist as it had all her life.

During the first year of therapy this confluence which minimized our contact opportunities was disturbed by two incidents. In the first, Emily learned of a group I was starting and felt angry and hurt that I had excluded her from membership. A woman that she knew was in the group and the fact that she was in and Emily was not re-enacted the old triangle in which mom and dad shut Emily out of their relationship. In the second, I moved my practice to another community and Emily had to drive further to see me. She experienced a sense of abandonment and was irritated that I could just move away and she was expected to change her schedule to come see me at a different office. Through these incidents, the tranquility of our relationship was inadvertently challenged by my actions. Emily was drawn into contact with me, in both cases, to express her unhappiness with me. In both cases, the confluence between us was quickly restored. Emily was extremely ill at ease with her feelings toward me and clumsy as she attempted to express them. Despite my encouragement she would lose her momentum through self-deprecatory comments like, "It's silly for me to have these feelings so let's drop it," or "Why should you take my feelings into consideration when you make decisions."

Moving into our second year of therapy, a series of sessions took another turn away from confluence, this time initiated by Emily. Her previous experience with men had led her to conclude that men were critical, judgmental, and demanding. Her experience with me was different. Emily was in a bind. She had resigned herself to the notion that men could only relate to her in one way. She had developed a type of confluence with this notion — men are always this way; it would never change. My behavior and way of being with her was disturbing that notion and, over time, making Emily more and more uncomfortable. She attempted to reconcile her dilemma over a series of meetings in which she tried to pick a fight with me. She would say that I must have criticisms of her that I was withholding, probably because I thought she was too weak to hear them. I must disapprove of her relationship with her mother and daughter and other aspects of her life, so go ahead let her have it.

Emily was compelled to disrupt the comfort of the confluence in our relationship because the way I was relating to her was beginning to unnerve her. She had fully expected that eventually I would attempt to seduce her or I would tell her that she must move away from her mother. During these sessions, I would hold my ground and report my present awarenesses to her. I would say "I'm not aware of any critical feelings toward you about that. What I am aware of is …" Emily was compelled to disrupt the confluence because she was beginning to sense that something different was possible with me. In Gestalt therapy theory, the organism has an inherent wisdom about these matters, about what can occur as the surrounding environment shifts and contact is supported.

During this series of sessions (which lasted for several months), I painstakingly continued to clarify my field of awareness. In doing so I was making my contribution to sharpening the edges of the contact boundary Emily and I shared. I observed that Emily was less "comfortable" during our meetings. She was experiencing the kind of excitement, shyness and anxiety which herald the emergence of contact.

At this point in the therapy, my efforts to challenge the confluence became more purposeful. Emily was demonstrating, through her interest in our differences and her growing tolerance to conflict, that she was self-reg-

ulating to her therapy environment. At her initiation more contact opportunities had been created in our relationship. Now it was my turn to find a
more intentional avenue which would help Emily move beyond a confluent
adaptation to a more contactful one.

I will conclude this case example with a description of another series
of sessions that occurred toward the end of the second year of therapy with
Emily. During these sessions "silence" became that avenue to further exploration of confluence and contact in my relationship with Emily.

One day Emily acknowledged that she became extremely uncomfortable around people who did not talk a lot and keep conversations going. She
admitted that she would sometimes ask me my opinion or experience with
some issue just to keep me talking. This admission led us quite naturally to
a period which lasted several months during which we would experiment
with silence whenever Emily had the urge to talk or have me talk "just to kill
time." What she discovered sitting in silence with me was a very uncomfortable level of self-consciousness.

Fritz Perls (1969) discussed self-consciousness in his earliest work
on Gestalt therapy. He described self-consciousness as the projection onto
another of critical and disparaging attitudes we have of ourselves so that at
that moment the criticism is experienced as coming from others (p. 253).
It is a consciousness of our own despised or condemned features and behaviors. Very frequently self-consciousness is related to the inability to say a
clear "no" to the demands of others. Emily cannot say no to the expressed or
assumed demands of others because to do so would bring about a change
in her world. A grudge forms against the person who makes these demands
and leads to feelings of weakness and impotence. In self-consciousness there
is always something unexpressed (retroflected in Gestalt therapy language).
Perls wrote that the correct method of addressing self-consciousness is to
undo the retroflections or promote spontaneity and expressions and to
assimilate the projection or take ownership of the critical attitudes (pp.
253–257).

In our early explorations of silence, I would suggest that we be silent
for relatively short periods of time. In one session, Emily reported that in the
silence she became aware that I was angry at her, bored by her and punish-

ing her by not speaking. In another session that followed, Emily literally squirmed in her seat and began to assume a closed body posture. She later told me that I had "filthy eyes" and she felt completely exposed. In yet another session she told me, after a period of silence, that I enjoyed watching her discomfort and that I felt superior to her. In a fourth session, she reported that I was able to see all her faults and was critical of her. In that session she became so agitated that half way into our agreed upon time period of silence she blurted out that she "would do anything to make this stop."

In these silences, I was transformed in Emily's eyes. I became the torturer, the voyeur, and the judge. I was looking through her, seeing all the faults, imperfections and deficiencies. Being unable to end her intense discomfort by expressing her needs or feelings to me (taking action toward contact) she would accede to any demand I might have if only I would agree to speak again. The peaceful confluence which had characterized our therapy relationship had ended. These were stormy times. I attempted to regulate the level of tension Emily was experiencing by adjusting the amount of time we would spend in silence. I fought off her projections by telling her what I was actually experiencing to contrast with what she thought I was thinking and feeling.

In a previous article (Frew, 1992), I outlined three types of intervention styles which Gestalt therapists can employ as they serve as an environment for their clients. The therapist may impose his needs at any moment upon the client, typically to heighten the client's awareness. The therapist may choose to compete with the needs of the clients through a process of negotiation and experimentation. The client wants to do one thing and the therapist another. The therapist may follow the needs and experience of the client, deciding to stay out of the way for a time so that the other's experience can be confirmed or validated, not challenged or overrun. Whatever posture the therapist adopts, the client mayor may not experience the therapist or the interventions in the way they were intended.

For example, when I was quiet too long Emily experienced me as being very imposing (even punishing) even though it was not my intention to impose on her. By not talking, I was doing something to her. Individuals locked into confluent systems frequently feel imposed on regardless of the behavior of the other simply because they are powerless to say "no." Conversely Emily experienced me as a very confirming environment when I would fill the silences and protect her from the pain and tension of being in the limelight of self-consciousness.

One other session stands out as Emily and I experimented with silence to challenge the confluence and increase our contact. On that day, Emily was particularly uncomfortable with the silence and asked me to end it by saying something. My intervention that day was competing. I said, "I have nothing to say right now. I want to be quiet. You will need to take responsibility for your own discomfort." Emily was used to being imposed on. She was used to being around others who talked enough to minimize her self-consciousness. She was used to being alone. She had very little experience with someone whose words sent the message "I'm taking care of myself right now; I suggest you do the same." This session rattled Emily like no others we had had to that date.

The following week she told me that she had been angry at me all week. She contemplated cancelling our appointment. I encouraged her to express her anger and she did. How dare I not protect her from pain and discomfort? How could she ever depend on me or trust me again? A contract, indeed the confluence contract I had never signed, had been irrevocably broken!

The following week Emily seemed more self-assured than I had ever seen her. She marched into my office and told me that she was tired of faking it with me; tired of talking just to fill the air, tired of worrying about boring me. "If I'm not entertaining enough for you, tough!" I wrote earlier that contact is difficult to describe. During this session I experienced a quality of contact with Emily that I had not previously experienced with her. It was as if Emily was finally in the room, as if I had finally found her.

After the session our formal experiments with silence ended. Emily became more aware of her own criticisms of herself. She would tell me that she felt empty inside and that she had nothing to offer in relationship. She wasn't smart and she wasn't funny and she wasn't well-read. How could anyone other than her mother and her daughter possibly be interested in spending time with her. As she owned and attempted to assimilate those aspects of her self, she hardly noticed the silences which more naturally punctuated our sessions.

Some months later something quite remarkable occurred. Emily planned a vacation to Hawaii and bought two plane tickets, one her herself and one for her daughter. She told her mother that she wanted to spend some time exclusively with her daughter. The conversation with her mother was difficult but when it was completed, Emily felt strong and excited about being on her own for two weeks. She was planning to do quite a bit of swimming in Hawaii.

Emily never got to Hawaii. A week before she and her daughter were scheduled to depart, her mother was diagnosed with cancer. Further testing revealed that it was a rapidly spreading cancer and that with or without treatment Emily's mother would die in several months.

As I conclude this chapter, Emily and I are meeting weekly as we have for over three years. Emily is facing the loss that she had dreaded her entire life. Once she said, "How could you help? You wouldn't be feeling the same thing I am feeling." I sit with her, often in silence. I am different than she is. I hand her Kleenex to catch the cascading tears. I sit with her in contact. My sense is that I am helping.

POSTSCRIPT

As I prepare to submit this chapter, ten months have passed since I completed my first draft. I saw Emily several days ago for our regular weekly appointment. We noted the six month anniversary of her mother's death. My daughter just turned five and two weekends ago swam for the first time without dad nearby to grab onto. Now Emily and I are in the water and she is learning how to release and touch. She is grateful to be near the surface after many months of drowning in her grief. A part of Emily died with her mother. In confluence, healthy or unhealthy, a part of us dies with those we are attached to. Another part of Emily is beginning to swim, like my daughter, for the first time. The strokes are unnatural, tentative, and frantic. But there is a confidence in both of their eyes, anxiety is supported by excitement and curiosity, and I know they are on their way.

REFERENCES

Frew, J.E. (1992) From the perspective of the environment. *The Gestalt Journal, 15*, 39–60.

Jacobs, L. (1989) Dialogue in gestalt therapy. *The Gestalt Journal, 12,1*, 25–67.

Latner, J. (1986) *The gestalt therapy book.* Highland, NY: Gestalt Journal Press.

Perls, F. S. (1969) *Ego, hunger and aggression.* New York: Vintage Books.

Perls, F. S., Hefferline, R. F. & Goodman, P. (1951) *Gestalt therapy.* New York: Bantam Books.

Polster E., & Polster M. (1973) *Gestalt therapy integrated.* New York: Vintage Books.

◊

2

BILL: FINDING ROOTS IN THE HIDDEN GROUND OF LOSS

John Mitchell

◆◆◆

*"Negative capability, that is when man is capable of being in
uncertainties, mysteries, doubts, without any irritable reaching
after fact and reason."*
— John Keats

BACKGROUND AND FIRST IMPRESSIONS

Bill is a teacher, age 30, married to Lucy, with a daughter aged four and a
son aged 2. This was a self referral, Bill having previously been in therapy in
Sussex with a therapist whom his older brother had been seeing. He found
the distance impractical, hence was seeking a local therapist.

In his previous therapy Bill had been working on his relationship with
his mother who died when he was 4. His original presenting problem had
been his general sense of inadequacy and anxiety in relationships, which he
associated with this early loss.

After his wife's death, his father married again, and encouraged him
and his brother to bury their feelings about their mother's death. Bill had
tried recently to talk to his father about his mother, but his father seemed
reluctant to do so.

Bill hoped that through therapy he might develop some sense of relationship with his mother and improve the quality of current relationships,
especially with his wife and his father.

He was worried about his wife, Lucy. She was unhappy in her work and given to fits of depression. Bill seemed uncertain about what therapy could achieve, but impelled by a sense of past and current unhappiness to seek help.

At the end of the first session we made a contract to work for a minimum of six further one hour sessions.

Bill is of medium height, but the thinness of his build makes him appear tall. The crown of his head is bald, and his hair trimmed short at the sides and back. His face has a youthful look which contrasts with his bald head. His eyes looked nervous, even frightened, and often avoided mine. He dressed neatly and casually in subdued colors. He seemed anxious on first entering my room. His movements were uneasy, his eyes wary. He seemed careful, if not to please, at least not to displease me. However, my general sense was of an openness and preparedness to make contact within limits set by his initial anxiousness and mistrust of a stranger in whom he had decided to confide.

Early Hunches

I sensed at once that Bill might take fright and/or offense easily, that his openness (he was quite disclosing of his feelings about his parents and his wife in the first interview) might conceal a vulnerability and defensiveness which I had only glimpsed so far. I was interested by his semi-formal manner and meticulously casual dress (his shoes were usually carefully polished) and my sense of a turbulence beneath this exterior. Though I did not feel personally drawn towards Bill I was curious about this contrast, and aware of the possibility that he might bring to our relationship some of the ambivalence he obviously felt towards his father. This might mean that while he would look to me for support in his search for some sense of relationship with the mother he could barely remember, he might at the same time push me away and call this support in question. I did not, however, anticipate in this first meeting, the degree to which another relationship, that with his wife, would occupy center-stage in many of our sessions, in spite of Bill's resentment of this apparent distraction (in his view) from his stated purpose of working on his relationship with his mother.

Emerging Themes

This theme (his wife as a "problem") became clear in the second session, when Bill reported that she had "gone into a deep depression with sudden outbursts of anger." We spent much of the session on what support he and his wife could find to help them through her difficulties.

I carry, as part of the essential ground for my work, the importance of what Perls called "involvement in the total field" (Perls, 1973, p. 104), of giving attention with sensitivity and responsiveness to the client's process and my own; while at the same time refusing attempts to manipulate me into colluding with his/her position of helplessness: "[The therapist] must then learn to work with sympathy and at the same time with frustration. These two elements may appear incompatible, but the therapist's art is to fuse them into an effective tool" (p. 105).

Toward the end of the session Bill acknowledged resenting his wife, and me for his having spent time on this: "I came here to talk about me, not her." I told him I was very willing to go with this, and highlighted how he had repeatedly returned to the topic of his wife's problems. He was open to taking some share of responsibility for how he used the time. Here we touched on what was to emerge as a major theme: Bill identified a child part within who didn't get enough of his mother; and his resentment of the demands of living as an adult. In these opening sessions I often had a sense of being with a petulant child who would emerge for a while, sometimes with tears in his eyes, and then would quickly, and often with embarrassment, be put away in favor of a not very convincing display of adult responsible behavior.

Sometimes I was moved by the sight of this "inner child" as when, in our third session Bill talked with deep sadness about the part of him which felt the loss of the mother he hardly remembered: "I don't even have a sense of who she was." I encouraged him to stay with these feelings. (He tended to become embarrassed and tidy himself up quickly.) By the end of the session he had begun to sense that he had some choice as to how deep he would go, and an awareness of when he had done enough for the time being.

In our fourth session Bill got angry and embarrassed as he talked of his sunburn-prone skin, which, in contrast to his wife's, turns pink instead of golden brown. I acknowledged his embarrassment, and suggested a fantasy dialogue between his angry part and the part which thought he shouldn't care about such things or feel envious of his wife's beautiful skin. He began from the parental position, and quickly became aware of his need for attention, touch and care, from Lucy in particular, and how this gets confused in their relationship with sexual needs, an area of conflict since the birth of their second child two years previously. I gave support and validation to the part of Bill which wanted to accept this need for care and touch and at the same time began to open up the distinction between having this need satisfied and his attempts to make his wife into the mother who was taken from him.

Initial Diagnostic Picture

As I thought diagnostically about Bill at this stage, I considered him in terms of a personality style which tended towards dependency. He seemed ill at ease in the world of adults, with a sense of inadequacy in personal relationships which meant that he often felt out of things, especially in groups of friends. His capacity for being meticulous and organized meant that he normally kept his head above water at work, though this seemed to be at the expense of much personal contact with fellow members of staff. In his work with his students he was successful, though reluctant to acknowledge this to me at first.

Bill's dependency needs seemed to be focussed largely on his wife, who seemed unable or unwilling to meet them. I describe the dynamics of their relationship later. At this stage it seemed to me likely that both Bill and Lucy were making inappropriate demands on each other as a result of their projections. By the time Bill entered therapy with me he had already recognized that he displaced his early unfulfilled need for mothering onto his marriage. It seemed to me understandable that much of his attention should, to his annoyance, be taken up with his difficulties with his wife. However, while I was prepared to look at these difficulties with him, I was aware that he had a tendency at times to disown his neediness and project it onto his wife: "She's the one who needs help." It was thus important to remind him frequently that he had come to me to talk about himself. Therefore, when Bill opened up the possibility of he and Lucy together seeing a counsellor, I supported this suggestion as I thought that this might: 1) ease some of the pressure he felt to do something about their difficulties; 2) challenge his tendency to see either himself or Lucy as "the problem"; 3) provide him with a sense in our session of having space to deal with the area which he felt underlay his difficulties, his relationship with his mother, and with his father and stepmother.

Other strands in Bill's personality, faint at first, began to emerge. He experienced sudden changes of feeling, in particular a tendency to become tearful when his "child" needs were recognized. This vulnerability often seemed just below a calm exterior. Sometimes resentment or anger would break through, and he often felt surprised at his own hidden aggressive energy. He also had a flamboyant and excitable aspect which he found hard to admit to and secretly cherished. He told me with pride of an incident where he had ridden on the roof of a friend's car and jumped into the sea fully dressed.

However as our work progressed I began to see these outbursts of feeling and excitement as emerging from a background which prevalently displayed characteristics of an avoidant personality style.

Generally in my work I find this kind of diagnostic approach useful in avoiding potentially damaging interventions with dependent, avoidant and narcissistic clients, where an early confrontation of their life-position may irreversibly damage the prospects of forming a working relationship, and may be experienced by the client as a "re-run" of old hurts. (Delisle, 1989)

In Bill's case I initially made an impressionistic diagnosis and intuitively took an approach of acknowledging his experience and only gently confronting, while focussing on building relationship through what Yontef (in Corsini, ed., 1984, pp. 281–282) calls "commitment to dialogue," "allowing contact to happen rather than 'making' contact and controlling the outcome." Delisle, (1989), advocates increasing the avoidant client's ability to be passive in order to balance his/her tendency to an "active style in situations that generate anxiety." I found that my emphasis on "being" rather than "doing," though anxiety-provoking for Bill at first, gradually created a space in which he could let go of some of his anxiety about being rejected or humiliated. For example, I would frequently draw attention to his process in the moment, showing interest in how he "was" rather than in what he might "do" in therapy.

This space in which to develop relationship was essential for Bill. I made an assumption that his mother's death had constituted a major interruption in the process of his forming a developed sense of self, through his system of contacts in relationship, at the moment when he began to confront the uncertainties and challenge of relationship with his peers, and when the continuance of nurturing was crucial. In addition, Bill was not supported by his environment to acknowledge and grieve for his mother's death. It was not talked about, and he never knew the whereabouts of her grave. Yalom draws attention to the implications of inadequate support:

> Exposure to death in the child's environment is an important event; some types of contact with death may — in proper dosage and in the presence of already existing ego resources, salubrious constitutional factors, and supportive adults who are themselves able to deal adaptively with death anxiety — result in inoculation, whereas some types may exceed the child's capacity to shield himself or herself. (Yalom, 1980, p. 104)

Bowlby (1981, pp. 292–294) has emphasized the influence of the behavior of the surviving parent: "a substantial proportion of the special difficulties which children experience after loss of a parent are a direct result of the effect that the loss has had on the surviving parent's behavior towards them."

Yalom has illustrated the reluctance of adults in our culture to acknowledge the realities of death out of their own existential anxiety[1] (Yalom, 1980, pp. 80-82), an anxiety greatly accentuated by the death of a

---

1   This anxiety is described by Perls in terms of a break in the "confluence with everything we are fundamentally unproblematically or irremediably dependent on: where there is no need or possibility of a change. A child is in confluence with his family, an adult with his community, a man with the universe. If one is forced to become aware of these grounds of ultimate security, the 'bottom

close relative or friend. He traces this death denial to early childhood (pp. 95–96) and maintains that children give up their inquiry into death in the face of adult denial (ibid, pp. 87-88). A great deal of energy must be invested in this "giving up" in the case where the child is not supported to acknowledge his/her own parent's death, and this must have powerful repercussions in childhood and later life (p. 106).

Bowlby also stresses the importance of recognition and mourning, opposing the traditional opinion that children cannot mourn and that emotional problems following parental loss can be understood as due to an arrest of development at the phase thought to have been reached at the time of loss or at some earlier phase (Bowlby, 1981, pp. 317–318).

These views are in keeping with the Gestalt perspective which takes into account the total environmental field: in considering Bill's mother's death it is essential to consider the context, which was one that gave him no support to contact, know and assimilate it as part of his reality.

When a client reports an event whose significance seems beyond doubt, and specifically orients himself in that direction, it is tempting to see the work of therapy as directed towards the completion of whatever unfinished gestalts cluster around the event in question. At this point I know I need to be wary, for in pursuit of the chimera of this completion, we may lose touch with the present systems of contacts of the client and his/her characteristic interruptions (Perls, Hefferline, and Goodman, 1973, pp. 509–518; Polster & Polster, 1974, pp. 70–97; Latner, 1989, pp. 86–93; Zinker, 1978, pp. 97–113). This focus is central to the formation of dialogue and relationship in Gestalt therapy inasmuch as it offers a way through the maze of interruptions to moments of transparent contact and awareness which together begin to constitute relationship. This also offers the client a model of possibilities for his/her wider existence.

The difficulties around diagnosis (and therefore treatment planning), whether on an etiological or symptomatic basis, are considered by Perls intrinsic to a structural as opposed to a functional view of the world. The

---

drops out,' and the anxiety that one feels is metaphysical." (Perls, et al., 1973, pp. 510–511)

model which they offer is a "description of the neurotic 'ego' in process," and it is the therapist's role to "help the patient develop his creative identity" through this very description i.e. through drawing his attention to those moments when he interrupts, thus providing a context where the old behaviors "no longer achieve anything: their meaning has changed from technique to obstacle." For Perls "diagnosis and therapy are the same process" (Perls et al., 1973, p. 509).

However, they do acknowledge that "the therapist needs his conception in order to keep his bearings, to know in what direction to look. It is the acquired habit that is the background for this art as in any other art" (p. 507).

Thus part of the ground for my work with Bill, as with other clients, was a sense of his movement through a sequence of interruptions as the failure of each to produce its customary effect led to the deployment of another.[2]

This movement showed an oscillation between two polarities: the need for contact and affirmation and the fear of engagement. As the meaning of each interruption changed in the therapy context "from technique to obstacle" the possibility of contact became momentarily real, and would give rise to an anxiety-based reaction in the other direction.

So, after a session where Bill tearfully acknowledged to me that he's a good teacher and allowed me to see this, as opposed to his usual "I'm not competent in the adult world" introject, he reacted in the next session by

---

2   An instance of this occurred in a session where he talked about his difficulty in acknowledging to himself and others what he wanted. Fear showed in his face. I asked him what he was afraid of "Antagonizing other people," he replied, "especially Lucy." He went on to talk about his conflicting sense of guilt at wanting "unreasonable things" and "resentment at not getting what I want." He looked at me squarely, momentarily relieved as he said this, and then becoming afraid again, his eyes glistening and avoiding mine. He had undone a habitual retroflection in acknowledging his resentment, and now quickly reverted to projection, imagining me to be disapproving.

reverting to talking about his wife's difficulties and leaving the session without payment, having forgotten his cheque book.

CHARACTERISTIC PATTERNS OF RELATIONSHIP

I will conclude my description of Bill's way of being in the world with a summary of my sense of his characteristic patterns in relationship.

I had a sense that Bill's difficulties centered around managing the contact boundary (Perls, 1973, pp. 274–282; Polster & Polster, 1974, pp. 98–127) without adequate systems of internal or external support. He was in a perpetual double bind — feeling a desperate need for contact, yet unable to tolerate the threat which he felt from the inevitable difference of others, a difference which was sometimes oppositional, critical and rejecting and often became more so as Bill's demand for confluence increased.

This pattern could be seen most obviously in his relationship with his wife, which was dominated by his fear of being abandoned. He would take care of Lucy in the hope of getting his needs for intimacy, care and touch met and of lessening the likelihood of her leaving him. Lucy would often repel his "attentions," a row would ensue, Bill would withdraw hurt, frightened, anxious and privately critical. Lucy would then go into depression, which would increase Bill's anxiety and intensify his need for contact. He would then renew his efforts to help her, and so on …

With friends Bill reported feeling anxious, that they were more grown up than he, and that he was not supposed to have fun. His stepmother had discouraged him from having friends visit the house when he was a child. He was aware that he was habitually critical and intolerant of friends behind their backs, often making them into parental figures.

In a fantasy dialogue with George, a close friend, he identified how he projected a parental introject onto him, and hence reacted to him either with exaggerated deference or unexpected outbursts of rebellious anger. This in turn opened up his relationship with his father and stepmother for attention.

Bill yearned for better contact with his father, partly because he saw this as the key to unlocking his relationship with his mother. However, because his father had discouraged any talk about, or expression of feeling for, his mother after her death, Bill did not trust his father to be helpful. (He had already made an approach to obtain photographs and information about where his mother was buried, and received a promise but not action). He also felt acute embarrassment about even broaching the subject. However, his father had been warm and playful at times during Bill's childhood, whereas his memory of his stepmother was of her strictness and emotional distance. Currently he saw her as self-congratulatory about her work, something he strongly disliked. He mistrusted any efforts to be friendly on her part. During the course of his therapy he realized a strong similarity between his perceptions of his stepmother and of his wife. On the other hand he remembered with great sadness a former lover, Jenny, who had left him before he met his wife, whose qualities of being "safe, normal, and fun" he also associated with his mother, from brief references made by his father.

Bill's children featured in his work mainly in as far as their care was a source of conflict with Lucy. Though it was clear that he was kind and caring for the most part, I had the impression that their presence was a frequent reminder of the miseries of his own childhood and that at some level he resented the fact that they received more love and attention than he had.

Bill was proud of his ability as a teacher and found it easy to get on with his students. (This contrasts with the difficulties he experienced with his peers, whether friends or colleagues.)

CHOICE OF THERAPY FORMAT

I want to say something about my choice of work format with Bill. He originally approached my for individual therapy. His level of confidence with his peers was low, and my sense of him was that, at least for a while, he would be better able to use the one-to-one situation. We agreed on weekly one hour sessions, to be confirmed after six sessions.

Soon after he came into therapy he asked if I would see both him and his wife together — he was experiencing a lot of difficulty in that relationship.

I thought it inadvisable to bring his wife in at that stage, as I anticipated difficulty in working in a balanced way, in view of my early assessment. (See above) Also, I saw it as important to support his original wish for a space of his own where his wife would not take up too much of the session. I therefore agreed that they should see a couples counsellor (providing Bill informed him/her that he was in therapy with me) while I continued to work with Bill. They continued to see this counsellor for five months, and later recommended after a four month break.

Towards the end of his therapy Bill suggested he go into group therapy with me. A place was not available at that time, and the question was complicated by the fact that the colleague with whom I co-ran the group was his wife's therapist, and we had an agreement not to discuss our work with them together.

Any inclination I had to re-negotiate this contact was offset by my suspicion that Bill's frequent consideration of different therapy formats was a sign of his fear of accepting our relationship as really significant — an attempt to deflect the closeness which he saw as a possibility between us, and an example of the polarity to which I have referred above.

PHASES OF THERAPY

As I review my work with Bill I distinguish three major phases: an opening phase, roughly three months, in which we laid the foundations of a working relationship; a middle phase, lasting eight months, characterized by increased turbulence in Bill's, personal life and in our relationship as he encountered his fears and frustration more intensely and struggled with his "problem" and with me; and a final phase of 2 ½ months of increasingly definite and confident action ending with a sense of closure and satisfaction. Although the progress of the therapy could be schematized in themes of the Gestalt cycle of experience (Zinker, 1977, pp. 97 – 113; Hall, 1976, pp.

53–57); or in terms of Perls' "layers of neurosis" (Perls, 1970, pp. 25–30), I am aware that the therapy process, even the relatively simplified and selectively viewed form in which I have recorded and recollected it, consists of a complex series of cycles within cycles, of approaches to and retreats from the impasse, which happen throughout the work, moving towards a crescendo as the foundations of sensation, awareness, mobilized energy and experimentation come gradually to be trusted by the client.

I hope to give some sense of this in the following account of Bill's therapy.

OPENING PHASE — CREATING A SPACE FOR DIALOGUE

In the opening phase I identify several ways in which I played a part in establishing a relatively safe and potentially exploratory working environment:

1. listening to his story
2. receiving criticism — not insisting that he re-own responsibility
3. "staying with" him through uncomfortable feelings, e.g. embarrassment, anger
4. discussing and suggesting options
5. introducing experiments
6. giving guidance, e.g., about frequency of sessions, consulting a couples counsellor
7. working with sensation, awareness, breathing and physiological self support
8. affirming and satisfying his need for attention, closeness, and for someone who will receive his criticisms
9. supporting his self compassion (focussed mainly on himself as a child)
10. overall, frequently bringing the focus to his process and our relationship; being sensitive to his need for and fear of close-

ness; being aware of the danger of challenging too harshly or too quickly.

It may be noted that in several of these interventions I "accepted" the manipulation (e.g. requests for advice about his marriage; critical remarks in which he disowned responsibility for his therapy). Later I would be more challenging in similar situations, thus grading interventions in a way that is largely intuitive against a background of assessment, and an awareness in the therapist and client of his/her ongoing responses to previous interventions. Grading of interventions and systems of support in therapy are discussed at length by (Polster & Polster, 1974, pp. 165–167, 203–207), and by Zinker (1973, pp. 132–133). The following passage sounds a keynote for my work with Bill.

> Another source of support is the expectation and the assurance that one's movement into the previously unassimilable — unthinkable — experience will be gradual and faithful enough to the individual's needs. He needs to know that his I-boundary will be extended without irreparable risk and he will find retreat avenues available, should he need them. He may not need to retreat a great distance, but he must sense that he could back up as much as he might need. (Polster & Polster, 1974, pp. 203–204)

During the first twelve sessions this approach made it possible for Bill to experiment with challenging me, testing the boundaries of our relationship in a way that the had felt unable to do with his father and stepmother as a child. He also became aware of the projection mechanism by which he distorted his current relationships.

MIDDLE PHASE — MOBILIZING ENERGY, EXPLORING CHOICES AND BEGINNING TO ENGAGE

Our work now entered a turbulent middle phase. Several themes began to emerge as a result of this concentration on our interactions and on Bill's own sensations and emerging needs.

He encountered his difficulty in acknowledging to himself and others what he wants; his fear of antagonizing others; his guilt at wanting unreasonable things versus his resentment at not getting what he wants; and his need for closeness with his father.

I suggested he draw up at home a list of "wants." He missed the next session, and when I challenged him about how much priority he was giving to our work, he became very angry. He agreed to make another appointment. During the following session he complained that our work had consisted of crisis counselling and stress management and that he wanted to look at "deeper issues." Also, his anxiety about his appearance re-emerged.

He also found a key phrase which expressed his prevailing sense of unease about his internal state and his experience in relating to others. "There always has to be something wrong." Although this had the flavour of an introjected message (perhaps reflecting his stepmother's critical and punitive stance in relation to him as a child), I sensed that it also denoted a more deeply-rooted sense of "wrongness" which Bill associated with his unfinished business with his parents, most especially with his dead mother.

Our clash over the missed session had stirred Bill's awareness of his difficulties with friends. Our work now entered a phase when he talked about his tendency to criticize and be intolerant, and I encouraged him to come out with his criticisms during our sessions. I suggested that he begin by describing what he found hard to tolerate in Lucy: "She's no sense of humour. She's always analyzing and philosophizing. She doesn't enjoy my silly side — she disapproves if I fool about." In the next session he focussed on his suppressed need to play ("I'm not supposed to have fun") and talked about his sense of being younger than his peers. I was hearing from the Bill who had not been allowed to play as a child because of the dominant influence of his stepmother, who, he reported, also inhibited his father's playfulness. Bill was tearful with sadness and held-in anger as he contacted aspects of his being which had been cut off from the nurturing which they needed to become fully assimilated into his sense of self.

At this point I suggested he make a list of his childhood introjects. This may have encouraged him to go into a detached, cognitive mode, for in the session which followed he talked in an unemotional way about how his stepmother had discouraged friendships and made his friends unwelcome. He recognized that this still influences his current friendships which he tended to sabotage. I shared how out of contact I felt when he described his experience in that flat, uninvolved tone. We began to focus on how he sabotaged our relationship. Here, as often with Bill, I was struck by the power of simply drawing attention to what was happening between us. He became tearful and acknowledged having "set up" a recent clash with me on the telephone. He was beginning to recognize the possibility of relationship with me, and the fear and anger which this evoked in him.

Bill's questioning of the work we were doing intensified from about this time, often in response, it seemed, to a previous session in which he had felt particularly acknowledged, or had begun to explore a "forbidden" area. After a session in which we had focussed on breathing, grounding, and awareness of sensations, he talked about how hard he found it to be aware in this way. He likened this to his difficulties in concentrating both in his life "out there" and in therapy, which he saw as sabotaging our work. Delisle (1989) has noted this cognitive distraction, and also the "active process" involved in avoidance. To heighten Bill's awareness of his active role in this I encouraged him to articulate his wandering thoughts, which he did. As a result he seemed to feel "seen," and to be more open than previously to the possibilities of relationship. However at the beginning of the next session he talked again about ending therapy; he then went on to open up a new area — his relationship with Jenny, his lover before his wife. He became very energized. We agreed to continue our work together, and to keep under review when therapy might end.

In a fantasy dialogue Bill now explored his relationship with Jenny, feeling his sadness and sense of how his continuing yearning for Jenny and the playful, easy relationship he remembered was getting in the way in his marriage.

This heightened awareness was followed by an intensification of his difficulties with Lucy, in reaction to which Bill absented himself in imagining a more playful and lively Lucy. A fantasy dialogue with her highlighted his split between his critical and placatory, self-blaming aspects.

At this point Bill became interested again in going to couples' therapy with Lucy (they had stopped counselling there four months previously), and when he returned to therapy after the Christmas break, he said that he and Lucy had arranged this, and that his job was in jeopardy and that he might have to end therapy.

I brought to his attention what I saw as an established pattern in our work: Bill's touching on significant themes in a vividly felt way and then calling into question the continuance of our work. I agreed to a three week break until his employment position became clear, after which we would re-negotiate our contract. In the meantime I suggested he write letters to his stepmother and father (without necessarily sending them) about what he didn't get that he needed from them as a child.

During this phase I needed to hold a balance between giving my authentic responses and maintaining a non-judgmental receptive attitude. I sometimes felt irritable and impatient with Bill, and was aware of the danger that I might reproduce either the "non-presence" of his father or the punitive authoritarian behavior of his stepmother, which had been an outstanding feature of his childhood experience. I found it essential to be able to "call up" the ground of our interactions, including Bill's history and my working hypotheses, as well as areas of my experience which might be restimulated, in particular my relationships with remote male figures (father, teachers) and domineering and punitive female figures (teachers of my childhood and adolescence). At the same time I needed to maintain a "phenomenological trust in immediate experience" (Yontef and Simkin, in Corsini [ed], 1984, p. 281) which would ground me in the here and now and model for the client. In supervision I talked through my feelings of impatience and irritation with Bill, and this played an important part in my ability to stay with him.

FINAL PHASE — ACTION, SATISFACTION, WITHDRAWAL

Now we entered the final phase, which I think of as the phase of responsible, embodied choice and action.

Bill came to the next session more energized than I had often seen him. He had written a letter to his father ("for the wrong reason: to please you" he told me) and had realized how much he needed facts about his mother, and "something solid that belonged to her," as well as recognition from his father of his need to "realize" his mother. (I was reminded of the many times Bill had reported not feeling solid and grounded in his life.) He had a strong sense that information and memorabilia would help in the process of making his mother real to him, so that he could grieve for her and hopefully move on.

After some discussion we agreed to make a contract to terminate therapy after six more sessions. In retrospect, I think that it would have been useful to propose a longer period, say 10-12 weeks (see below). Bill was clear that he wanted to move towards an ending and said he would find a definite termination date supportive because of his tendency to put things off. I had discussed the question of how and when Bill's therapy might end in supervision. What stood out for me was the shift in Bill's energy which had begun to happen at the time when he started to explore his relationship with Jenny and now showed in his excitement about the letter to his father. He was still talking of ending therapy, but now in a mood of mounting creative excitement coloured, as it must be, by uncertainty of outcome. It was in the spirit of support of and engagement with his excitement that I agreed and made it clear that I would not re-open therapy after that date.

I was concerned then, and still am, that I may have been over-rigid in this, indeed that by parallel process we may have reproduced an ending too reminiscent for Bill of the arbitrary finality of his mother's death. I took the decision with this awareness, and I think that the sense of finality had an important part to play in the mobilization of energy which followed. I discuss below the drawbacks in terms of Bill's grieving Process and with regard to the satisfaction and withdrawal phases of therapy.

Bill had now been in therapy for eleven months. My work during this concluding phase was largely to provide him with a supportive environment in which to explore his options, report on his decisions and actions and begin to assimilate their significance. In tandem with this went an increasing awareness and recognition on his part of the significance of our relationship.

This first became a clear figure for him at the end of the first session of our termination contract, when I suggested he make a brief statement of where he hoped to be by April 22nd (our ending date). Earlier in the session he had been preoccupied with the fact that his former lover Jenny had recently had a baby. I asked him to imagine what it would be like to be Jenny's baby. He became tearful and replied: "Safe, normal, fun." He said these were qualities he associated with his mother and realized how he'd split himself between his memory of Jenny and his experience of Lucy, thus seeing his relationship with Lucy as unsafe, abnormal and devoid of play.

He went on to read the letter he had written to his father and acknowledged wanting to cry in his arms. During the following fortnight he struggled with his fear of sending the letter. This was paralleled in his conflict about how to act in relation to Lucy, where he saw his only options as to capitulate and appease her, to walk away, or to complain and whine. When I suggested another — to say clearly and firmly what he wanted — he remembered having done this recently with some success. His image of himself as ineffectual and unassertive had yet to catch up with the changing reality of his increasing sense of himself and his needs and wishes.

In the next session he reported having sent the letter to his father who gave him a sensitive and understanding response and agreed to help him in whatever way he could. "I feel as if a weight has been lifted from me," he said. "I feel more real, more here." I shared with him the warmth I felt towards him, and my sense that he was there in a fuller way than I had experienced before.

When I next saw him he reported having had a boundary dispute with a neighboring property owner, in which he was pleased to have been clearly assertive without feeling an aftermath of resentment. In our next, and penultimate, session Bill told me how the previous day, his mother's birthday, he had visited her grave. He was tearful, deeply moved, and seemed to me more substantial, rooted, than I'd ever experienced him. His skin glowed with aliveness and he looked me fully in the eye, with none of his former evasiveness.

Later in this session Bill was wholehearted in his appreciation of our work together. We shared our warmth and excitement and sense of completion. It was a moment of recognition in which Bill made open to me his process of re-owning and letting go, as he described simply what had happened by his mother's grave.

In our final session we reviewed our work. I was aware that our termination contract allowed little time for satisfaction and withdrawal. Bill was clearly moved to believing and ambivalent about letting go of a relationship whose significance he had so recently recognized.

CONCLUSION

In retrospect, I think his ambivalence about ending may also have been rooted in an organismic need for the support of a significant other in the grieving process on which he had embarked. I regret that I did not respond to the discomfort I felt at this point by suggesting that we re-examine our contract in the light of what had emerged. It is difficult to see how, in the Gestalt approach, the commitment to contract can be separated from the fundamental commitment to honour one's own and the client's process.

Had I been more alert to the unity of this field, I would have opened up the possibility of bringing the work of therapy to a more satisfying closure. The following passages underline the importance of the phases of satisfaction and withdrawal: "The goal of this phase (satisfaction) in counselling is to facilitate the client in experiencing satisfaction and Gestalt completion, allowing herself to be fully and finally gratified with the contact which has occurred" (Clarkson, 1989, p. 122).

"It is very important for the counsellor to support and encourage the acceptance and exploration of the withdrawal and isolation which is a necessary part of the transition process" (Clarkson, p. 133).

In thinking about likely future developments in Bill's process I come back to my strong sense that the uneven process of our developing relationship provided firm enough ground for the explorations and risks of the final phase. By establishing the feasibility of contact and a relationship which could encompass conflict and compassion, we set up a model for other contacts (for example his relationship with his father), and nurtured a tolerance for uncertainty and an appetite for the undiscovered.

I trust that the momentum we generated continued to inform Bill's experience after our work ended:

> "For the creative meaning of the situation is not what one thinks beforehand, but it emerges in bringing to the foreground the unfinished situations, whatever they are, and discovering-and-inventing their relevance to the apparent present lifeless situation. When in the emergency the self can keep in contact and keep going, the therapy is terminated." (Perls et al., 1973, p. 526)

APPENDIX

Characteristic Interruptions Of Contact/Blocks In Awareness Cycle

Confluence
Makes demands for confluence in marriage out of fear of abandonment. Avoids friendships, maybe because he can't see any possibility short of the confluence and total security he craves. This is reflected in his efforts to keep me at a distance and terminate therapy.

Desensitization
Is often unaware of his environment and his responses to it.

Deflects
Care and attention and praise (is embarrassed, or does not seem to hear).

Introjects
I mustn't get emotional
I shouldn't have and enjoy friends

I shouldn't be playful, have fun (father was playful, stepmother serious)
I shouldn't feel needy and vulnerable
I shouldn't be angry
I should work hard
I should be a good father and husband
I shouldn't indulge myself, e.g. in therapy
I'm not competent in the adult world

Projects
Playful impulses (onto friends, his children etc.)
Anger (imagines others angry with him)
Good feelings about his appearance (sees others as attractive, not him)
Need for care, attention, touch (sees Lucy as vulnerable, needy, father unable to cope with his need to discuss mother)
His capacity for surviving in the adult world (sees others as more grown up than him)
Responsibility (is critical of others)

Retroflects
Impulse to play, behave spontaneously
Need for care, attention, touch
Need for friendship, intimacy
Sexual needs
Anger
Sadness
Joy (feels embarrassed instead)
Fear
Creativity (doesn't give enough time to his music)

Egotism
This may be involved in the form of excessive sensitivity to the approval/dis-approval of others (arising out of his stepmother's harsh treatment) which

interferes with his ability to be spontaneous in play, to express emotion and to his own sexuality.

REFERENCES

Bowlby, J. (1981) *Attachment and loss. vol II.* London: Penguin Books.

Clarkson, P. (1989) *Gestalt counseling in action.* London: Sage Publications.

Delisle, G. (1989) *A gestalt perspective of personality disorders.* Montreal: Centre d'Intervention Gestaltiste.

Fagan, J. & Shepherd, I.L. (Eds.) (1970) *Gestalt therapy now.* New York: Science & Behavior Books.

Hall, R.A. (1977) A schema of the gestalt concept of the organismic flow and its disturbance. In Smith, E. W. L. (Ed.) *The Growing Edge of Gestalt Therapy.* Secaucus, NJ: Citadel Press.

Latner, J. (1989) *The gestalt therapy book.* Highland, NY: Gestalt Journal Press.

Perls, F. (1970) Four lectures. In Fagan, J. & Shepard, I.L. (Eds.), *Gestalt therapy now.* New York: Science & Behavior Books.

Perls, F. (1973) *The gestalt approach & eye witness to therapy.* New York: Science & Behavior Books.

Perls, F., Heffeline, R., & Goodman, P. (1973) *Gestalt therapy.* Harmondsworth: Penguin Books.

Polster, E. & Polster, M. (1974) *Gestalt therapy integrated.* New York: Vintage Books.

◊

3

THE BROKEN DOLL:
A SURVIVOR'S JOURNEY INTO LIFE

Ruth Wolfert

❖◀❖

THE SURVIVOR

Dora[1] was 26 years old when she came to see me, an Orthodox Jew living at home with her mother and the uncle who had raised her.[2] They lived alongside other relatives in a close-knit Orthodox community with traditional values. People rarely traveled outside for any reason, much less for therapy. Only Dora's determination to survive led her to venture forth in response to an announcement for a self-esteem workshop. I was later to discover she was a survivor in other ways as well. But first she had to awaken to life.

When Dora walked into my office in the fall of 1978, she had big blonde hair and a beaten look. Her face was tight under her glossy make-up. She hunched forward in her chair, her voice moving with restless fluency. Almost no breath escaped her closed chest; no sense of contact showed in her wide, unfocused eyes. Her disconnected words rushed out ceaselessly, filling the void with desperation.

---

1   I want to thank "Dora" for her help in reconstructing the therapy sessions and for her account of her therapy with me which appears after my report. We chose "Dora" as the Americanized version of her Jewish pseudonym "Deborah" (pronounced DeBORah) and have altered some biographical details to protect her identity.

2   Her father had died before she was born.

"I've been in therapy a year and nothing's happened. Everything's just the same. I don't know if anything can help me. I'll come if it'll do any good." She waved her right hand despondently. "But I need special work — individual counseling. You do that, don't you?" Dora glanced in my direction for the first time since she started to talk. Her eyes showed the strain of struggling to think about the difficulties that were overwhelming her.

I acknowledged that I did individual work. She exhaled and sat farther back in her chair and, with her head down, launched into another spate of words: "There's something wrong with me. I'll never get married. My old boyfriend just got married. He was right, I'm no good. I'm a loser." Dora seemed removed and hopeless as her eyes began to tear. No access point there.

My eyes went to her hand. As she was talking, her right hand had closed and was moving slightly with her words. Could that motion be a sign of incipient life? I suggested she exaggerate the movement and experience what she was doing. It turned into a punch, and I asked her to speak with the motion.

In a voice that sounded connected for the first time, Dora said: "I'm not married." Punch. "I'm not thin." Punch. "I'm not popular." Punch. "I'm not doing anything." Punch. "I'm stupid. I'm a loser." Punch. Punch.

At last, I thought, some possibility of life. But her voice, although more emotional, sounded constrained, almost strangled; and her breath was still shallow. I asked her to change chairs and put her "I" statements into the "you" form. After a moment of confusion, Dora came alive in the role of the aggressor.

Her eyes flashed as she punched out at the "Dora" in the empty chair, roaring triumphantly: "You're not married! You're not thin! You're not popular! You're not working! You're stupid! You're just a loser!" Then rising to a scream, "A LOSER!"

Dora's lip was curled, a faint flush colored her face and her breath was coming in rapid bursts. I asked how she felt. "Cruel, vicious and very powerful," she answered without hesitation.

I thought Dora would immediately recognize the speaker; but when I asked who it was, she seemed puzzled. Her head had sunk back down, her eyes moved from side to side, blindly pleading — who could it be? She seemed on the verge of defeat, of falling back to her image of herself as a stupid loser. If she slid back now, the work would not crystallize for her. "What about people from the past?" I prompted. It was an immediate click.

Dora sat upright for the first time and gasped out, "It's Dode,[3] my uncle, Dode!" Then her eyes clouded over. "No, it can't be," she mumbled as her head sank. She wavered for a while between seeing her uncle clearly as the harsh critic and drooping in confluential blankness. At last she settled forward in her chair and said, "It's definitely Dode!" Dora seemed amazed, but quickly saw the implication. If the critical voice was her uncle's, it was possible she wasn't just innately, irredeemably a loser. Perhaps her life could be turned around after all!

AWAKENINGS

Dora's desperate search for esteem told a sad story of neglect and betrayal[4], so it was particularly important that I always dwell with her contactfully. In the safety of the Ruth-Dora field, she often did experiments that enabled her to experience her blocks directly. Then in every session, we would meet as Ruth and Dora, at least for a moment or two.

In the beginning, our work centered on Dora's awareness of her body, breathing and images. It was vital she expand the grounds of her self-support. She had never focused on her body before, but took to the work at once. From her first body scan[5], she got in touch with streamings, burnings, pains and energy surges — experiences she learned to support with her breathing. Dora was on her way to becoming somebody.[6]

---

3   Pronounced DOHdee, Dora's name for the uncle who had raised her.

4   For those interested in diagnosis, Dora's DSM IV classification would be
     Narcissistic Personality Disorder.

5   A process of scanning body sensations inch by inch.

6   Laura Perls used to say that without a body you were nobody, so now Dora was
     becoming somebody.

She often felt inchoate energy streaming down her legs both in session and at home. This fascinated her. What was it trying to tell her? It didn't answer. After months, Dora heard her energy's voice at last. "I want to make you notice now," it said, but still would not give specifics. The content was all in her images.

From the start, Dora had vivid images, so I often asked her to draw. At first, she would take a big black crayon and move it back and forth across the paper, angrily intent on blackening every bit of white (see fig. 1). She would say uninformative words like "dark" or "black" in response to my questions about the pictures. But I knew her excitement was strong, so I kept suggesting she draw and watched for a new gestalt to form.

One day she put a blue dot in the sea of black (see fig. 2, circled). "The blue dot is ME!" she told me, awed by the presence of her existence. Now Dora was becoming more than a somebody. She was starting to sense herself as a unique individual with her own reality.

figure 1

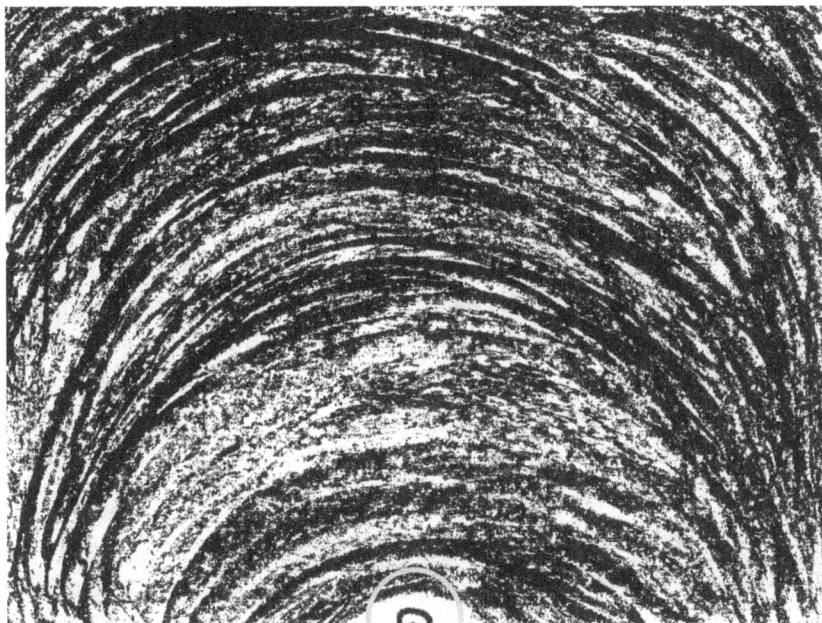

figure 2

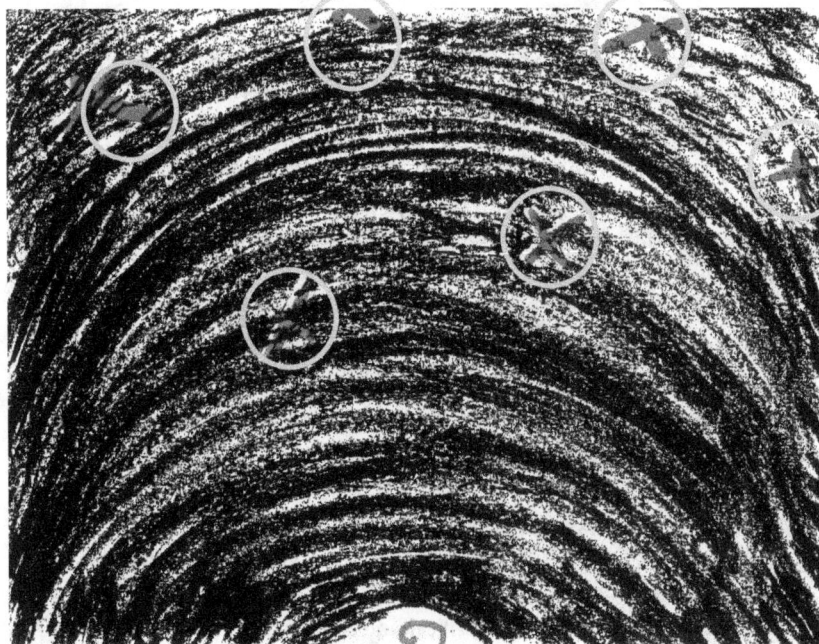

figure 3

As time went on, her drawings slowly changed. The black became less prominent; the blue took up more space. Then Dora started adding red crosses (see fig. 3, circled). It was some time before she understood their meaning, but one day she was able to say, "Mistakes." She had finally told me what she was so afraid of, what she kept diminishing herself about. In ensuing weeks, she got in touch with her fear of being punished if she made mistakes or was wrong or bad in any way.

Dora was the shame of her family for being unmarried at 26 — most 26-year-olds in the community were long married with several children. She often went on arranged dates[7] with men from appropriate families, hoping to find someone to marry.

After each of these dates, her uncle would be waiting to quiz her on the possibilities for marriage. When I asked Dora to play the scene, she attacked as her uncle and squirmed as herself, and would not go further. But she was growing, and I soon asked her to play the scene again.

"Well, little one," Dora chortled as her uncle in a tone of artificial jollity. "So how did the date go?"

"I don't know," she responded plaintively.

"What do you mean, you don't know?" "her uncle" boomed. "I, who have had dinners in my honor, can't hold my head up in the community because you are unmarried. And you tell me you DON'T KNOW how the date went. What have I done to deserve this? You are bad, VERY BAD!"

"I'm bad," Dora said in a low voice with her head drooping. "I can't find anyone to marry. There's something wrong with me."

"Nonsense! There are plenty of boys to marry, just pick one."

Dora exhaled with force and fell silent. She had reached a dead end.

To open the impasse, I asked her to take the role of a judge. She began jabbing a finger at the "Dora" in the empty chair as she became the judge: "You are bad!" *Jab.* "You make your family suffer!" *Jab.* "You deserve to be

---

7   Traditional Orthodox dating is directed toward marriage. Family background and reputation are considered critical, and couples often marry after a few months.

punished!" *Jab*. "You will NEVER get married!" *Jab*. "You are a LOSER!" *Jab!* "BAD! BAD!" *JAB! JAB!*

Dora sat erect with flushed cheeks, breathing rapidly. When I asked, she said she felt "powerful and triumphant."

I thought she might go further, so I asked her to play the judge toward her uncle. Dora gasped and turned pale. "Toward *Dode?*" she asked in a small voice. "He's so big." Her eyes widened as she looked up — a fearful child in the presence of a threatening adult.

I asked her how big the judge was. Dora pointed high above her head, but stayed small, gasping that Dode was the judge. I asked her to be aware of her breath which was shallow and irregular. Her breathing began to deepen, and she soon strengthened enough to judge her uncle. Dora stood and pointed her finger down accusingly at "Dode." "*You* are bad," she declared as the judge. "*You* make everyone suffer! *You* deserve to be punished!" She started jabbing her finger. "You are BAD!" *Jab*. "VERY, VERY BAD!" *Jab! Jab!* "I HATE YOU!" she screamed at the top of her lungs and sat down, breathing heavily.

We looked at one another for a moment in silence. Then Dora smiled at me and said, "Very, very powerful," without waiting to be asked. "I feel on top of the world."

Dora had always been Dode's favorite. He would caress her lovingly, calling her his little doll, his lollipop, but at any moment his mood could turn. He would often go into fits of rage — shouting insults, beating her sister and slapping back her mother as she was yelling at him to stop. Through the battles, Dora always stayed silent, removed from the uproar, not taking sides.

Now she began speaking up to her uncle at home. Once when her mother and sister were screaming back at him, she joined in. She took sides and screamed at her uncle for bullying them. It hurt him deeply. He had been ill for some time; now he got worse. Dora was often asked to sit on his bed in his darkened bedroom, something she had always hated. Now she dared to refuse. Soon his weakened body gave out. She was numb during the mourning.

POWER AND COLLAPSE

After the shock of her uncle's death wore off, Dora had a great burst of energy. "I'm going to Switzerland for the summer," she announced triumphantly. "I can see some of my relatives there."

I was concerned about what might happen and suggested experiments to allow her to probe her high-energy state, something I had done before with little result. This time also, her experience did not deepen. Over and over, Dora strutted around the room, exuding power — nothing could stand in her way. I was uneasy, unsure how she would meet the challenge ahead, but there was no way to protect her from herself. To try to stop her would have been an act of violence.

So Dora went to Switzerland and, sadly, collapsed. She developed a perforated bowel that required an emergency operation and returned home with thinning' hair, meager periods and severe constipation.

It was her hair loss that alarmed her. Dora would point to her head and say sorrowfully, "Look at that spot. My hair is falling out." She kept focusing on the damage and her desolate hope that I would save her. When I asked how she felt, she would ignore me and wail, "But what should I do? I'm becoming bald!"

I persisted and kept asking for her feelings. After some weeks, Dora finally got in touch with her intense disappointment in me. "Why didn't you stop me going to Switzerland?" she asked. "I couldn't take it, all alone with those strange doctors."

At last we were talking directly. I told her of my unease and unsureness before she had left. Dora's eyes widened as she took in that I had not known, that I could not know, what would happen. Her desperate insistence that I restore her abated. She started expressing the depth of her despair and rage at the effects of the operation, and even touched on her shame. As she released her feelings from her body bit by bit, her energy rose.

Now Dora wanted to do everything. This was a modulation of her high-power state, not as out of contact as before, but still immoderate. She wanted to go back to school, get a job, get married, get thin, study Torah. When I asked her to prioritize, she said she wanted to do them all. Then next time, she'd come in with nothing done, pale and down-trodden once more. Gradually Dora was able to feel out the meaning of each plan and sense what was primary to her.

College and work were most important. Going to college would mean she was intelligent and could make something of her life. Dora had been sure she was stupid — failing all through school, unable to concentrate, being kicked out of classes since kindergarten. She experienced herself as intelligent for the first time in therapy. She grasped things quickly and people considered her capable. Now she wanted to go to college to see if she really had ability.

But getting a job was also critical. It meant independence. For some time, Dora had worked in the family business, going in once or twice a week without specific duties. She sat there doing nothing, feeling bad about herself.

Dora decided to get a "real job" immediately and also go to college when the new term started. She took a high-pressure sales job part-time and started in high-energy mode. She got plenty of prospects, but was rarely able to close.

She began dragging herself into sessions barely breathing, hunched over and anxious. I would ask her to sense her body, and Dora would hear her colon moaning: "Please stop. Go slow." But she wouldn't listen. Selling was the only way she could support herself part-time. I kept focusing on the impasse, with little apparent result.

Then one day, she came in looking calmer than she had in a while. She had caught a glimpse of a bag lady in a mirror on 42nd Street. When she looked again, Dora saw it was herself. She couldn't believe it; she looked so down-trodden and wrinkled. As she had stood there in shock, she heard her colon say: "Too much stress. Go slow." Shaken, she left her job.

I asked her to talk with her colon. It moaned, "Pity me. Take care of me."

"But I quit the job," she answered.

"It's not only the job. Yes, you quit, and I'm glad. But I need gentleness. You stay out late every night. You binge on sugar. Please stop. Take care of me."

Dora began crying. "It's true," she said to me. "I'm abusing my body. I keep running to doctors about my body, but I need to start taking care of me."

We smiled at one another in silence, delighting in the moment.

TAKING CARE OF HERSELF

Now that Dora was paying attention to the messages from her colon, she realized she needed a low-pressure routine. After some vacillation, she decided to delay financial independence and take a low-level, part-time job while in college.

Once that was settled, she wanted to focus on her eating. Since childhood, Dora had binged and then starved herself to control her weight. I had suggested Overeaters' Anonymous, but did not insist on it. By now she understood she was in charge of her therapy as she was of her life. I would not tell her what to do.

When she came to see me, Dora was bingeing most of the day. She was ashamed of her eating and had worked on it periodically. She had experimented with chewing[8] through binges, giving her feelings a voice, accepting her appetite and transforming her energy by breathing and walking. Each time she had taken a step and binged less. Now she was no longer motivated by shame, but by a genuine desire to take care of herself. Was she ready to stop bingeing completely?

To start the work, I asked Dora to reexperience a recent binge moment by moment. She hunched over, squeezing down on her breath and began gnawing on her fingers. "I'm very, very anxious thinking about marriage-about to explode. I say to myself, 'I swear I'll only have one ice cream, that's all.' I run to the car and drive to the store. I grab up an ice cream and run back to the car. I rip off the paper and jam it in my mouth." She breathed

---

8   "During each and every meal, take one bite … and liquify the food completely by chewing." Perls, Hefferline & Goodman (1951, 1994) p. 444. The experiment allows people to assimilate introjects.

deeply. "Ahhh, ecstasy. I'm melting into the chocolate. The relief is enormous. I have no more anxiety, only bliss."

Dora clamped down on her breath again: "Now I have a gnawing pain inside, and a voice says, 'Stop.' Another voice says, 'Don't listen,' and I bolt it all down and run back to the store. I grab up a Kit Kat, rip the paper and gobble it. More joy. The voice stabs me again, 'Stop! What are you feeling?' I go blank inside and shut it out. I run and take another chocolate and cram it in my mouth. This time the voice is speaking even while I take the first bite: 'Stop! You're hurting yourself!' "

"The pain is great, but there is still some joy. I take up another Kit Kat and stuff it down. 'STOP! YOU'RE KILLING YOURSELF!' The pain is everywhere. There is no more joy. Bloated and queasy, I drive home. The binge is over." Dora sighed.

She was so alive to her experience that a short dialogue with the chocolate allowed her to realize there was no way it could ever take her pain away. But what could she do instead?

Dora decided on several experiments[9]: dialoguing with her food every time she wanted to binge, walking briskly for an hour several days a week, breathing deeply for five minutes twice a day and chewing to liquification once a meal. She did not stay with the breathing or chewing for very long, although she did return to them later. But she continued the walking for years and, most impressive of all, talked with her food through every binge from then on.

In the beginning, the food would tell Dora to breathe and walk. After a while, it told her to have her feelings. "You don't want me," the food would say. "You just want the pain I give you. Go to the real pain. Feel the feeling." And when she would get to the deepest feeling, the binge would stop. "Binges are like therapy sessions," she said one day. "I learn something from every one."

---

9   Prom the beginning, I had suggested many home experiments to Dora, mainly focusing on body and breath, to allow her to keep contacting her process and give her a sense of independence from me. She tended to do them for a while and then lose interest.

Now that Dora was working on her own so much, I was able to successfully solicit her criticisms. When pressed, she would disparage my scuffed furniture, my gloomy office, my unstylish clothing. And she began telling me of her hurt and anger when I was late, failed to smile at her arrival or ignored her in group. She was asserting herself more, increasingly becoming her own person.

GROUP

Since we had been working together, Dora had been in a women's group that focused on contact among the members. I participated as openly and transparently as possible, expressing my point of view and facilitating contact.

In the beginning, Dora remained isolated. When she was not talking about herself, she seemed to be daydreaming, and sometimes actually dozed off. Then one day, it came time for someone to leave the group, and the others all crowded around to hug her good-bye. Dora stood apart, looking at them from a distance. I smiled at her, and she met my eyes with a look of longing. She later told me that at that moment, for the first time in her life, she thought she might some day become part of, might some day belong.

After that, Dora began relating more to the women in the group, gradually becoming intimate with people outside her family for the first time. When she had wavered about becoming "the judge" to her uncle, she was emboldened by recalling how aghast the women were at his treatment of her. She had imagined their voices cheering her on as she told him off. Now that she was part of the group, she was no longer completely insulated within her community with its rigid view of authority.

It was a new experience for Dora to be with a group of people who honestly communicated their thoughts and feelings. Our openness helped her let go of her idealizations of me and become more assertive. At the same time, the group's view of her as capable and deserving encouraged her to find her own way and make something of herself.

INDECISION

But whatever advances she made, Dora would sink into indecision. She would come in pale and hunched over, barely breathing, scraping her teeth across her nails and scoring lines in them — an experience we repeatedly focused on. One day she burst into tears, suddenly recalling[10] what she had done during the horrific fights of her childhood: "When I couldn't take all the screaming and hitting at home, I'd run into the closet. I'd sit there in agony in the dark, hearing the screaming, unable to move, unable to take sides — rocking, stuffing my ears, crying and biting myself."

Now that Dora had remembered her agony in the closet, she realized she was constantly recreating it. Just as when she could not choose between her mother and her uncle, she would sink into the anguish of the closet whenever she had to make a choice between two contesting possibilities, living in what she began to call "nowhere land." She would decide and re-decide the same things over and over in a tormented frenzy. Should she or shouldn't she get her own apartment? Should she or shouldn't she choose her own career: be a teacher (her wish) or go back to the family business? And most desperate of all: should she or shouldn't she be with this or that man?

Dora had gone out with Samuel for several years, on and off. Now she wanted to decide once and for all whether to marry him. She saw him alternately as good-and-supportive and rigid-and-controlling, mirroring her childhood division of Dode into thrilling savior and terrifying persecutor. None of our work with polarities had much effect. Dora continued to maintain her divided view, hoping to keep sheltering in Samuel's perfect goodness while renouncing his rigid control.

Should she or shouldn't she marry him? She pulled at everyone to tell her what to do — but was never satisfied with the answers. One day in a frenzy of indecision, Dora called people non-stop without finding an answer. That night she dreamed her answering machine was broken. As we

---

10   When Dora started therapy, she had a few childhood memories.

worked on the dream, she saw that no one could save her from being her own person. She had to find her own answers.

So Dora began allowing her different views of Samuel to come together and started integrating her feelings for him. One day she asked someone to role-play her, while she took Samuel's part, positioning "Dora" this way and that, arranging and rearranging her. But no matter how she was placed, "Dora" never looked right to "Samuel." Dora realized she could not marry someone so critical of her. Or could she? She kept reopening her decision, tantalized by the hope of being accepted, but in the end, she left the relationship. It had become primary to be herself.

Now that Dora was resolved about Samuel, she began focusing on her weekly crisis about where to spend Shabbas[11], an enormous energy drain. Should she or shouldn't she be with her mother? With this friend or that? Away or in town? Every week she tormented herself trying to make the perfect decision. She was usually buffeted by uncertainty until the last possible moment. As she came into contact with her hope of finding a perfect Shabbas of ease and joy, Dora saw that wherever she went, she was anxious —wherever she went, she took herself with her.

We decided on an experiment: Dora was to make Shabbas plans by Tuesday night and keep to them, no matter what. It was not easy; appealing possibilities would arise late in the week. But then she'd remember she would be taking herself with her and would be able to keep to her plan. Her weekly mind-changing was over!

SMALL STEPS

Now Dora's energy rose again. Our challenge was to integrate it. She started in college full-time, rented an apartment near her mother's and decided on a more feasible way of making money than high-pressure selling: market-

---

11   The Jewish Sabbath, sundown Friday to nightfall Saturday, is a ceremonial time when the Orthodox often stay overnight at the home of relatives or friends as they can travel only by foot.

ing her own special cake. But her colon was so blocked she rarely moved her bowels. In session it would plead: "Go slow. Please slow down." Dora would listen, touched by its plea. "Small steps," she would say. "I have to take smaller steps." And then she'd get enthusiastic about an even more plausible venture that would also, ultimately, come to naught.

I stayed with her through all these turns, trusting our process to allow her to find her way. In the end, Dora reluctantly gave up money-making schemes and took a part-time, low-pressure job. She borrowed money for expenses and moved to Manhattan; college remained her top priority. In sessions, she kept experiencing the necessity of taking small steps. She was now meditating and doing the chewing experiment as well as talking through binges and walking daily. She seemed on her way.

COLLAPSE

Then, *smash!* Dora got caught cheating on a test — a remnant of her old view of herself as incapable. In a frenzy of agitation, scraping her nails with her teeth, she was back in nowhere land with a thud. As we worked, Dora got in touch with feeling hurt and vulnerable. She seemed more open, but could not maintain it. Soon she was in full retreat, saying she was no longer sure about college – maybe she should return to the family business and not become a teacher. I was surprised by the severity of her collapse and realized there was some ground we had yet to discover.

It gradually emerged that Dora was staying stuck "in the closet" to save her family, refusing to abandon them to go out and live her own life. One day I suggested she re-experience how she had been stuck as a child. Dora got in touch with her torment at being trapped in her horror-filled house. She sounded desperate as she said: "I can't go out and open my family secret. No one can know how horrible my uncle is … No, I won't stay here anymore! I want to go out into life, but it's too scary to go alone … I know, a special friend will come in and get me. Only she will know the family horror. I see her leading me outside to the other children where we all laugh and play in the sunlight."

After that, we created a separation ritual in which Dora placed her family in a row and took her formal leave of them, one by one. At the end of the ceremony, she bowed and said: "I'm going into life now."

She registered for school the next day. By that time, however, she had missed more than a month of classes. Dora was open with outsiders as never before: she threw herself on the mercy of her teachers and got permission to make up her assignments slowly. She seemed to have entered more fully into life, but could not sustain it, and again began coming to sessions blanked out.

What were we missing? Dora would come in pale, blank and drooping, although she no longer wounded herself. Each time she would convert this stuck collapse into alive fear and pain. She would express her feelings and sense the necessity of breathing and taking small steps, but next time, would again arrive drooping. She drifted away from her job and began staying at her mother's much of the week. She walked less often and no longer chewed to completion or meditated. Dora said that between sessions she felt "weak and insubstantial against the turbulence of events."

She kept calling for emergency phone work. I would suggest she draw or write her experience, but she appeared incapable of working alone. It seemed harsh and unproductive to refuse her. But what of the next day, or even the next minute? The calls did not seem to be fostering self-support. So I began requiring that Dora leave her mother's house to speak to me. It seemed like a variation on her fantasy of a special childhood friend coming in and freeing her from being stuck in the torment of her house. And she did take strength from being out: walking vitalized her, and her breathing deepened. The phone calls trickled off.

Now that Dora was stronger, she wanted to make her own way again. But then she would get terrified at the thought of living in her own apartment. "I'd be all alone," she'd cry, feeling too weak to be so separate. Although she would strengthen in each session, next time Dora would again dissolve in terror at the thought of venturing forth on her own. What deep ground had yet to be revealed?

THE HOLOCAUST

At this point, Dora had a fantasy in a breathwork workshop: "I was in a camp, in the line to be cremated. It was me, but I was older and careworn, and dressed like people in the old days. As the guards dragged me to the ovens, I told my two young sons I would come back to take care of them. I swore: 'I'll come back as your daughter.' And I did, in the fantasy anyway. I was Raisa, mother to Dode and my biological father, and now I'm Dora, their daughter."

As we worked on the Holocaust material, Dora began having nightmares. She would wake up sobbing with horror at not being able to save her family. "It's the agony of the closet," she told me. "I want to save Dode, but I can't. It's too horrible out there with the fighting, like the camps almost. I can't save anyone … Dode had a horrible life and now he's dead. I didn't save him." She wept for a long time.

To allow her to finish the experience, I asked Dora to imagine life in the camps. She said: "The horror is beyond belief. Death is everywhere: the long lines to the ovens, corpses left lying in the dirt, emaciated creatures falling over while they do hard labor. And the brutality is overwhelming. Beaten with gun butts, spit on by guards; and over and over: 'Dirty Jew.' 'Rotten scum.' Knowing that a flicker of resistance means instant death. Endless torment with nobody to save us." She sobbed and sobbed.

After that session, Dora woke up and became appalled about living in the past. I asked her to talk to the Holocaust people and she started to cry. "I feel scared to tell you, but I want to leave you now and get into life. I know you died in the worst horror imaginable. But now I want to live. Do you think I'm terrible?"

"It doesn't help us if you stay here in the darkness," she answered as the Holocaust people. "Then the Nazis will have another victim. We are dead; nothing can change that. But if you go out and live, some spark of us lives on. Go, my child, and create new life."

After that, Dora stopped mourning. She started going out and having fun.

At last, we had found the deep ground for her repeated collapses. Her family's horrific Holocaust experiences had resonated with her anguish at her uncle's brutality and the shattering family battles to make the world seem unsafe indeed. Dora had been too fearful for her safety and too guilty about not saving her family locked in perpetual torment, to escape to her own life. But was it the only deep ground? Could she now finally be in life?

DAN

I went on vacation for a month, and when I returned, Dora was on the verge of becoming engaged. She was excited by his charm, his looks and, above all, the intensity of his love for her. "His name is Dan. Dode's name was Daniel. Isn't that a riot! They're so different, like night and day. Dan is light and funny! I don't want to keep wondering about it and get stuck in 'should I or shouldn't I?' I want to jump into life and get engaged!"

And jump she did, hesitating only briefly before agreeing to marry him. But their relationship started degenerating right away. Within a week, Dora was agonizing about whether to break it off before the public announcement the following month. Swamped, she was back in "should I or shouldn't I?" with a bang.

"Sometimes I think Dan really cares," she said. "He tells me he can't live without me, that I'll never want for anything. But he keeps undermining me, like when he looked at my face carefully in the sun and said marriage would smooth my wrinkles away. I never noticed any wrinkles before, but now I keep checking the mirror." Dora sat upright. "Yikes, just like Dode giving me money to 'fix myself up,' as if something was wrong with me. I always hated that."

As she told me her experiences with Dan, Dora often recalled her life with Dode. But she kept asking: was Dan saving her or undermining her? One day, I invited her to take a position that embodied the attitude of the question. She sat as if in the closet, but with her eyes peeking out from between her fingers. She realized she both wanted to know and didn't want to know. Either answer would bring her more into life. She had wanted to jump into the heart of life. Now she was holding tight to the periphery.

And then their relationship took a darker turn. Dan began to question Dora's interest in men they saw in the street or at restaurants. He kept hammering away at her, no matter what she said. I asked her to dialogue with him.

"Stop badgering me!" Dora said. "There's nothing to tell, but you're never satisfied. Leave me in peace!"

"But it's for your own good," she responded as Dan. "I need to know everything about you in order to save you."

"I want you to save me," she answered. "But I don't want you to keep picking at me!"

Dora would speak up to Dan like that in session, but never in life.

Then just before the engagement was made public, she had a dream: "I walked into the ocean, first into the shallow margin, then into the deeper water. The ocean rose up until I couldn't stand; I could barely tread water. Then the waves came crashing down on my head in torrents, swamping me, shaking me awake." She sighed. "I knew I couldn't come out of the engagement alive." But she still didn't speak up, so their engagement was announced.

Dora was in agony. Dan was becoming more and more possessive. He didn't want her spending time with anyone else. Friends were forbidden. Therapy was evil, the cause of all her problems. Dora began sneaking her phone calls to friends and her sessions with me. I was becoming increasingly concerned, but both of us realized the only way to move through the impasse was to keep focusing on the powerful forces pulling her in opposite directions.

Then one day, she came in bellowing. "WHAT IS WRONG WITH THIS THERAPY? I HAVEN'T GROWN AT ALL! YOU ARE HOLDING ME BACK."

I went into shock. It was like being battered in a maelstrom. I went blank as I had in my childhood when I was assaulted for no reason I could ever figure out.

Dora was still yelling: "YOU ARE ONLY HOLDING ONTO ME FOR THE MONEY. YOU ARE KEEPING ME DOWN, NOT LETTING ME GET MARRIED!"

I just sat there, unable to say anything or even to think clearly. Eventually she stopped shouting and spoke in a more moderate, although highly irritated tone: "Why don't you help me get married?" Unable to deal with the assault, I responded by focusing on her desire to get married, and soon Dora was talking about how she was trapped into staying with Dan. "If I leave, he'll tell my family secrets. I can't have everyone knowing about my uncle screaming and hitting." Then she spoke to Dan: "I HATE your pounding at me! You are SICK with your demands." But she still did not confront him in person.

Then two sessions later, Dora came in screaming again: "THIS THERAPY IS BULLSHIT! YOU'RE HURTING ME, MAKING ME SELFISH AND DEMANDING!"

I went into shock again, just barely able to stay with her under the barrage. Finally, her abuse trailed off, and we made the transition into a regular session. This time, Dora got in touch with the thrill of being saved: "It's thrilling when Dan looks at me. It's as if his eyes go right through me. Even being afraid is thrilling. I have to watch every word. It's all so dramatic … Yikes, just like with Dode."

But regardless of what happened in our work, Dora would often start sessions by screaming at me. I never got used to it and went into shock each time. On occasion, I had fantasies of her leaving therapy, but never asked her to go. In my calmer moments, I heard her pleas for help underneath the abuse. I could not turn her away.

I was working intensively in my own therapy on what remained unfinished from my childhood abuse. I had stayed open to those original assaults partly because I had sensed them as pleas for help. No wonder I was caught now. But I was getting desperate. Not only did I keep going into shock in Dora's sessions, but she seemed stuck in endless, fruitless turmoil. I had to find a new approach.

Then, one day when Dora was in a frenzy of agitation about Dan, I suggested a new type of breath meditation. I invited her to focus on both her breathing and her agitation at the same time, and then asked her to feel her connection to the universe. Dora breathed in from the universe, letting it touch all of her, then breathed out to the vastness of all that is, deepening her connection with each breath. She was silent for a long time, breathing deeply. At the end of the session, she said: "I am totally at peace for the first time in my life. I have come home to myself. Now I am at home in the universe, like the Little Prince."

I knew what made Dora's experience so strong was her growing spirituality. As a child, she had turned inward out of desperation. She had been trapped in "nowhere land" until reading *The Little Prince* (St. Exupery, 1943) opened the possibility of voyaging in a universe beyond — a possibility that later became ground for her spirituality. Dora had begun opening a spiritual connection early in the therapy; now she strengthened it.

She soon became aware of an "inner voice," a spiritual dimension distinct from her throng of introjected voices and surface thoughts. This opened a new possibility. I would suggest that Dora ask her inner voice to guide her in a process of experiencing her blocks to taking more and more responsibility for whatever she was working on, going deeper and deeper until the issue dissolved. Soon she was doing this work both in session with me and at home herself. Her assaults had lessened with the new breathwork, and now they stopped entirely.

During the course of our therapy, Dora had remembered much that was previously blank from her school years. As she entered more powerfully into the inner voice work, she began seeing images along with the words. And then she began to recall events from her early childhood — wonderful moments of being petted and caressed by Dode, horrible scenes of being pushed away by him, sad experiences of being excluded by her mother and sister, uncomfortable memories of Dode lying on her bed, of his questioning her about her games of doctor.

But Dora still could not decide about Dan. Should she or shouldn't she stay with him? By now she was speaking up more, yet he still wouldn't listen. She kept at it, hoping to get him to regard her. Why couldn't she resolve the situation? I kept working with the impasse, watching for new ground to emerge — but it never did.

Then one day, her sister handed her a quiz in a magazine: "Does Your Man Hate Women?" Dora answered "yes" to all the questions. Yes, he was jealous and possessive. Yes, she had to walk on eggshells. Yes, he was preventing her from seeing friends. Yes, yes, yes, to all the questions. Now she realized that he would never accept her as she was.

Dora made up her mind to break the engagement. Each time she started to tell Dan, though, she would become doubtful, overcome by his view of her as bad and the thrilling prospect of being saved. But her hope kept diminishing, and eventually Dora stopped seeing Dan and began to find her own way again.

HEALING

In the peaceful silence of her life after Dan, Dora concentrated on healing. Now she was finally ready to join Overeaters' Anonymous and focus on her eating with a sponsor. Although she had shortened her binges by consistently dialoguing with her food, she still started many of them — a pattern she continued in OA.

But Dora loved the meetings. She basked in their free atmosphere, soaking in the permission to expand. She had been so pounded that she only opened her constricted feelings by degrees, and remained weak and shaky for months. She slowly converted her stuck pain and shame into living experiences and assimilated them bit by bit, growing sturdier and more robust. During this time, Dora turned to Judaism with a new sureness. She had long been uncertain about how observant of the laws she wanted to be, or even whether to remain Orthodox. Now she committed herself. Her spirituality took root in Judaism where she found a life-affirming identity. She even started using her Jewish name, Deborah[12].

---

12   Pronounced DeBORah.

THE BROKEN DOLL

Deborah yearned to experience love without pain, but for her they were always intertwined. One day as she was focusing on how they were linked, she suddenly began to shake with a memory. She had long remembered her discomfort at her uncle lying on her bed. Now she recalled sucking his penis as a baby. "What a combination! A sour taste mixed with the sweet warmth of being loved. And worst of all, I would suddenly be thrown down on the cold floor. Loved and thrown out!" Deborah burst out sobbing and then became confused and doubtful. "Maybe I'm making it up," she said. "It couldn't have happened." She decided to ask her mother.

The talks with her mother made her more sure of the incest. Her mother thought her uncle selfish enough about his needs to be capable of it, and recalled often seeing Deborah as a toddler on the floor next to a bed where Dode was lying. Then too, there was Deborah's delayed development. She didn't speak until after she was three, and for years had seemed lost in a fog.

I asked Deborah to speak to Dode. She sighed and said: "I loved you. How could you do this to me, your little doll?" Her jaw tightened, "You used to call me 'lollipop.' Ugh, what a sick joke! You abused me! And I thought I was so special." She bowed her head and added in a low voice: "But maybe I'm making it up. Maybe I'm the bad one." She turned to me and asked if I thought it had happened.

It was crucial that Deborah find her own truth. I suggested she tell Dode the value of being doubtful. "If I'm doubtful," she said, "then I don't have to decide what to do. I don't have to speak. I can keep your secret … Ohmygod, just like when I was a baby."

She turned to me sobbing. "I was so confused," she said. "Dode belonged with Mommy, but he was with me. He loved me, but when Mommy came, he threw me away. I didn't know what to do — bite it or love it. It was horrible; but it was the only love I got, so it was wonderful. Without Dode, I'd have nothing. I'd be stuck with Mommy, and she was so cold." She burst into tears again. "All I could do was retreat into nowhere land." Deborah sat up in her chair and spoke directly to her uncle: "How could you do this to me?"

"I didn't mean to hurt you," she answered as Dode, "but my life was so brutal. Everyone was so mean. Then you came along, an adorable pink and white baby. You were my ray of sun, the only thing I had. And I didn't think you'd realize. You were so young."

When she remembered the incest, Deborah had already assimilated some of her deep pain and shame, so her feelings did not completely swamp her. She was able to sob and rage freely, crying out her disgust and shame at having sucked her uncle's penis; shrieking out her devastation at his betrayal, at being violated, used and abandoned. These were the feelings, along with her forlorn yearning to counter them and be valued — be saved, be special, be loved, that were the deep ground for her impasse with Dan, with all men. They were the feelings she had fogged out in nowhere land, acted out in worthlessness and indecision, and had tried to swallow down with food — only to have them surface as self-blame about her bingeing.

Once Deborah's feelings about the incest settled down, she took a big step and joined Gray Sheet, a 12-step eating program that had a strict diet. Deborah followed the regimen, stopped bingeing on food completely, and became healthier and more present. She found something else to binge on, however. Artificial sweeteners were allowed on the diet, and she would bolt down 40, 50, or even 100 packets when things got bad enough.

JOSEPH

Since her engagement to Dan, Deborah had been too shattered to date anyone seriously. Now she met Joseph. She was entranced by him. He was so gentle, moving slowly and delicately through life. She blossomed in his company, and the first few months were idyllic.

Then, *crash!* Joseph told her he didn't have any money. She came to session in distress, but in a different way. Deborah had not wounded herself for some time. Now she did not sag either. This time her teeth were clenched, her jaw set and her lips pursed. I asked her to feel her mouth, and she began to snarl at Joseph: "You don't have any money! Grrr. What am I doing in this relationship? Grrr. YOU CAN'T MAKE IT! GRRR! GRRR!" She imagined Joseph remaining silent, his head bowed. But that did not stop her. Deborah kept attacking him until she ran out of words.

This was how she had looked when she had blasted me during her engagement to Dan. But I had grown since then and could now be with Deborah's fearsome onslaughts. I asked her to focus on her face, and she imagined it as stone: "I feel myself stiffening against Joseph, refusing to be open. That way he can't hurt me."

As Deborah spoke, her face softened, and she spoke of her disappointment. "If he doesn't have money, then I'm not special. I'm not saved. I'm just one of. So human, ugh." Being human felt like being a worm on the ground with everyone treading on her. But Deborah was also attracted to being real and letting her humanness show. It was her growing edge. For some time, she had been wearing little make-up and jewelry. With Joseph's encouragement, she even stopped bleaching her hair.

So Deborah would come forward, entranced by Joseph's realness, his gentle steadiness. Then she would see him as too withdrawn, not grand enough or not PAYING ATTENTION to her, and would abruptly shut down and berate him.

Deborah began calling for emergency sessions again. We had agreed that she would not ask me for extra sessions, but would instead attend additional 12-step meetings when she was in distress. Now she explained that in meetings she always got feedback to drop Joseph. "Therapy is the only place I get a sense I can work things out with him. No matter how impossible I think he is when I come in, by the time I leave, I see my role and have hopes for the relationship." We decided that, for the time being, she could call for extra appointments.

I knew it would be critical for Deborah to start working more on her own again. When she called for an emergency appointment, I suggested inner voice work or a breath meditation. I would stay on the phone with her for a few minutes until she could take off by herself. She saw she could get in touch with herself on her own and began doing spiritual work at home again.

At this point, Deborah and Joseph started coming to see me as a couple once or twice a month. They were polar in many ways: most importantly in Deborah's tendency to self-involvement and Joseph's other-directedness; in her emphasis on momentary feelings and his concentration on a through line. I often suggested experiments in which Deborah was to pay attention to Joseph and listen for his underlying messages, while Joseph was to express himself and focus on fluctuations in feelings. As the two of them became more flexibly various, they developed more appreciation of each other and grew closer.

They began mentioning the possibility of marriage, although neither was ready to commit immediately. But by now Deborah was being pressed. For some time, there had been an ever-louder chorus of relations telling her to either get engaged to Joseph or drop him. Her family seemed to have no concept of developing a relationship. Either a person was a match for you or not, something that should have been evident in their first few months of dating.

When Deborah was lambasted by her relatives, she would see Joseph as flawed, and become stone-faced and abusive. He would gently turn her abuse aside, and she would melt toward him and push her family away. Then there would be relative peace until the cycle of pressure and abuse started again. At last Joseph put his foot down: No more abuse! She stopped for a while, but was soon berating him again. It was too much for her to stay in contact with him consistently.

At other times, Deborah had a "fake voice" with Joseph, a variation of not speaking up. It was a voice of exaggerated sweetness, polar to the snarl of stone face. As we worked, she found the middle ground of her true voice, a way of expressing herself to others in keeping with her inner voice. She began speaking truly to Joseph as she never had to a man before, but would still revert to her fake voice and to abuse, the modes in her family. Before Deborah could become more authentic with Joseph, she had to separate from them.

SEPARATING

For years, Deborah had realized she would have to leave her mother's side to get married. It seemed as if her mother wanted her to marry — indeed, was continually pushing her into dates with "great guys" solicited from the far-flung Orthodox society. But no one was ever good enough. "Drop him," her mother would say at the first sign of difficulty. "With your looks and background, you could have anyone."

Her mother was also disdainful of her career. Deborah had graduated from college soon after breaking her engagement to Dan and had gone on to get an MA in Education. She was now teaching in a special school for Orthodox girls with learning disabilities. Her mother kept talking of a woman who owned a large school, "She's a millionaire, really someone." Then Deborah would become ashamed of being a lowly teacher, but would quickly rebound and realize she liked teaching.

Yet Deborah could not stand her ground with her mother about men; she would often get swamped and take on her mother's contemptuous point of view. So Deborah asked her to say nothing negative about Joseph. But he kept getting dismissive waves of the hand, while a parade of "great guys" was offered as dates.

One day when Deborah was swept up in daydreaming about one of these wondrous creatures, I asked her to imagine the perfect man. She thought of a millionaire: a handsome, smiling, outgoing man giving her a life of ease in a luxurious house. She saw that her pain did not go away. It grew ever larger as she imagined herself forever locked in an answering smile. She sighed with relief at the comfort of being with Joseph, as hidden and hurt as he was. For she was hidden and hurt too. They could share their pain.

But between sessions, Deborah would often blank out her affinity with Joseph, tightening into stone face to shut him out. One day I asked her to feel how she was tightening in her body as well as her face, and then to exaggerate it . She sensed herself getting smaller and had a flash of being a little child holding on tightly to her mother's dress. Deborah burst into tears, declaring: "I won't ever leave you, Mommy."

I asked her to sense what she wanted by holding on. "To be safe," she said. "My mother was cold to me, always. She and my sister and aunt are the world of women. They talk and talk to one another, but never to me. They sneer at everybody who's alive. Only the dead seem loved — especially my mother's dear little blonde sister lost to the Nazis." Deborah sighed. "I want to join in, but I'm an outsider — ignored. I hold on to my mother, so I can belong. But if I speak up, I'm treated with scorn."

To belong with her mother, Deborah would often retreat to the safety of stone face. One day as she was focusing on her stony face, it felt dead. She started weeping: "For your sake, Mommy, I wish I was dead. That way you could always keep my ashes with you and never be alone … But I'm also angry at you, Ma. I want to live my own life!" So the Holocaust was still reverberating in Deborah's attachment to her mother. Now that it was surfacing, would she separate more?

Soon Deborah started to have a sense of being tied to her mother by invisible strings. One day, she explored being a puppet, moving back and forth, this way and that — pulled by her mother's strings. The experience was so complete, I suggested a ceremonial separation. Deborah used her fingers as a scissors to cut the strings; her breathing deepened, and she felt her love for Joseph. Although she would revert to stone face, she would cut the strings, and her heart would again open to Joseph.

Now that she was separating from her mother more, Deborah started focusing on her uncle again. She came to see his brutality as part of the original stone face[13] and got back in touch with her terror and rage at being attacked by him. She didn't mention the incest, however, so I asked her to talk to him about it, and resolved to keep alert to opportunities for completion in the future. Deborah screamed her pain and rage at Dode for incesting her and then got in contact with her fear of refusing his "yucky" loving. I suggested she imagine what might happen.

---

13   Stone face was an introjected amalgam of her mother's contempt and her uncle's assaulting, which in turn, were probably introjected from Holocaust experiences.

In her fantasy, Deborah heard her uncle saying: "If you don't give me what I need, you won't be special anymore. I'll beat you just like the others. You won't be saved from my punches." Deborah shivered. Then she saw her mother disdainfully wave the outside world away, saying: "Uch, uch. Never trust anyone. Stay with me." Her uncle again: "I'm good to you and keep you safe. Stay with me." Deborah hesitated, sinking lower in her chair. Then Joseph beckoned to her. "Come out and play with me," he said, echoing her childhood friends. She knew that if she stayed in the house, she would molder and die along with her family. Deborah shook with fear, but she went outside to Joseph where they started laughing and playing.

Meanwhile, Joseph had also been growing. For a long while, he had been reluctant to commit himself to marriage, but more recently had wanted to become formally engaged. Now Deborah agreed.

MARRIAGE

Even after their engagement, Deborah wanted to move into marriage gradually, getting used to each little step. But each time she was on the verge of setting a wedding date, she would panic. All of a sudden Joseph would seem too withdrawn, too much of a risk. As we worked, she would re-own her projection, sensing her own withdrawal and feeling her pain underneath. Then she would edge toward marrying him, only to flare up in panic a short while later. She was moving forward perceptibly over time, but with such turmoil, it was critical to find a way to open the cycle.

I turned to the spiritual use of will, creating experiments in which Deborah could embrace the whole of her experience and choose whether to let go and allow a new figure to emerge. On experiencing herself as shut down, for instance, she could choose either to remain safe in that way or to let go and be with the present actuality. When she let go, Deborah would sense herself as free and whole, separate from her introjected pattern of shutting down, separate from her mother. Soon she was working with these choices on her own as well as in session and proceeding toward marriage with more resolution.

Meanwhile Joseph was slowly growing and had developed a solid business. Deborah realized his tiny steps were carrying him forward and became less apprehensive about entrusting herself to him. Then too, she had grown more buoyant, more willing to enter an imperfect situation. So Deborah gave herself over to friends who became like a loving family. They steadied her with gentle assurance at each move forward, carrying her tenderly toward marriage.

And so Deborah and Joseph got married. During the first few months of their marriage, Deborah continued to feel ignored by Joseph's lack of fervor. But if she could bear to stay with her pain, her perception would shift, and he no longer seemed so distant. And over time she became more attuned and was able to feel his love in his small murmurs.

Deborah had not binged on food for quite a while and had even graduated from the strict diet of Gray Sheet to a more moderate program. But she kept gorging on artificial sweeteners. She had tried cutting down several times unsuccessfully. Now she decided to stop completely. At long last, no more bingeing!

Then Deborah's challenge was to face, unbuffered, her raw vulnerability. In the beginning, she often retreated into stone face, shutting Joseph out, even abusing him at times. Then she saw she was afraid of becoming too close to him: he was bound to die, like the people in the Holocaust. Over time, she realized she had a choice between living with death and opening to life. So Deborah let go by degrees and opened her heart more fully to Joseph, allowing herself to trust in life. And soon she was rejoicing; she was pregnant with new life.

And then tragedy — a miscarriage. Deborah was heartsick. One more death to add to the endless deaths of the Holocaust. It was almost unbearable, but she did not collapse. For the first time, Deborah faced a crushing blow without shutting down.

As she grieved for her lost baby, she began mourning her uncle again, but without mentioning the incest. I suggested she picture the whole Dode, incest and all. She saw a large ailing dragon covered with bandages, still massive, but lonely and no longer able to breathe fire. As she looked at him, Deborah felt sad for him and his death and also hurt and angry at his abuse.

So she had come to an integration, but her initial avoidance showed me I needed to become even more active in working toward completion. I suggested writing regularly about the incest. Although her feelings were often too raw to face alone, she did write in fits and starts, and we continued our occasional work in session until her pain lost its sharpness.

TERMINATION

Then Joseph got a remarkable business opportunity in the West. As Deborah struggled with the issue of leaving her family and friends, I suggested the chewing experiment[14] again, which she did consistently for the first time. As she chewed, her eating become more self-regulating, and she began eating healthy meals without placing restrictions on herself. At the same time, she examined her confluential ties to her family and separated more from them. So in 1986, Deborah and Joseph moved out West. The first year, she came back so often and had so many sessions, it was almost as if she had not left. But gradually, she let go more. Ultimately, she settled into a pattern of visiting New York twice a year and coming to see me then.

Soon after the move, Deborah began teaching in an Orthodox girls' school. She kept getting closer to Joseph in her usual back and forth fashion, and then got pregnant again. All her old fears came up, but she was able to face them and bring the baby to term. At last, Deborah brought forth new life into the world! Now death lost much of its hold. Shortly afterwards, she got pregnant again and had four children in all. Although her days sometimes seem a series of crises, she is usually happy to be with the bustling life at home and in the school where she continues to teach part-time.

As we worked on preparing this chapter, Deborah told me how she felt about our therapy. She saw the stuck pain in which her sister and mother were living and recalled how she had felt before. Her profound gratitude toward me and the therapy moved her to tears. She told me how she had

---

14   See note 8.

been inspired by my own journey of discovery and growth, a journey to which she is now dedicated.

NOTES TO THE READER

In this chapter, I wrote of sessions that were pivotal in Deborah's growth, so the reader may get a sense of our work as a series of dramatic scenes based on role-shuttling. But the therapy was built on our relating, and we ordinarily focused on the details of process, small awarenesses of body and breathing: the work of ground-building and assimilating, with small shoots of growth.

I elected to write about a long-term therapy with many difficulties as a way of showing the importance of continuing to grow as a therapist. Although it seems more coherent in writing than in the living of it, I have tried to give a sense of how puzzled and distressed I was at times. Then my challenge was to grow, to stretch beyond my comfortable known to find new ways to fully meet Deborah.

THE WAY OF A SURVIVOR

I also offer this therapy to further understanding of survivors. I saw immediately that Deborah had a tenacious will to survive, although I did not recognize it as a reaction to having survived horrific events. Without it, she might have sunk. Over time, I came to understand Deborah as a survivor of deep and abiding effects of the Holocaust, allowing me to see the extent of the suffering that endures to this day.

I also came to see her as a survivor of family brutality and, ultimately, incest. Deborah recalled the incest in the early 1980's, long before the controversy about the validity of retrieved memories. The facts behind such recollections are never as important to me as the emotions, which are real, and invariably a reaction to something. In this case, I had no doubts. Deborah's memory came without prompting in ordinary awareness and made her history comprehensible. Her doubt was part of her perennial uncertainty, itself a reaction to the abuse. As she faced the issue, she became more confident in all respects, and later found her uncle had also approached her sister. Although Deborah's pain has not completely ended and may always have ripples, the incest is no longer of central concern to her.

When abuse is horrific enough, a child cannot encompass the wound. With such a massive breach in the grounds of security, the loss is metaphysical. The world is no longer safe; the coming self does not emerge. And Deborah was doubly unsafe as she was locked into the abuse by her paralyzing dread of the Holocaust lurking outside, dread made real by her uncle's brutality and her mother's perpetual mourning — so she could not escape to live in the world of school and friends.

In extremis, unable to move forward or backward, with no other recourse, survivors of abuse are usually driven inward in their pursuit of safety. There they can remain, languishing on the margins of life, ever-ready to fragment or withdraw. With the ultimate grounds of security shattered, survivors must find a new connection to the universe to heal the destruction. As in the therapy with Deborah, their ossified flight inward can be transformed, step by step, into a spiritual connection (Wolfert, 1989), healing the metaphysical breach and developing new grounds of fundamental safety, so they can emerge fully into the world.

REFERENCES

Perls, F, Hefferline, R., & Goodman, P. (1951) *Gestalt therapy*. New York: Julian Press, (1994) Highland, New York: Gestalt Journal Press.
St. Exupery, A. (1943) *The little prince*. New York: Harcourt, Brace & Co.
Wolfert, R. (1989) "The 'Perennial Philosophy': Spiritual Aspects of the Stages of Contact." Paper presented at the New York Institute for Gestalt Therapy.

FORAGING FOR EXISTENCE:
SOME HIGHLIGHTS OF MY THERAPY
WITH RUTH WOLFERT

BY "DEBORAH"

I was dead. Not actually, of course, but emotionally and spiritually I was dead. I was all of 26 years old, but I felt like I had lived several lifetimes — none of them good. My childhood was sad, my school years pathetic, my college years the worst. I was the prettiest girl, or so everyone told me — the boys, my girl friends, and there was even a teacher who passed me for my looks. On the outside, I was blonde, blue-eyed, shapely and well-dressed. But on the inside? Dead.

Bingeing all the time, my chin nearly scraping the pavement and my shoulders caved in, I somehow managed to notice an announcement about a self-esteem workshop. G-d knows I needed that, so I called and made an appointment with the kind-sounding therapist, and so I had something to look forward to for the week. Then came the appointment. I had been in therapy before and did not have high expectations. I sat there telling my story, recounting all my terrible mistakes, all the ways I had ruined my life. I imagined that the therapist would pity me as I spoke on and on and then ask me to pay. But something quite different happened. This therapist had me role-play the "bad voice." At first I couldn't understand why and it seemed weird. I went along with it though and got into it. All I can say is that it changed my life. It was as though I had been living in a dark room without any windows, and all of a sudden there was a crack and some sunlight pierced through.

I saw that it wasn't necessarily all my fault — that somehow, in some way I did not realize, my horrible childhood had actually had an impact on me. My relief was enormous. All of a sudden I had hope. I can say without exaggerating that it was like being born. It was the first day of my aware life.

The rest was a rocky, uphill climb. There were countless times I came into sessions feeling hopeless, at my wits end. I had just binged or broken up with a boyfriend or had some altercation with my family — and the list goes on. I'd come in with my head down and my eyes all cried out, in what I came to call "nowhere land." I'd be overcome with self-hatred and then somehow I'd begin to get in touch with myself. I'd express things I didn't even know I was feeling and begin to breathe again, and before long I'd be feeling better about myself. More often than not, I'd walk out of the session ready to cope with what was bothering me.

My whole life, it seemed like I could not make a solid connection with anyone. Every relationship was wrought with pain and guilt. With Ruth, for the first time I was allowed to express myself freely, open up my mind and heart and soul to another person and not have to worry about taking care of her. At last it was safe to be me.

During the beginning of the therapy, I did not have a job or commitments of any kind. There was only one person I had steady contact with, only one place I wanted to be every week, and that was at Ruth's. Those years, I might be at the family business on Monday, shopping for clothing on Tuesday, at the ocean on Wednesday, and G-d knows what I'd be doing for the weekend, but on Thursday, it was a sure bet that I'd beat Ruth's, and on time, for my weekly session and therapy group. Therapy was my lifeline, the real moments in my week of running around trying to dodge whatever horrible things were going on. Now I had a priority — growing — and someone who was committed to helping *me* flourish. I knew I could rely on Ruth. I could love her freely and trust that she would not turn on me. She didn't demand that I give myself up and do what she wanted the way my family always had.

My family always considered me wonderful if I did what they wanted and an uncaring idiot if I didn't. It was horrible to love them because they extracted such a heavy price. If I cared for them I was supposed to follow their lead. If not, I was bullied into submission. By the time I came to therapy, I had lost all sense of my own voice. What I wanted was answers ASAP. But Ruth never gave me answers — and that enraged me. Life often seemed impossible, and I spent a lot of time trying to make her see I was an emotional amputee who couldn't manage without her guidance. But way below the surface, I loved her confidence in me, and I did grow to find my own voice.

From the beginning, I loved the focus on me in the sessions, and also in the homework when I could be in touch with myself. But in the early years, life often seemed too difficult, and I would frequently be desperate and call Ruth begging her to save me. Perhaps I was in a binge state, or had just got kicked out of class, or fired from a job. I had no way to support myself and no clue how to begin to get back in touch with myself.

Over time, I learned to pick up the pieces on my own. I learned how to become calm in the midst of a whirlwind and how to stop binges in the act. As I became more consistent and grounded, I learned to prevent disasters before they happened. At the beginning of therapy, a desperate phone call would be met with a therapy session on the phone — sometimes very brief, sometimes more lengthy, until I felt I could cope once again. Later in the therapy, Ruth would respond: "You have the tools, what could you do now to support yourself?" I both hated and loved Ruth for that response. I hated not being saved, but I loved finding myself.

Before I entered therapy, I had careened back and forth between my safe world inside and the "real" one outside. Whenever things got difficult, I would have a temper fit or cut off- dropping friends, boyfriends or work or school — and do whatever felt easiest at the time. So with Ruth, there was a period when I veered back and forth between loving her and the therapy and cursing her out, thinking I should quit. It was the worst time since I began therapy. My fiance kept pounding at me about how horrible the therapy was until I couldn't take it anymore. I just couldn't stand up to him. So I began exploding at Ruth.

After a while, she actually began answering me back. This was wonderful. In my family whoever yelled loudest won the fight. The only thing that mattered was to have the last word. Ruth showed me a real way to communicate and I saw I couldn't just bulldoze to get my way. I learned to face my anger, to love someone and not run away because I couldn't tolerate the feelings. When I first entered therapy, I ran away from people a great deal because pretty much all my emotions were intolerable.

The thing I hate writing about even now is being incested. I had no memory of it before the therapy, but of course, I had no early childhood memories at all until therapy. I knew that I was painfully aware of my over-developed sexuality, and I did recall times in my teens when my uncle got into bed with me and made weird sexual comments.

In my early years of therapy, I began to remember a good deal of my childhood and would occasionally get hints of something sexual with my uncle. I never wanted to focus on it, and nothing was clear until a session when I suddenly recalled sucking on my uncle's penis as a baby. It later turned out that my sister was also approached by him.

It still hurts when I think back to that time when my small, vulnerable mouth had a penis shoved into it and no one protected me. It was so horrible I had no place to go but inside. I escaped into the only safety I could find by cutting off. No matter what was going on outside, I could be in MY world where I heard nothing, saw nothing, felt nothing going on in the unsafe whirlwind around me. No one understood — they just punished me for not paying attention and so I retreated even more.

It was like a miracle that Ruth could meet me in that nowhere land. She didn't demand that I come out, but somehow I learned to communicate from that place. The pain was so deep and my retreat so total that I sometimes wonder I could open. The only way was by finding a spiritual sanctuary within, a meditative space that was a second cousin to nowhere land. As I got a sense of my spiritual nature, I no longer needed to retreat from the whirlwind around me so much. I gradually developed a sense of peace with awareness which took the place of the cut-off I had created as a child. Gently and slowly Ruth allowed me to find my voice in even the most profound of retreats. I learned how to merge my world with the outer one, how to *create* my own safety in the real world.

Each little step has been difficult, but I have been able to let go of the endless circle of pain and blankness. Slowly and with a lot of backsliding, I have found a career as a teacher, married a sweet, gentle man, and now we have 4 wonderful children.

Sometimes in the evening, as I look across at my husband and children, or in the day at my students in school, I feel blessed in my peace and joy, and marvel at how far I've come. When I think of how I used to spend all day bingeing and running away from the horrible pain of my life, I feel great love and gratitude to Ruth and the therapy. From the first session to the last, I have been on a journey of discovery, a journey into life. And I have continued to grow on my own. Now when things bother me, I can usually breathe and get in touch with what is going on, and even use it to expand. I am glad for my life, glad to be on a lifelong path of exploration and growth. Thank you, G-d and thank you, Ruth!

◊

4

THE INTEGRATION OF SELF PSYCHOLOGY/ INTERSUBJECTIVITY THEORY INTO THE PRACTICE OF GESTALT THERAPY

Stephen G. Zahm, Ph.D. and Elaine K. Breshgold, Ph.D.[1]

❖◆❖

CASE HISTORY

Jean was referred to me for psychotherapy by her family physician. Her first appointment was preceded by a letter from him indicating that she was 37-years old and had a recent history of increasing use of pain medication, as well as a long history of "multiple tension type symptoms including headaches, spastic colon, etc." As I worked with Jean I came to see these symptoms as merely the tip of the iceberg. In terms of a traditional diagnosis, she had Borderline Personality Traits, with recurrent Major Depressive Episodes. From a Gestalt therapy perspective, I initially saw Jean as a retroflective process personified. She held her breath for long periods of time, and after a while I began to move with her rhythm and found myself holding my breath in unison with her. We would both exhale together in relief, only to hold our breath again a few moments later. She suffered from a variety of psychophysiological problems. She complained that she was tense "all the time," and that she struggled with depression. She had taken anti-depressant medication in the past which afforded her some periodic relief from these symptoms, but the depression would always return. She described herself as having been overweight since she was a child and reported that she continued to compulsively overeat. Recently her depression had gotten the best of

---

1   Stephen Zahm is the therapist in this case. He wrote section I and II; section III was written in collaboration with Elaine Breshgold.

her and she was often unable to get out of bed and was crying a lot. She had been married 15 years, had three children and hadn't worked outside the home for ten years, choosing to focus her energy on homemaking and raising her children. She felt ambivalent about having given up a professional career, but was fearful of getting back "into the world," lacking confidence in herself and her abilities.

Jean was a very angry woman who sounded irritated all the time. She was almost completely unable to express her negative feelings to the appropriate person — contact forever retroflected. A typical psychotherapy session would include Jean raging to me about an incident such as a woman cutting in front of her in a shopping line, and Jean boiling inside, but saying nothing. She retroflected her anger and blamed herself for being "such a wimp." She was extremely self-critical. It was painful for me to witness her self-flagellation.

Jean's father had died when she was eight. Her mother was unable to cope with her four children. Consequently, Jean was "shipped out" to live with an aunt for a year. This had a powerful effect on Jean, heightened by the painful fact that her siblings got to stay with their mother. This and other experiences of abandonment had contributed to an ingrained sense of herself as "a nothing — a zero." Over the course of the therapy a pervasive theme was how she would compromise herself in a variety of situations in an effort to avoid the possibility of experiencing herself as worthless, unimportant, inconsequential and in her words, "a zero." Avoiding conflicts, letting people abuse her, saying yes instead of no were typical strategies that Jean used to escape the potential humiliating experience of the other's slightest displeasure with her. Jean had a world class radar system, finely attuned to pick up the most subtle forms of criticism, displeasure, or discontent from other people which would be reflexively translated into confirmation that she was in fact (once again) proven to be "a zero."

Jean's mother had died about five years prior to her beginning therapy. In the beginning of treatment, Jean grieved the death of her mother, at times idealizing her. After several years of painful exploration, insight and new awareness, Jean began to see her mother and their relationship more clearly. She began referring to her mother as "the ice woman." Jean could not recall ever being hugged or held by her mother. The injury was deep and hidden, but the clues were obvious in her behavior and her deepest feelings about herself. The creative adjustment of various forms of retroflection had worked in the past to avoid the dreaded experience of herself as "a nothing." Much later in therapy Jean was able to describe herself as having her heart broken by her mother. She had a fantasy of an infant with needs not met who then turns to stone. She saw herself as the fragile inside of an egg, with a hard protective shell. Jean came to understand that she was hardened and guarded with me and others to protect her fragile inside.

Jean had few memories of her father. She stated he "wasn't around much." After his death, her mother was single until Jean was fifteen, at which time her mother remarried. Jean hated her stepfather who was an alcoholic and she experienced this marriage as another abandonment by her mother. Her stepfather died when she was nineteen. Jean's description of her mother indicated that she was withdrawn and depressed. Her mother threatened suicide when Jean was sixteen, an illustration of her inability to consider the needs and feelings of her children who had already lost one parent.

COURSE OF TREATMENT

Over the course of therapy we covered many themes, celebrating together Jean's personal victories, and commiserating about her setbacks. For example, we saw her growth reflected in her beginning to open up to people, letting them in, learning to be more contactful in a variety of ways including expressing her anger directly, and setting limits that truly reflected who she was. She was eventually able to confront her husband about her dissatisfactions in that relationship and to insist on starting couples therapy (with another therapist). Jean came to understand more about her violent moods swings, became aware of her needs, and was more able to act on them. Her initial presenting symptoms such as frequent crying spells, chronic tension, psychophysiological problems, need for pain medication, long periods of isolation and intense depression gradually decreased and were mostly resolved by the fifth year of treatment. She also became aware that her overeating was an attempt to avoid feelings, and to nurture herself. She would eat when she felt deprived or to soothe herself rather than going after what she really needed. With this awareness, and as she became more skillful at getting her needs met, this behavior ceased to be problematic.

There were occasions when Jean experienced major set-backs and reexperienced periods of regression and despair. The most striking of these occurred in the sixth year of treatment. Jean never sat in the waiting room and waited for our appointed time. The possibility that I might be late and that she would feel abandoned and forgotten was too threatening. We had a set time for her appointment which never changed. She needed to be able to count on that. She would always show up for her appointment five or ten minutes late and simply walk into my office through the open door, avoiding the anxiety of waiting. One day, due to a scheduling error I had the office door closed thinking her appointment was a half hour later than it was. Normally, we met at the same time every week, but this particular appointment had been rescheduled from her regular time. She ended up waiting in the waiting room for twenty minutes after facing the dreaded closed door. The felt hurt and betrayal was intense. She immediately slipped into seeing me as an all bad person who had duped her into trusting, and she perceived herself as once again worthless. We had worked on her loss of perspective and "splitting" many times, and had looked at the way she held grudges for long periods. This issue had come up in our relationship in smaller doses in the past. The most important lesson had been that she needed to be aware of the hurt and to be able to express it to me. Her loss of perspective was primarily the result of this missing contact function. With the expression of hurt and my genuine acknowledgement of how I did hurt her, she would begin to integrate and experience herself and me as whole people, that is, she would regain perspective. This situation was, however, qualitatively more intolerable, painful, and wounding for her. It seemed no amount of rational understanding, expressing the hurt and anger or my being with her, could soothe the fire and pain of this event. She regressed, became angry and depressed and later talked about how this incident almost ended our relationship. During this period of about five months, it was important for me to understand her experience and unspoken needs. She needed attunement to her deep sense of despair and disappointment in me. My own sense of frustration was retroflected … unexpressed. (I felt like screaming something like "Come on now, I did not do that on purpose — how can you close up on me and yourself over this? I'm really an okay guy you can trust.")

During this time, Jean needed me to be attuned to the injury that I precipitated, to understand the meaning this had for her based on her history, and to repair our relationship (selfobject bond) through discussion and understanding (Bacal, 1985). Stolorow's (1990) concept of the intersubjective field is useful in conceptualizing the dynamic between Jean and myself during this period: Jean noticed my frustration and impatience in my tone and body language which had an effect on her. It reinforced her sense of her self as in some way worthless and unwanted. She in turn would pull away more. This vicious cycle was the result of our mutual interaction and influence. My subjective experience and behavior were influenced by Jean's subjective experience and behavior and vice versa. Over the course of several months, as we came to understand all of these issues together, our relational bond was gradually repaired.

The idea that somebody in this world would care enough about Jean to invest in her well-being was novel from the beginning of treatment and constantly being tested. Over the years of treatment, the subtleties of how Jean dealt with this issue changed, but the core issue remained alive along with the important meaning to her — was she someone who could be cared about or was she a "zero"? In the beginning stages of therapy Jean would present life problems to me in a way that bordered on aggressively hostile and challenging behavior. The attitude — usually reflected in the metacommunication, but sometimes actually overt — was something like "Okay now, I've got this problem, see, and I'm waiting for you to do something about it and your had better hurry up because I'm paying you good money." Her aggressive, tough position with me became palatable and even touching for me as I started to understand that under the bravado hard line, there was its polar opposite — a last ditch hope that I would come through for her and maybe something would be different than ever before. In this space which I could feel residing very close to the surface, she was exceedingly vulnerable and exposed, perhaps even in a state of panic around the high stakes of this issue for her.

During the initial stages of therapy, I would invest myself in whatever issue or problem she presented. My sense was that for the most part, talking about her desperation and need for me to come through would not be an appropriate therapeutic choice. I needed to just do it. When we couldn't get closure on a particular issue or figure out a problem, Jean would leave with two different messages to me. First, "Well we didn't figure out what to do — we didn't accomplish anything." And then she would pause, look at me, and say sincerely "thank you," in a contactful way that seemed to have a lot of meaning in back of it. She seemed to really mean "thank you." My interpretation of the thank you was "thank you for being present, thank you for absorbing yourself in my problems and for investing yourself in my interests, thank you for helping me feel important even for one hour, and especially thank you because during most of our time I didn't feel like a zero." As Jean progressed in therapy she was able to express these feelings more directly. The life problems Jean presented were much less important than these unspoken, unaware needs. These needs represented developmental deficits, or incomplete gestalten that seemed to scream for attention and closure. That I would invest myself in her problems, be absorbed and interested in her, was very meaningful for her. As the intensity of the charge reduced, she was more capable of and more interested in understanding the dynamics surrounding her previously unspoken demand to me. At first we could only talk in retrospect about her needs. Later, we could deal with this process as it occurred.

Jean had strong negative feelings about "dependency" and "dependent people." In an irritated tone, she would complain about friends and relatives who needed too much, couldn't take care of themselves, and expected others to pamper them. She swore up and down that she would never, ever be a "clinging vine" like so-and-so. It took a number of years for her to come to grips with the true feelings surrounding the issue of dependency and the need for others. Significant introjects were "never ask for help" and "never feel the need for help." If one is stoic, suffers in silence then eventually, some day, true love will arrive. Jean would become furious when telling me about friends who didn't follow this edict, but somehow got the "goodies" anyway. She had learned her lesson well with mom, "the ice woman," when as a child, although desperately needing attention or holding, she never let on. Our work followed a progression of 1) focusing awareness around this issue, 2) experimenting with asking for something, 3) exploring the feared responses from others, 4) risking more as she started to let others in on what kind of nurturing she really wanted. All of these steps were difficult, held a sense of danger, and were accompanied by a deeper understanding of her makeup and a new, expanded sense of herself.

The relationship issues, of course, evolved over time in the therapy. At first, Jean made it clear that ours was a clinical relationship. She was simply using me, just like a person uses a dentist or physician to do a particular job, say to pull a tooth. After all, she explained, she "could always get another shrink." My initial attempts at exploring her objections to needing me were stonewalled and blocked. No discussion. Next topic, please (in an irritated tone). Over the years of therapy the conversation continued. My attention frequently focused on how much I could overtly explore and experiment around this issue (e.g. "What is your objection to needing me?" ... or "Imagine you are a clinging vine") versus her need for me to simply be attuned to her, and be with her in her experience of these feelings. My need and desire for her to become more aware of herself and for her to do something more contactful with me (for example, tell me she needed me for something specific or tell me she would not need me) was put on the back burner.

Jean knew intuitively how much anxiety she could tolerate. As her sense of self became firmer, and she developed increased self-esteem and confidence (bolstered and supported in small steps by my acceptance of what she could do and who she was), she eventually became easier with the topic. One day, prior to my vacation, she wondered what would happen to her if my plane crashed and I died. After all, she said "you know more about me than anybody else in the whole world." I thought, "Eureka!" but kept my cool as we began a deeper level of exploration around her need for me, and her fear of that need.

As Jean became more aware of her fear of needing me and her need for me, we explored the various aspects of this issue which ranged from her irritation with herself for such "weakness," to the historical underpinning and reasons for these feelings. We explored her feelings toward me (ranging from distrust to appreciation) and her very primitive longings, extremely soft and vulnerable. For example, Jean described a longing to be so perfectly taken care of that she "wouldn't even notice it." Jean had fantasies of fusion with a "presence" which would take care of her. Being taken care of in reality was too risky, but it was safe to stay with the fantasy. Jean began to awaken to aspects of her nature that were rigidly buried in her emotional survival mode of existence. I was frequently touched by her as our work ranged from her feelings toward me to memories of past experiences, to internal awareness. My interest was always rubberbanding back to what type of contact Jean could manage with me around these issues. She needed constant support as she ventured out into uncharted emotional regions. I found that as she expanded her sense of self, one important source of support was my opening up to her with information about my own feelings and needs for other people. We talked about different types of needs and began to categorize them. We differentiated Jean's "adult" needs (like feeling she needed encouragement, a hug, or support) from her more "primitive" child-like needs (like wanting someone to read her mind, know exactly what she required and give it to her).

As Jean began to integrate her dependency and "neediness," she actually became more independent. About the seventh year of treatment she wanted to "take the summer off" which we did. Prior to this, our therapy sessions had been very consistent, with few interruptions. When I did take a vacation Jean's reaction was fairly predictable as she responded to the felt abandonment and particularly her objection to caring about it. Her behavior would range from anger at my being gone when such and such was going on in her life (but of course, she really didn't need me), to emotional withdrawal with her own special form of rigidity, criticalness, and coldness — "ice woman" returneth.

Two years prior to the termination of treatment, Jean set a goal of ending therapy by the following summer. As we explored the issues related to termination, new issues emerged, and Jean decided to continue a while longer. As the issues which termination had raised were resolved, Jean was able to take periods of time off from therapy over summers and holidays. She experienced these breaks as "practicing" being independent and experienced the sense of security that she could still need me and always come back. She would return from a one or two month hiatus radiating with a pride in herself that was almost palpable. Typically she would start the session with something like, "Well, I didn't think of you once!" I would celebrate this achievement with her and keep to myself whatever narcissistic injury this created within me.

Three months short of ten years of therapy, we ended treatment. Jean had been taking more and more time off — the latest being a two-month break while she studied for an important licensing exam. Her self-esteem significantly improved, she had decided to "get back into the professional world." During the last session Jean made the comment that her experience in therapy had "changed my life." I took this opportunity to find out, from her perspective, how she had been affected by this experience and what she had gotten from it. She said that she felt good about herself, and had confidence in her abilities, for the first time in her life. She described being aware of needs and feelings, and feeling entitled to having these needs met. She was able to ask for what she wanted and needed. She said her relationship with her husband, as well as with her family and friends, had changed now that she was no longer critical of herself for having needs, and believed her feelings and wishes were important. Also, she no longer got lost in and overwhelmed by negative feelings and depression, and she was able to keep perspective about herself and in relationships. She was no longer angry at others for needing, was able to be dependent and independent, and did not feel scared or angry all the time. The "ice woman" had melted.

DISCUSSION

Gestalt therapy and self psychology/intersubjectivity theory have been described as compatible approaches to psychotherapy. They have similar and compatible views of basic theoretical concepts such as resistance, the unconscious, and transference (Breshgold & Zahm, 1992). The therapeutic stance in both orientations is phenomenological and looks at the relationship and the patient-therapist interaction as opposed to the isolated mental apparatus of traditional psychoanalysis. Further, we have proposed (Breshgold & Zahm, 1992) that a Gestalt therapist may benefit from integrating the developmental theory of self psychology/intersubjectivity into the practice of Gestalt therapy. Jacobs (1992) discusses the insights which self psychology/intersubjectivity theory offer Gestalt therapy. She states "… after one understands the concepts of selfobject functions and selfobject relatedness, one never views clinical material in quite the same way again" (p. 26). She goes on to state that assimilating these newer psychoanalytic constructs may encourage a shift in emphasis in Gestalt therapy and move us toward focusing on some of the less developed aspects of our theory. However, she sees these two approaches (Gestalt therapy and self psychology/intersubjectivity) as differing to a certain extent in what processes are important in therapy. She describes the psychoanalytic theories as focusing on developmental processes related to the development of self structures, while Gestalt therapy focuses on the here and now awareness process, using the lenses of Gestalt formation and contact to elucidate how awareness supports and refines self regulating capacities (Jacobs, 1992).

We will use our discussion of this case example to highlight 1) the compatibility of Gestalt therapy and self psychology/intersubjectivity theory in practice, 2) the benefit for the Gestalt therapist of integrating this developmental theory and 3) how doing so provides a different lens for viewing clinical material. Gestalt therapy directs the therapist's focus and attention to the processes occurring at the contact boundary. The therapist interventions are geared to address the patient's organismic self regulation. The therapist focuses on the obstacles to contact which prevent the patient from obtaining what is needed from the environment. The objective is to increase awareness and restore ego functioning, resulting in a change in the patient's experience of self. What self psychology/intersubjectivity theory contributes is the idea that there is a parallel process occurring simultaneously relating to developmental needs and strivings. This process involves the patient's selfobject needs and developmental deficits and the ways in which the selfobject ties with the therapist are established and maintained in order to assist in the development of self structures (self regulating capacities).

Throughout the course of treatment with Jean there was a blending of focus on boundary processes and focus on the selfobject dimension of the relationship. Initially the selfobject dimension of the therapeutic relationship was prominent. Later, as Jean became more integrated, less fragmented, and developed more intact self structures, there was a foreground shift and it became more possible to look directly at the contact-making process with the therapist. As the work moved into dealing more directly with the themes involving Jean's character issues, the therapeutic relationship, and contact boundary processes, the selfobject tie became background providing support for the explorative work. When an injury occurred resulting in a rupture of the selfobject tie, such as the closed door incident, Jean would regress, become fragmented, and require work focused primarily on selfconsolidation and reestablishing the selfobject tie. At these times the relationship itself and the selfobject needs were once again foreground. From a Gestalt therapy perspective, this illustrates basic concepts such as the importance of attending to what is currently foreground in order to achieve closure, and the usefulness of trusting the patient's own self-regulatory process. For example, when Jean initially refused to discuss her neediness, or objections to needing, it was important for the therapist to accept this "no" which included her unwillingness to discuss what the "no" was about. Jean knew how much anxiety she could tolerate, and as she became more confident of her ability to tolerate such exploration, she was ready to move on to the next "figure" which was her interest in her difficulty needing the therapist and her fear of needing in general.

Jacobs (1992) points out that self psychology and intersubjectivity theory can influence the Gestalt therapist to understand phenomena from the point of view of the experiencing subject (patient) rather than from the point of view of the observer (therapist). She maintains that this leads to focusing on what the patient requires from the therapist in terms of developmental needs. The focus is tilted away from what the patient may be avoiding, defending against, or manipulating for. The therapist is oriented toward seeing developmental deficits rather than a conflict-defense dynamic.

This is compatible with the Gestalt concept of creative adjustment which looks at behavior as a creative response to environmental requirements or constraints. Jacobs sees Gestalt therapy theory as containing both perspectives. "The influence of Frederick Perls and Wilhelm Reich leads us to look at neurotic processes as avoidance" (Jacobs, 1992). However, our view of personality development, and belief in organismic self regulation, does not support the conflict-defense position which views people as wanting to avoid maturity and having to be persuaded to give up infantile longings (Jacobs, 1992). If the therapist is more oriented toward seeing conflict-defense (or avoidance and manipulation), the therapeutic interventions will be more geared toward confrontation. In the work with Jean the influence of self psychology and intersubjectivity theory shifted the therapist's foreground toward seeing developmental deficits and longings. As a result, interventions focused more on her phenomenology, for example, Jean's longing for the therapist to read her mind, to know exactly what was needed and to provide it for her. At those times, she withdrew into depressions and silence, her overt attitude indicated anger toward the therapist that served to initially push him away — the opposite of what she really needed. For the therapist, understanding this process in terms of selfobject needs/developmental deficits, and as a response to a fear of re-injury (because of therapist's failure to meet a developmental need) oriented the therapist to try to understand her subjective world. The interventions were consequently geared less toward observing, and commenting on her silences, pouting, or biting remarks, and more toward understanding with her what her current experience was which resulted in these behaviors.

Prior to therapy, Jean had lived a life which involved countless power struggles and grudges she would hold for long periods of time. In many cases she had abruptly terminated relationships. Interestingly, and with theoretical significance, the therapy relationship did not suffer from these difficulties. There were periods of withdrawal after an injury, but never the power struggles which had characterized Jean's life. Gestalt therapy and intersubjectivity theory each provide similarly useful perspectives on dealing with these issues. Gestalt therapy theorists have put forth the idea of therapy without resistance (Polster & Polster, 1976) and have further explained that the concept of resistance is actually antithetical to the tenets of Gestalt therapy (Breshgold, 1989). We point out that so-called resistant behavior is:

> ... viewed as the patient's expression of what is currently figural and the goal of the therapist is not to dissuade the patient from his/her position, but to help the patient explore and become aware of whatever the experience is which is being expressed. In Gestalt therapy, the therapist does not have the goal of getting through something to get to something else. The focus of the therapy is whatever emerges and becomes figural for the patient. Once the therapist and patient have attended to the forming figure, it will be completed, and patient will naturally move on to the next emergent figure. (Breshgold & Zahm, 1992, p. 78)

Therapy with Jean was replete with situations illustrating this. For example, her initial refusal to engage in certain experiments, or to talk about certain topics. In each case, she required closure of one figure before moving on to the next. A major illustration of this is the incident involving the closed door. Jean withdrew, was hurt and angry and was unwilling to continue discussion around the therapy topics which were previously being explored. The injury had caused a foreground shift to the injury itself, the relationship, what the injury meant to her and whether she could continue in the relationship at all.

According to Stolorow (1990), resistance in therapy occurs when the patient expects that his/her emotional states and longings will be met with the same traumatic response from the therapist that he/she received from the original caregiver. Resistance is always stimulated by some quality or activity of the therapist that for the patient indicates an impending recurrence of traumatic developmental failures. The patient is responding to something such as a therapeutic intervention or personal quality or behavior of the therapist that lends itself to the patient's expectation of repetition of developmental failure. Negative therapeutic reactions and impasses are a property not of the patient in isolation, but of something gone awry in the intersubjective system, contributed to by both patient and therapist (Stolorow, 1990). The working through of resistance "requires careful investigation of the specific intersubjective contexts in which the defensive/resistant reactions arise and recede" (Stolorow, 1990). Over the course of therapy, there were numerous occasions when Jean felt injured due to something the therapist did or said. At these times what was required was understanding what the therapist had done to stimulate the felt injury. In the closed door incident, it was obvious; in other situations, less so. In this case she needed to understand what the injury meant to her, her expectations around future developmental failures, her feelings toward the therapist, the genetic/historical roots causing the sensitivity, and the resultant introjections and feelings about herself. The selfobject bond had to be repaired before the therapy could proceed. The intersubjective approach was particularly useful in enabling the therapist to explore "resistance" from the *patient's* perspective.

Jean had a deeply rooted sense of herself as "a nothing" or "a zero." She was quick to react to the slightest form of rejection by reflexively attaching this meaning to it. Stolorow (1990) refers to this type of reflex as representing an invariant organizing principle. In Gestalt therapy, this would be seen as reflecting a predisposition to a particular figure formation or gestalt in response to specific environmental stimuli. Many times over the course of treatment, Jean reacted with sensitivity to the ways she experienced the therapist as emotionally abandoning her. In each instance the abandonment was unintentional and in some cases unavoidable. However, the meaning she extracted from these interactions was that she was worthless. For example, the therapist's attention wandering, the therapist being tired or "off" on a particular day, or a glance at the clock, all had this result. The necessary therapeutic steps required for healing and growth to occur are outlined more specifically in self psychology (Bacal, 1985) while the Gestalt therapy perspective provides the general theoretical guidelines involving figure formation, awareness, and closure, leading to natural healing process and growth.

Each incident of experienced emotional abandonment resulted in Jean's stony ice cold anger and withdrawal. In the beginning of treatment, Jean was more inclined to remain fixated on her anger at the therapist. As the work progressed, she was able to identify softer, more vulnerable feelings residing below the anger. As long as she remained stuck with only her anger at the therapist and at herself, she was trapped, seeing both of them in a completely negative light.

During the initial stages of therapy, Jean was unwilling to participate in traditional Gestalt experiments. She was a no-nonsense kind of person and rejected such experiments as "role playing," in her typical irritated, stubborn manner. She also declared discussion about her objections off limits. She needed to tell her weekly stories and express her rage toward others to the therapist. In providing these selfobject functions for Jean, the therapist was attending to developmental deficits, and this was usually primary in terms of her hierarchy of needs. What was foreground was her need for the therapist to "come through" for her in specific ways. These included: being present, understanding her position, understanding her emotional needs, and maintaining an attitude of confidence and calm in the face of her anger, anxiety, or fragmentation. Later, it was possible to discuss her needs and longings for these relational experiences. Earlier in treatment, Jean could not tolerate confrontation of boundary processes. Her primary need was for affective attunement and satisfaction of mirroring and idealizing selfobject functions. Work on awareness of her retroflective process had to be carefully titrated into the sessions. For example, it was more important, in fact paramount to her, for the therapist to understand her subjective experience when she felt victimized, and only after she experienced this understanding was she interested in looking at what her contribution may have been to the situation she described. Generally, any initial focus on her own process made her irritated and angry, and disrupted her momentum and what was foreground for her. As the work progressed, it was possible to integrate more direct focus on here and now awareness and more traditional experiments. From a self psychology perspective, Jean was more receptive to this as she internalized specific functions and acquired structures which were previously missing in her development. From a Gestalt therapy perspective, there was a shift in her needs and a change in foreground.

Stolorow (1990) makes the distinction between self consolidation needs and self differentiation needs of the patient. Initially in treatment Jean required the therapist's attention directed toward her fragmentation and general heightened and sometimes overwhelming sense of anxiety. The therapeutic task at these times was to help her develop a consolidated sense of self. When she felt unsupported and overwhelmed with anxiety, interventions which were supportive and functioned primarily as a "verbal holding" were needed to help her establish more order and less fragmentation. Later in therapy more interventions were geared toward self differentiation work. That is, as Jean became more consolidated in her self experience, the focus shifted to exploration, experimentation, and internal awareness work. This type of focus requires the supportive background of a consolidated sense of self as well as an intact selfobject tie with the therapist. Selfobject needs were not figural at this time. She was ready to explore and experienced sufficient self and environmental support to do so.

Toward the end of treatment, Jean required less of the therapist in terms of providing selfobject functions for her. Her ability to take time away from the therapy relationship indicated her internalization of these functions. From a Gestalt therapy perspective this might be described as movement from environmental support to self support. Jean became more self supporting via the therapist providing these functions for her over time, and her increased awareness of feelings and needs made it possible for her to do a better job of being dependent (that is, getting her needs met) as well as making her more independent (providing more self-support).

Stolorow (1990) describes the goal of psychotherapy from a self psychology/intersubjectivity perspective as "the transformation of self experience." Isadore From (1984) describes psychotherapy from a Gestalt therapy perspective as resulting in a "new experience of the self." While Jean's most debilitating symptoms may have subsided earlier on in her therapy, the therapy was completed (from both a Gestalt therapy and self psychology perspective) when she was able to experience her self in a new way. She was no longer enslaved by her old patterns of relating to herself and others. She was able to make contact in a different way. Via the therapeutic relationship, her relationship with herself and others transformed.

This case example provides an illustration of the possibilities for integration of self psychology/intersubjectivity theory into the practice of Gestalt therapy. It illustrates the benefits of this integration both in terms of clarifying what the appropriate focus for clinical intervention may be at any given moment, and in terms of understanding theoretically the various processes which may be occurring simultaneously as the therapy takes place. Integrating these psychoanalytic insights enables the therapist to have a broader perspective in viewing the therapy process and gives the therapist a wider array of therapeutic choices.

REFERENCES

Bacal, H. A. (1985) Optimal responsiveness and the therapeutic process. In Goldberg, A. (Ed.) *Process in self psychology, vol. II, pp. 202–227*. New York: Guilford Press.

Breshgold, E. K. (1989) Resistance in gestalt therapy: An historical/theoretical perspective. *The Gestalt Journal XII, 73-102.*

Breshgold, E. & Zahm, S. (1992) A case for the integration of self psychology developmental theory into the practice of gestalt therapy. *The Gestalt Journal, XVI, 61–93.*

From, I. (1991) Gestalt therapy. Unpublished lecture material.

Jacobs, L. (1992) Insights from psychoanalistic self-psychology and intersubjectivity theory for gestalt therapists. *The gestalt journal. XV, 2. 25–60.*

Polster, E. and Polster, M. (1976) Therapy without resistance: gestalt therapy. In Burton, A. (Ed.) *What makes behavior change possible?* New York: Brunner/Mazel.

Stolorow, R. D., Brandchaft, B., & Atwood, G.E. (1987) *Psychoanalytic treatment: An intersubjective approach.* Hillsdale, NJ: The Analytic Press.

Stolorow, R. D. (1990) Presentation at self psychology and creativity conference, Santa Fe, New Mexico.

◊

5

A GESTALT APPROACH TO FOOD INTOLERANCE IN ADULTS

Ray Edwards

❖

FOREWORD

The Gestalt therapist gives attention to figure development, his or her own and the client's, and most particularly to the manner in which the client interrupts such development. Attention will now be focused on problems in the physiological ground as the origin of distorted, non-functional figures.

It is obvious that the very ill, febrile patient is unable to form figures, including the need for food, which would normally develop. Lesser states of illness may likewise be accompanied by malfunction; when afflicted by nasopharyngitis the affected person may have considerable difficulty in concentrating on the processes of everyday life although well enough to be out and about in the world.

My present contention is that the debilitation accompanying the above febrile and other states and, more pertinently, the symptoms of the specific adaption syndrome (Selye, 1956) include aspects which may be considered to be defects of the ground, out of which emerge distorted figures. The particular example of the specific adaptation syndrome to be discussed and illustrated by case description is the occurrence of food intolerance in adults. Sluckin (1993) has demonstrated the value of attending to dietary food and chemical intolerance in children when considering Gestalt therapy for "bad behavior."

THE GESTALT CONTEXT

The importance of the symptoms of food intolerance for Gestalt therapists, or any other kind of psychotherapist, lies in the mimicry of what are usually regarded as psychological symptoms, hyperactivity, depression, persistent fatigue, irritability, disorientation (Mackarness, 1976, p. 108) and confusion (1980, p. 72) and all these symptoms can be the result of foods. As discussed above and emphasized by Sluckin (1993), the important focus of therapeutic attention is the food and it is important to evaluate each patient's diet.

What Is Ground?

By definition, anything out of awareness is ground and the very act of anything coming into awareness is an emergent figure. A hunger figure is related to gastric phenomena which are normally out of awareness and thus is ground. The patient with a gastric ulcer may feel very hungry with no relationship to real need, aware only of the hunger figure and not of the physiological change in his stomach.

Events in the physiological ground are thus of paramount importance when considering psychological symptoms.

The Physiological And Psychological Boundaries

Boundaries are not, in general contiguous. For example, when vinegar is toxic this toxin is taken across the physiological boundary where it exerts its deleterious effect. This toxin also effectively crosses the psychological boundary, behaving metaphorically like an introject and is only dealt with adequately when, in full awareness, the decision is made as an organismic figure to take the necessary action of avoiding ingestion of the toxin.

With these two levels, physiological and psychological, running simultaneously, the stages of the contact and action cycle cannot be completed satisfactorily unless the toxin is avoided. At first all goes well because the food plus toxin is ingested. At the action stage, i.e., digestion, the cycle fails; the toxin takes effect, hyper- or hypo-activity supervenes, the cycle is not completed as there is no satisfaction stage; diversion to a new anorganismic cycle occurs with distorted figures, initiated by the toxin process.

Therapy

As emphasized above, the essential therapeutic move with people suffering from the effects of food intolerance is to deal with the ground state rather than the figure. With clients such as those discussed here, therapy that takes no account of non-tolerance to dietary factors is as useless as trying to cure a brain tumor with psychotherapy.

For me a consequence of the holistic approach is to find it natural to include a consideration of physiological aspects in my field of interest. Put very briefly and historically, whereas Freud focussed on sexuality and Reich on breathing, Perls extended his interest to include food ingestion. Perls et al., (1951) used dietary factors metaphorically. The present study is on a different level: actuality, rather than metaphor. Food intolerance, a physiological phenomenon, is accompanied by changed behavior.

The most telling argument relating to the treatment of the five clients presented here is the observation of changes that occur on eliminating a noxious stimulus from the diet. Anyone who has seen the resulting behavior change marvels.

FOOD INTOLERANCE

Mackarness generalized and discussed clinical ecology (1980, p. xv) and was also concerned to found his ideas on scientific (reductionist) theories of allergy (p. 22), on Cannon's homeostasis theories (Mackarness, 1976, p. 49) and on Selye's generalizations about stress (p. 107).

The observations and conclusions of Mackarness (1976, 1980) indicated that there are four main and possible features when food intolerance occurs; 1) the symptoms include hyperactivity with excessive, somewhat compulsive movements, 2) the symptoms include periods of hypoactivity, lassitude, night sweats and catarrh, 3) the person tends to want to ingest excessive amounts of the non-tolerated substance — a vague form of "addiction" occurs and 4) the symptoms disappear on elimination of the non-tolerated substance from diet. The range of symptoms from hyper — to hypoactivity is at first sight confusing and, as noted above, can be clear for a Gestalt practitioner who is aware of polarity phenomena.

Mackarness (1976) described food intolerance as ecological illness (p. 37) which will be interpreted here in Gestalt terms as dis-ease in the field, in the ground of the sufferer. Ingestion is transfer of non-tolerated substance from external to internal field.

The altered reaction aspect of allergy theory begs the question — altered from what? The non-reactive person can eat peanuts, strawberries, shell fish, etc., with no problems. The reactive person reacts. Symptoms appear and the symptoms vary, depending on the nature of the tissue or organ which reacts. Modem immunological explanations depend on dem-onstration of production of an antibody to the substance causing the reac-tion. Other substances do not produce antibodies, are not allergens, and are toxic. Thus the botulinus toxins are not allergens, they are nerve poisons. However, ingestion of toxic substances in very low doses produce similar reactions to those of allergens and, as an extreme example, arsenate has been traditionally used as a tonic. It is convenient to discuss here the effect of both allergens and toxins as if of the same category and refer to non-tolerance.

Some of the allergens discussed here, wheat, milk, peanuts, are well described in the literature (King, 1984; Schauss, 1984; Yunginger, 1980) whereas others are not well documented and are concisely summarized in the table.

OBSERVATIONS

One of the most important features of non-tolerance provides the reason for the failure of generally aware, intelligent, observant people to make the causal connection. There may be a one to three day delay between ingestion of the non-tolerated substance and onset of symptoms. It is, however, clear that the non-tolerance shown by these people can be described as the spe-cific adaptation syndrome, each person having a different causative agent.

Case Examples

The five clients described came to me over several years during which I dealt with the order of one hundred other clients.

Mathew, a carpenter, aged 27 presented on recommendation from a friend and in preliminary interview complained of long term "depression." He appeared to me to be puffy rather than fat and was diffident when talking about himself. On questioning, in the therapy group situation, he said that depression for him was a state of inactivity during which he could not rouse himself to be interested in anything. He had occasional jobs but failed to keep them for more than one week or two as his employers wanted more activity and interest from him. His parents would not have him live with them, he could not keep a girlfriend and male friends quickly got bored with him. He didn't want to get up in the morning.

After some months of lack of concentration in group the subject of favorite foods came up and I was surprised at the energy Mathew exhibited when talking about his love of fish and chips. This energy contrasted with his usual hesitancy. Remembering the tendency of people to enjoy ingesting large quantities of substances which were non-tolerant for them I suggested he observe how he felt in the hours after enjoying his fish and chips. The next week he reported feeling very depressed the morning after the ingestion so I suggested that he take the fish and the chips separately. Some weeks later he reported that fish alone and chips alone did not upset him. Instead he suspected that the upsetting factor was the liberal quantity of vinegar he usually put on his food.

Over several weeks he conducted and reported many experiments with or without vinegar confirming that this substance was the source of depression. He tried many varieties of vinegar — including natural fermented, malt, white and cheap diluted acetic acid plus caramel — and it became apparent that the noxious constituent was acetic acid. I found this surprising since acetate is a central entity in carbohydrate and energy metabolism though I did not share this observation with him.

On seeking a substitute for vinegar he found that lemon juice satisfied him with no deleterious effects. On the final occasions in the group the relationship with fellow members benefitted him in providing feedback about his improved appearance, relationships with people and in providing support whilst he made his dietary experiments. The key therapeutic change was, without doubt, abstinence from ingestion of vinegar. He left the group soon after feeling well and six months later, when I met him in the street he showed a marked change in his character. He had gained in energy. Got a job and held it. Got a girl friend and continued with her. Physically, he had lost weight, losing the bloated look he had about his face on presentation and presented a healthy, youthful face.

Peter, an accountant in his mid-30's, complained of harassment by his employer who was evidently dissatisfied by his slowness at work. He said that his colleagues at work were unfriendly and "pushy" and that, when he was at home, he paced up and down his room worrying about what might happen tomorrow and particularly if he lost his job. He frequently wakened from sleep during the night and had difficulty in going to sleep again.

Concentration on relationships with fellow group members seemed indicated. However, on asking him for more detail about himself he told of his "fidgetyness" at work, how he couldn't settle down to his books and papers and had to "keep going to the toilet" although he did not need to for excretion purposes.

The element of hyperactivity caught my attention and I asked about his favorite foods. He liked salads with raw onion (he emphasized these two words), tomatoes, grated carrot, lettuce, and mayonnaise. On request he spoke more about the onions, he liked the strong flavor of fresh onions and considered them to be ruined if cooked.

As an experiment he stopped eating onions. He reported that a change was apparent on the second day when he became quieter and enjoyed a good night of sleep. He continued therapy in group for four weeks to improve his personal relationships and until we felt confident the changes were permanent. He reported that his employer and work-mates seemed to like him better. He came to understand that something about his attitude had contributed to alienating them.

Bertha, a hairdresser in her 30's, came with her husband to couples counselling and each complained of marital disharmony. He said that she was restless at night and disturbed his sleep. She wanted continuous personal attention, conversation, light massage, and sexual activity. She said he was unkind, unsympathetic and would not help her when she asked. She was much more energetic in presenting her complaints than he was.

During the first session, in addition to talking over mutual problems, each partner learned relaxation techniques, including breath control. This approach was not beneficial.

During the third session Ian complained that Bertha was putting on weight, eating too much, mostly toast at every meal plus two rounds immediately before going to bed. Since it was possible that ingestion of so much toast indicated an "addictive" reaction I suggested that she experiment by eliminating toast and other wheat products.

Within two days she was sleeping well. Ian said that she was no longer restless and not nearly so quarrelsome. After four more sessions, in which they found more harmonious ways of relating, they agreed to end therapy. During a final review of events together in therapy Bertha said that she could eat one slice of toast for breakfast with no ill effect but generally ate only rice cakes during the day, and not many of them.

Robert, a young medical student would not agree with me to formal therapy sessions since such "would be undignified for a doctor." He sorted out his problems at the bar in a pub. After several sessions in which he complained, among other things, of his inability to "get his energy up," inability to concentrate on his books (he looked and could not see) and of falling asleep in lectures, he hesitantly admitted that he was very short of money and that his diet consisted mainly of bread and peanut butter. Suspecting that he might suffer from wheat germ allergy I suggested that he could experiment with modifying his diet. He did so and found that it was the peanut product that was having the deleterious effect on him. He became the usual bright medical student on using a cheap margarine.

George, a psychotherapist aged about 50 years, is in therapy as an aspect of his life as a therapist. He had been reading widely in the psychotherapy literature and suddenly wondered if his cyclic depression and elation was related to diet. He became much more relaxed, calmer and better engaged with his activities when he eliminated milk and milk products from his diet. This was his initiative.

SUMMARIZING DISCUSSION

Cause And Effect Versus Holism; The Field

I think of figure/ground theory as holistic with field centered overtones and yet regard food intolerance as a cause and effect situation in which figures effectively emerge damaged from a damaged ground. The state of the ground, the nature of the field, here as physiology, dominates and determines behavior. It would be obdurate to deny the cause and effect nature of the relationship of the non-tolerance symptoms and the underlying physiological lesion, whatever that is. For Mathew vinegar, or something in vinegar, causes the altered behavior and the bloated facial features.

In terms of holism the damaged figure and the damaged ground are effectively one entity. The emergent figure is defective and manifests symptoms of the defect whilst reinforcing the "bad" affect and ideas about the defectiveness of the ground.

A therapist's failure to recognized the casual relationship, discussed above, may be related to introjected reliance on holistic theory with rejection of all aspects of cause and effect relationships. To reiterate, the food intolerance situation is both holistic in the sense set out by Smuts and scientific in the sense deployed by Descartes and Newton. We are faced with a dilemma analogous to the wave versus particle controversy of sub-atomic physics.

In terms of field theory, the internal and external fields must be considered, including recognition that the alimentary canal is also part of the external field. Transfer in to the internal field of a non-tolerated substance occurs on crossing the gut wall and metabolism may occur then or at any subsequent stage. Reaction may thus not be to the substance itself but to a metabolite, perhaps of hepatic origin. However, metabolism is irrelevant for therapy. Only symptoms and eradication of non-tolerated substance are relevant.

The present arguments support Sluckin's contention (1993) that it is necessary to address the whole field when investigating the mood of clients.

Experimentation

The present work has employed the experimental attitude of Perls to great effect. With each client the suggestion about dietary change was put as an experiment and executed as such by the client of his or her free will. It was on this basis that little confirmatory evidence is available, no substitution or any other kind of blind study. Once the presenting symptoms were alleviated the clients were unwilling to experiment further. Pressure, beyond a simple suggestion or request, was not brought to bear; the clients were not objects of experimentation as animals might be.

Gestalt Theory

This paper directs attention from figure to ground. It has been established that, in the example of food intolerance, it is the ground that requires treatment; the noxious substance, which affects the figure, must be eliminated from the diet.

This maneuver is done in awareness and constitutes a curative figure, a model and metaphor for all subsequent figures, with all features of a healthy figure. Recognition of the need to change diet is followed by interest in doing so, in mobilization of energy leading to contact with the actual dietary constituents and action in eliminating one (or more) of them. Then comes recognition of the benefits of this action and expression of pleasure as part of the satisfaction stage. The therapy figure is thus completed and the client is free to go on and lead a fuller life.

Recognition of the deleterious effect of an ingestible substance is an increment of awareness; once again we have underlined the importance in therapy of simple awareness. Attention to ground in the form of changing diet is also clinical practice; Gestalt therapy thus exists in the context of general medicine. The holistic attitude of Gestalt therapists is once more reinforced.

SUMMARY OF RELEVANT PUBLISHED INFORMATION

Based on a medline computer search, 1986 to 1993.

Intolerance	Author(s)	Year	Observation
Vinegar	Aronov	1989	Kidney disease and blood coagulation disorders.
Onion	Lautier & Wendt	1985	Contact allergy to alliaceae in one person.
	Dorsch *et al.*	1988	Onions and other allium species have an anti-asthmatic effect.
Wheat	Ciclitira & Ellis	1987	A review of the connection between coeliac disease and wheat gluten ingestion.
	Armenita Medina	1992	Concerning the potentiation of the wheat reaction by physical exercise.
Meat	Reports are concerned with illness due to bacterial, worm or other infestation. No intolerance of meat as such.		
	Weinstein	1992	Patients with Creutzfeldt-Jakob disease react badly to meat in the diet.
Beer	All reports were concerned with ethanol intoxication.		
Hops	Mezner & Kajba	1990	Bronchitis in brewery workers.
	Stricker, *et al.*	1986	Idiopathic anaphylactic reaction in 7 out of 102 patients; confirmed by skin prick test.
Peanut	Settipore	1989	Peanuts ingestion is the "most common cause of death by food anaphylaxis in the United states."
	Burks, *et al.*	1989	Peanut protein as a major cause of adverse food reaction in patients with atopic dermatitis.
Peanut	Donovan & Peters	1990	Demonstration that allergy to vegetable burgers was actually reaction to peanuts.

Intolerance	Author(s)	Year	Observation
Cows milk	Kleinman	1992	A review of the extensive literature concerning milk allergy in childhood.
	Norgaard, *et al.*	1992	Ditto and concerning adult patients.

REFERENCES

Aronov, B. (1989) Vinegar essence poisoning. *Feldsher Akush, 54,* 43–48.

Armentia Medina, A (1992) Wheat-dependent, exercise-induced anaphylaxis. *Ann. Allergy, 69,* 464.

Burks, A. W., Williams, L. W., Mallory, S. B., Shirrell, M. A., & Williams, C. (1989) Peanut protein as a major cause of adverse food reactions in patients with atopic dermatitis. *Allergy Proc., 10,* 265–269.

Ciclitra, P. J. & Ellis, H. J. (1987) Investigation of cereal toxicity in Coeliac disease. *Postgrad. Med. J., 63,* 767–775.

Donovan, K. L. & Peters, J. (1990) Vegetable burger allergy: All was not as it appeared. *B.M.J., 300,* 1378.

Dorsh, W., Wagner, H., Bayer, T., Fessler, B., Hein, G., Ring, J., Scheftner, P., Sieber, W., Strasser, T., & Weiss, E. (1988) Antiasthmatic effect of onions. Biochem. Parmacol, 37, 4479–4486.

Hall, R. A. (1976) A schema of the gestalt concept of the organismic flow and its disturbance. In Smith, E. W. L. (Ed.) *The growing edge of gestalt therapy.* New York: Brunner/Mazel.

King, D. S. (1984) Psychological and behavioural effects of food and chemical exposure in sensitive individuals. *Nutritional health, 3,* 137–151.

Klienman, R. E. (1992) Cow milk allergy in fancy and hypoallergetic formulas. *J. Pediat., 121,* S116-121.

Lautier, R. & Wendt, V. (1985) Contact allergy to alliaceae: Case report and literature review. *Derm. Beruf. Umwelt, 33,* 213–215.

Mackarness, R. (1976) *Not all in the mind.* London: Pan.

Mackarness, R. (1980) *Chemical victims.* London: Pan.

Meznar, B. & Kajba, S. (1990) Bronchial responsiveness in hops processing workers. *Plucne Bolesti, 42,* 27–29.

Norgaard, A. Skov, P. S. & Bindsley-Jensen, C. (1992) Egg and milk allergy in adults. *Clin. Exp. Allergy, 22,* 27–29.

Perls, F., Hefferline R., & Goodman P. (1951) *Gestalt therapy.* New York: Dell Publishing Co.

Schauss, A.G. (1984) Nutrition and behavior: Complex interdisciplinary research. *Nutrition health, 3,* 9–37.

Selye, H. (1956) *The stress of life.* New York: McGraw-Hill.

Settipore, G. A. (1989) Anaphylactic deaths in asthmatic patients. *Allergy pro.,* 10, 271–274.

Sluckin, A. (1993) Addressing the whole field: The implications of food and chemical intolerance for psychotherapy. *British gestalt journal, 2,* 10–18.

Stricker, W. E., Anorve-Lopez, E. & Read, C. E. (1986) Food skin testing in patients with idiopathic anaphylaxis. *J. Allergy. Clin. Immunol., 77,* 516-519.

Weinstien, M. (1992). Creutzfeld-Jacob disease. *Neurol. Res., 14,* 335–356.

Yunginger, J. W. (1990) Classical food allergens. *Allergy Proc., 11,* 7–9.

◊

6

"YELENA, YELENA, KEEP YOUR ILLUSION ..." A CRITICAL APPLICATION OF BEISSER'S PARADOXICAL THEORY OF CHANGE

Ruth Ronall[1]

❖◀❖

INTRODUCTION

I have written this chapter in the way I live and work. I first leap and then look, or, rather, I first do and then think ... but, that's not right either ... my leaping/doing is informed almost completely by my seeing/thinking, which I do with my whole self.

In the following report the left hand column contains the narrative of my work with Yelena. It is a description of our spontaneous interactions, it is our unedited dialogue, whereas the right hand column contains my thinking and reasoning and the theory on which I base my interventions. Thus reader, I have given you the whole: practice to the left, theory to the right.

---

1   I wish to thank Yelena, who after reading this chapter gave me permission to publish it, and my colleague and friend, Dan Bloom, who helped me through many a crisis, including the writing of this chapter (for me any writing is a crisis).

OUR SESSIONS

At the beginning of April 1994, I receive a telephone call from a former client saying "I would like to refer somebody to you, a woman who is here in Maine right now, but who is going back to New York soon and who needs therapy urgently. She is in bad shape. She is an artist: a writer, poet, playwright — very talented, very well known here and in New York, and really interesting. I think you will enjoy her, and I know you will help her."

A couple of weeks later this woman, Yelena, calls to make an appointment with me. She sounds depressed. Her voice is dark, her speech not quite clear. When she comes to her first appointment at the end of April, I am shocked at the way she looks. Her hair, cut in bangs, covers her eyes. Her face is swollen (from crying?). She looks disheveled. Her clothes don't seem to be fitting her. She often stops in the middle of a sentence, as she begins to tell me about herself, and her eyes dart all over the room, never resting on me.

She describes herself as "crazed," and that seems to me an accurate description. She says she

I observe that her behavior spells "interruption," principally retroflection, in the darkness of her voice, her muffled speech, her self distraction, self interruption. Her appearance (hair, clothes) suggest that she does not care about the impression she makes on her envi-

doesn't know what's happening. She is beside herself, she can't do any work, she can't do anything. All she can do is think of this man. "This man" is an artist, a set designer, whom she met about a year ago and with whom she started a relationship, both work — he is supposed to design the sets for a play that she is working on with him — and personal. He spent a great deal of time with her; sometimes at work and sometimes at romantic play. They even slept together, although they didn't have sex, because, he claimed, he was celibate. She describes herself as having been sexually active all her life, and missing sex a great deal since her husband died four years ago. This man, who is much younger than she, his name is Bernie, excites her and she dreams of living with him. Recently he suddenly withdrew from her. She had been away for several weeks, and when she came back he was gone. He had been using her apartment (she had given him the keys) and had left some of his belongings, but he no longer called her or answered her calls, and she just couldn't understand what was going on. When they had been working together

ronment. Her eyes avoid contact with me. She may, instead of looking at me and seeing who I am, be projecting some frightening person. She doesn't see the room she is in.

My image of Yelena's contact boundary is that of a very thin, porous membrane that allows everything from the environment to pass through and allows enough from the organism to flow out, all without discrimination.

on the play, he had stated at one point that he had never in his life experienced this, but he felt that his unconscious was in communication with her unconscious, and it was a very deep connection. How could he leave her so abruptly, and why? Was it her age? Was it something else? She puzzles and can't find an answer. She does know that she hasn't thought of anything else, and has been neglecting everything in her life. None of this is directed at me, but spoken into space. I feel no connection. The way she tells her story confirms my initial impression. And I wonder: This was the woman my friend had thought I could help? I would like? When she leaves, she seems a little bit relieved, possibly by having vented her feelings, but I am not sure what she is actually feeling or what part I have had in the process. She makes an appointment for two weeks later, as she is leaving town, and I am not sure whether she will return. Yelena does return. She still Seems quite "crazed," but a little less so. She repeats much of what she had told me in the first session, but seems more aware of me. This awareness is tentative. She states again that she doesn't know what is going on,

I, apparently, am not a figure of interest. She doesn't seem to see me and hardly allows me to say anything. She's not orienting herself in a field which includes me. Her awareness is severely restricted to her own obsessive concerns.

My lack of confidence in her returning is the result of my experience at the contact boundary of her being there and not being there, being with me and yet not being with me.

and I ask her if she would like me to tell her, because I think I can see what is going on. She agrees, and I tell her that I can see that she is in distress because a man that she has fallen in love with has left her. It is so painful that she won't allow herself to know it, but that was what had happened. He had left her. Even though she can see him occasionally in the neighborhood, she can not really talk to him or reestablish the relationship that she had enjoyed, and in her pain she is confusing the situation. She is listening, she is looking at me and I almost feel cruel, to tell her so clearly what is going on, to hear from me what I understand was her situation, as she had so carefully described it to me and yet concealed it from herself. I say, "I know it hurts. There's nothing you can do about it but allow the pain to be." She seems to accept my suggestion (at any rate, she does not protest). She leaves a little bit confused and sadder. When Yelena comes to her third session, she looks a little better, and seems able to be in fuller contact with me. We have a real conversation about what she is experiencing and what it means. She is moving toward me, and we are beginning to form a

This is the beginning of an experiment to help her get "unconfused." Her agreeing was a first clear recognition of me as another person. It means she sees me, she hears me, she opens up to someone else's different idea-these are elements of contact-making.

relationship. She complains bitterly that she knows her daydreams of reestablishing with Bernie are illusionary, but she can't give them up. She fights and fights, but she keeps daydreaming of the relationship. There is nothing else on her mind. "I can't give it up, I can't give it up. This illusion is killing me." Toward the end of our session, I say to her, "Yelena, you don't have to give it up. You can keep it. Only know that this is an illusion. Let yourself be aware that this is an illusion, and keep it." She looks at me with amazement, but seems to understand what I am saying, and on her way out plants a little kiss on my cheek.

Yelena comes back for her next session(she has been away again) looking a different person. She is dressed neatly, her hair is cut and combed, I can see her eyes and her face, she doesn't seem to be in utmost distress. She seems clearer within herself. She says, "That intervention you gave me last time was really powerful. It stayed with me all the time And it is painful and helpful." And again she kisses me on her way out.

During the next sessions, Yelena tells me about herself. Not

I had recognized the "illusion" as Yelena's creative adjustment to her loneliness. As long as she had the illusion she was not totally lonely. By supporting her illusion as an illusion, I gave her the opportunity to resolve the conflict between what she was doing and what she believed she should do. "Change occurs when one becomes what he is, not when he tries to become what he is not" (Beisser, 1970, p. 77).

I sense that I had spoken in language that she understands as an artist. She sees me as her therapist and her idea of the therapeutic relationship includes some friendly, personal element, such as occasional touch. It is certainly not a "cool" relationship; kissing me was her way of acknowledging the woman and the therapist in me. The problem of her infatuation was solved and the process of solving it had enriched her.

her family of origin, but herself as a young woman. She had a long affair with a very famous therapist and she was in therapy, in fact Gestalt therapy, with a woman. She tells me about her marriage to George, who, like her, was way out. Both of them earned a living teaching in public school. And she relates her experience as a housewife, mother, wife, writer and lover. She describes her marriage as having been very good. George had been protective and supportive of her and had admired her and her work. She misses him terribly. She recalls in her marriage there had been a triangle between her husband, herself, and the famous therapist who had not given up the relationship with her after she got married. She is proud of this. She had had a rich and adventurous life, an original life; she had not obeyed any rules, and she had benefited. She does talk sadly about her relationship with her daughters, who are both very talented painters. She describes them as extremely demanding and controlling, very often outright nasty to her and not appreciative at all. Before her husband died, the older daughter was antagonistic to him, and the younger empathized

When an incomplete Gestalt is powerfully and actively foreground little energy is available for anything else. The person, as here Yelena, is stuck, confused, and obsessive (or as she put it, crazed). By suggesting to her that she keep her illusion, be nourished by it, I unfroze a process she wasn't even able to identify or define, namely mourning, and ultimately to finish the Gestalt and move on. This intervention became a "turning point" as the most significant event in our contact.

Although I generally do not support "storytelling," I felt that Yelena was benefiting from telling me about her life. It was a way of restoring her personality function, the verbal repair of herself as she expressed who she was: a talented, successful, creative woman, a woman whose history supports her present being. By telling me about her past, she was putting into context her present pain and thereby allowing herself to heal from the hurts and wounds that she

with him a good deal. And the despair and sense of catastrophe about Bernie's abandonment is gone. It hurts her feelings, and that was natural, but it doesn't "craze" her to know that Bernie is looking for relationships elsewhere. In the next session she says, "I'm really through with him. He doesn't interest me anymore. I don't care what he does." And then comes a surprise. Yelena is leaving again for a two-week trip, and during our last sessions before the trip she leaves a manuscript with me, a play. When I take a look at it I am stunned. It begins as follows: A woman says, "Live the illusion and know it is an illusion. Live an illusion and know it is an illusion? When I lived the illusion and did not know it was an illusion, I was happy. The radiance shone from me. It illuminated the universe, my universe, I was ecstatic, in a state of euphoria, and now you say, live the illusion and know it is an illusion? Oh how can I do that? How can it be?"

had received from Bernie. She was restoring the picture of the competent, strong, creative woman that she actually is.

However, this is not all Yelena needs from me. The problem with Bernie was like the opening chapter of a novel which I offer the reader as a story which stands on its own as a discrete example of brief therapy.

Yelena had integrated the experience of letting go of her illusion into her artistic, creative self.

EPILOGUE

It is spring 1996. It is two years now since Yelena first came to see me. During this time she has come fairly regularly and worked intensively. Her intelligence has helped her not only to understand what is happening in therapy but also to transfer her experience into her daily life. She has gradually accepted that she cannot count on her daughters for company or practically anything else. And she realizes that this is not her fault. She has started again to write and derives great satisfaction from that and other professional activities such as giving readings and participating in committees. She has also been traveling and will spend four weeks this summer in Prague as a writer-in-residence. Her professional accomplishments have restored her sense of self-worth. She is less confluent and much more discerning about what she gives out and what she takes in. She no longer needs to see me as often as a year ago, and she has become more content with her life.

REFERENCE

Beisser, A. (1970) The paradoxical theory of change. In Fagan, J. & Shepherd I. L. (Eds.) *Gestalt therapy now*. Palo Alto: Science and Behavior Books.

◇

7

PSYCHIATRY AND GESTALT THERAPY: BEGINNING TO OWN PARTS

Ginny McFarlane

❖◀❖

I am not
prose
linear
straight
to the point
connections
I am not
story
beginning
middle
end
as one
totality
I am not
essay
thesis
proofs
conclusions
I am not
poetry
meter
rhyme
themes

I am not
word
letters
sounds
meaning
I am not
grammar
punctuation
distinction
linking
bits
I am not
them
I am scattered
No
not here
Now
I scatter
bits
outward
they --- NO
I come
at me.

I felt scattered, No. I scattered myself when I first studied Gestalt Therapy while continuing to practice psychiatry as a Physician Therapist. Gestalt Therapy dictated, "Work this way with the client"; Psychiatry dictated, "No, work this way with the patient." Now, I am aware that I project these dictates. I work both ways: I am beginning to own my seemingly disparate parts, or polarities, as a Gestalt Therapist and a Physician Therapist.

Whether or not you are a physician, you also may be grappling with these disparate parts. You may be trying to blend the best of Gestalt Therapy and Psychiatry. In many cases you may be doing this unawares, but you will serve better your patient/clients if you practice this hybrid therapy in awareness. To give you ideas of how to blend Psychiatry and Gestalt Therapy, I wrote these two case histories.

Why do I call Gestalt Therapy and Psychiatry polarities? Technically speaking they are not. Sharing many common roots, Gestalt Therapy emerged from mainstream Psychiatry[1] which continues to retain many of the elements of Psychoanalysis. However, mainstream Psychiatry has largely shifted its approach from Psychoanalysis to the medical mode[2]. On the other hand, Gestalt Therapy by leaving mainstream Psychiatry when it did, has not joined the march towards the medical model.

Consequently, history-taking, physical examination, investigations, diagnoses, and treatment plans are basic methods of Psychiatry. The methods of Gestalt Therapy are different. Consider the following two lists.

---

1   Mainstream psychiatry is meant here to include psychoanalysis as one of its components. However, this chapter is describing how the medical model of psychiatry, not psychoanalysis, can be combined with Gestalt Therapy.

2   At a Harvard conference in psychiatry in September 1995, I was impressed by the extent to which the medical model is dominating psychiatry: Psychiatry is beginning to look like a branch of Neurology.

Gestalt Therapy	Psychiatry
here and now	history
client	patient
response-able	not responsible
dis-ease	disease
person-to-person	doctor and patient
contact	examine
encounter	diagnose
I and Thou	*Diagnostic and Statistical Manual IV*
in the moment	
experiments	treatment plans
	medications
experiences	
integrate	symptoms
awareness	analyze
	insight
alive	
	cured
art	
holism	science
philosophy	dualism
of the obvious	brain research

Is there a way to blend these two polarities without losing their meanings, integrity, and usefulness? I believe there is.

The following two cases illustrate how Psychiatry and Gestalt Therapy can be blended. Each case is only a part of a human story which is complex, as are all human stories. And inter-woven with their stories is my story of working on integrating my polarities as a Physician Therapist and Gestalt Therapist.

CHERYL: PAPAYA JUICE AND COCONUT MILK

When I met Cheryl in October 1994, I encountered an intelligent, funny, articulate, warm, attractive, and accomplished woman. As a 38 year old, single writer she had written, and acted in, several successful plays. Currently she was majoring in English at The University of Toronto and doing very well. Despite this, she was complaining of low mood, oversleeping, overeating, weight gain, and grief over her recent losses of her boyfriend, and her psychiatrist whom she had fired. After the first visit, my psychiatric mind told me she was Manic-Depressive (or Bipolar 1, according to The Diagnostic and Statistical Manual of Mental Disorders, fourth edition[3]); my Gestalt gut told me she had a primary resistance of introjection[4], alienating her from herself. As time went by, I discovered that both were true.

Over the first several sessions, I heard Cheryl's psychiatric history. As a physician, I am obligated, by the standards of my profession, to take a psychiatric history, ensure that a physical examination takes place, conduct investigations, and make a diagnosis and treatment plan.

---

3   Bipolar 1 Disorder, or Manic-Depressive Disorder as I prefer to call it, is described in the *Diagnostic and Statistical Manual of Mental Disorders, fourth edition (DSM IV)*, on page 350. It is distinguished from a Unipolar Depression by the inclusion of at least one Manic episode. Bipolar II Disorder has a Hypomanic episode, rather than a Manic episode. Descriptions of Manic, Hypomanic, and Depressed episodes can be found in the *DSM IV* on pages 332, 338 and 327 respectively. The description of a Unipolar Depression, or Major Depressive disorder as it is now called, can be found on page 339.

4   By a primary resistance of introjection, I am referring to Ralph Hefferline and Paul Goodman's idea of the introjector as described by them in *Gestalt Therapy*, Chapter XV, and developed by JoAnne Greenham, my teacher at the Gestalt Institute of Toronto.

As Cheryl told me her story of her current and past sufferings, I became convinced that she had a chemical imbalance which needed to be dealt with before any imbalances in her personality could be addressed. I discovered that over the past twenty years, Cheryl had had recurring episodes of mania and depression requiring numerous admissions to hospital. When she was manic she had episodes of "speeding-up," being unable to sleep or eat, having delusions of grandeur, alterations in her perceptions and frank hallucinations. She would be treated with antipsychotics, released from hospital, and then she would sink into a deep depression with which she somehow coped. As far as she knew, no one had ever suggested she was Manic-Depressive, and she had never been treated with Lithium. (Months after I had made the diagnosis, when I got the charts from her previous therapist, I discovered that her most recent psychiatrist had diagnosed her as Manic-Depressive, and had unsuccessfully treated her with Valproic Acid, a less commonly used mood stabilizer.)

Like my predecessors, I had trouble making the diagnosis. I had never diagnosed someone as having Manic-Depressive Disorder. And I found it hard to believe that I could correctly diagnose someone when for twenty years more highly experienced therapists had failed to do so. I also found it hard to believe that Cheryl could be Manic-Depressive when she seemed to cope so well.

While the physician doubted, the gestaltist became intrigued with the human being before me. In an early session, Cheryl drew a picture of herself as a very mechanical-looking alien. She became aware of feeling controlled and not in charge of her life. I believed this reflected her difficulties with introjection. For awhile I forgot how Manic-Depressive illness is controlling too. And for several sessions, while my physician took a psychiatric history, my gestaltist made several observations.

I noticed how Cheryl seemed to have introjected her mother who had died of breast cancer when Cheryl was 18 years old. She was still grieving for her mother and at times would physically, emotionally and mentally emulate her: "Rise and shine. Greet the day. There's so much to do. So much to live for. Give everything your best." These credos were fine when Cheryl was hypo-manic and had the energy for them. Then she would organize her apartment, buy a new dress, throw a party, and write a new play. And she would do them all well, until she crashed. Being like hypomanic mom was "fine" as long as Cheryl was hypo-manic too.

When she was depressed, Cheryl slowed down, found life a drudgery, to be slowly plodded through to get to the next point of comfort, a good book, a tasty meal, and a long sleep. During these times, Cheryl would call her mother, "A shrew of the highest degree."

During some of the early sessions, as I took her history, I would periodically suggest a gestalt exercise which fit in with what we were discussing. Through different gestalt exercises — empty chair work, role-playing, drawings, and so on - Cheryl seemed more at peace with her father than her mother. He had lived a semi-retired life, working the stock market and reading numerous books; he had died when Cheryl was 27 years old. With her father, Cheryl was able to take him in, "chew" on him, "digest" those parts which agreed with her and make them her own, and "spit out" the rest. But her mother she either "swallowed" whole, or "threw up."

However, as I became aware of these connections, I was also aware that Cheryl was suffering. Without the appropriate medicine, she would never come to terms with her introjected mother, her manic-depressive polarity, or her grief over both.

Having to adhere to the standards of my professions as a physician saved me and Cheryl from missing the diagnosis. I completed the information-gathering, and very gently started discussing the possibility that she was Manic-Depressive in a depressed phase. Cheryl was very resistant to this diagnosis, and said she didn't want medication, she wanted Gestalt Therapy. So, putting on my Gestalt Therapy hat, I stayed with her resistance, and gently worked in a Gestalt Therapy mode, stressing basic principles of now-ness, awareness, and responsibility.

Perhaps through Gestalt experiments, or her own devices, Cheryl became more aware of her depression and need for medical help. So I put on my physician hat and educated her regarding different types of depression and treatments. Together we agreed to try an antidepressant, Sertraline, and continue to use Gestalt Therapy to work through her issues. Thinking that she had a Bipolar, not a Unipolar, Depression, and was therefore at risk of inducing a mania with the antidepressant, I watched her carefully. I also insisted, as my boundary in the relationship, that she see a psychiatrist to confirm the diagnosis, and get her blood work done, particularly her thyroid function which, if too low, could mimic depression.

Cheryl saw Dr. K., the psychiatrist, who firmly stated that she was Manic-Depressive, needed Lithium, and needed to go off the Sertraline or find herself in a manic psychosis. Cheryl felt "bludgeoned" and refused to go on Lithium, and off Sertraline. The gestaltist stayed with her resistance and left her medications as is, while the physician watched her closely. And when her thyroid function came back low, I suggested thyroid replacement therapy, to which she readily agreed.

Over the next two months, Cheryl got marginally better with only mild episodes of hypo-mania. These episodes gave further weight to the diagnosis of Manic-Depressive illness, for Cheryl and me. We talked extensively about Manic-Depressive illness, and Cheryl read several books about it.

At the end of March 1995, six months after she first started seeing me, Cheryl started Lithium. Over the next few months, her depression gradually lifted. And while her mood, energy, and relationships with family and friends improved, her problems with sleep, appetite and weight gain persisted. Cheryl blamed it on the Lithium, and still does. I wondered about the entire medicinal cocktail, as well as her difficulties with introjection. By eliminating the Sertraline (much to my relief as a physician). Cheryl's over-sleeping improved. Rechecking the thyroid showed it to be too low, likely contributing to the over-sleeping and weight gain. Adjustment of the dose helped Cheryl's over-sleeping, but she has continued to have problems with her weight. Why? My physician says: Because of the Lithium; my Gestaltist says: Because of Cheryl's difficulties with introjection. And I believe both are true.

And so in the past several months, as Cheryl's Manic-Depressive illness and hypothyroidism have gradually improved and receded into the background, her difficulties with introjection have emerged as the figure of therapy. And not surprisingly the polarity of manic versus depressed has been her main focus.

All along Cheryl has been ambivalent about being Manic-Depressive. "On the one hand it's good: I know I'm not aberrant. On the other hand, it's bad: I'm no longer special, unique." And it's the manic part of Cheryl that has made her feel special, and believe she can be creative, energetic, and excited about life. But it's also the part that she dreads — she's lost money, her house and relationships by being manic. Mania is desirable and unacceptable to her.

A few months ago, while working with her difficulties with her closest and oldest friend, Lee, Cheryl realized that to understand Lee's behavior — creative, energetic, and lively — is to "legitimize psychosis, and mania." Doing more chair work with Lee, Cheryl envied Lee's vitality, and realized, that for that day, she did not want to be as ambitious or single-minded as she. During a dream work exercise, Cheryl became aware that she missed Lee and could not forgive her behavior. I wondered if forgiving Lee would mean she'd be forgiving her mania, and her mother, for whom Lee's behavior was somewhat resembling.

The next week, after seeing again Dr. K. the psychiatrist, and being reminded of feeling "bludgeoned" by his diagnosis a year earlier, Cheryl became more aware of her grief over being Manic-Depressive, and missing her mania. She did a hot seat between "No-medication Cheryl," and "Medicated Cheryl." She noticed that the former was concerned with her outward appearance, whereas the latter was concerned with her inward feelings and well-being. I noticed that "No-medication Cheryl," wanting to look good, used a parental voice that I had heard Cheryl use when role-playing her mother. I wondered if she was caught in a dilemma which went far beyond simply coming to terms with being Manic-Depressive: to be untreated, to allow herself to be manic, was to identify with her mother, be the introjected mother, and keep her alive; and to be treated, to no longer be manic or depressed, but some blending of the two, was to be Cheryl, owning parts of mother and mania, and possibly parts of father and depression.

To some degree my suspicions were confirmed in the next few sessions. Cheryl continued to blame the Lithium for her lack of vitality, and put herself into a hypo-manic state by decreasing her dose of Lithium. Realizing she was slipping out of control- partly because Lee had expressed concern over her behavior - Cheryl also realized that her mother was probably Bipolar II[5]. She said, "This is what my mother must have felt like all the time!" Disliking her irritability, poor sleep, and super-sensitivity towards her environment, Cheryl resumed her previous dose of Lithium. I also rechecked her thyroid function, found it to be too high, possibly contributing to the hypo-mania, and decreased her dose of thyroid replacement.

In the next session, Cheryl came in emotionally split between manic and depressed. This was reflected in her appearance: blue nails, beautiful jewelry and a new hair style on the one hand; and baggy, comfortable pants, a T-shirt, and sturdy shoes on the other hand. Doing empty chair work with the two appearances, she realized she didn't want to be either way. But she was also unhappy being in limbo.

A few weeks later, when I mentioned the possibility of being neither manic, nor depressed, and blending what was good about both, Cheryl rejected this idea. She said, "To truly feel neither depressed or manic you have to believe that both are gone."

Does this mean that Cheryl will have to believe — accept — that both her parents are gone? I don't know. This is part of my theory, and not necessarily Cheryl's experience. I do know that she is still struggling, and getting closer, to coming to terms with being a human being with Manic-Depressive Disorder, and being manic and depressed, and with introjecting, and grieving for, her mother and father. Cheryl's own poem, which she wrote shortly after being diagnosed, and has recently revised, expresses best where she is at in terms of dealing with these polarities.

"Mania"

Mania is so seductive,
amorphous,
deceitful
like the devil
it slips in and out of guises:

---

5   The description of Bipolar II can be found in the *DSM IV* on page 359.

First it fills you with Aphrodite's charms
a soft Jasmine breeze lifts your dress
and all your fawning cupids
lie in wait to do your bidding.

Next Prospero appears,
his benevolent conjuring
allows feats of the impossible:
others freeze in mid-sentence,
their actions conforming blindly to your will.

They look at you with temerity
You master them with silent skill

Mania promises everything
success attention love
boundless energy
profound clarity of thought
extraordinary insights
things that can't be bought

Voila — you've invincible
Cleopatra on the Nile
but when you least suspect it
the serpent starts to smile
he says "You aren't Aphrodite,
your sorcery is cursed"

(And he says it like an actor
Whose lines have been rehearsed)

But what about the insight?
The vision? the call?

You talk about the ecstasy --
He leers "it's just the pride before the fall."

"Thanks for the tip"
I respond as I turn to run away,
but he commands me to wait
hissing
I've got one more thing to say

"Remember Faustus"
with that he gathers up his huge black cloak
and vanishes

As a cloud of sticky black vapor dispersed
I thought I heard a hoarse voice warn
"I'll be back."

So the moral
my manic-depressive friends
is painfully, sadly clear
look out for the wily serpent
for his tricks are always near

He'll give you a world called Euphoria
so he can add you to his list
then he'll take your manic-depressive soul
and vanish in the mist.

When Cheryl and I recently got together to discuss her story in this chapter, she treated me to a fruit drink that she had concocted. I was unable to discern the parts of the drink. So she told me, "It's papaya juice and coconut milk. Isn't that the perfect combination of yin and yang?!" I agreed, and secretly hoped that she would one day experience herself that way, a perfect combination of yin and yang.

Cheryl's story demonstrates how she needed and benefited from Gestalt Therapy and psychiatry. Without psychiatry, and especially its diagnostic and treatment tools, Cheryl would have been unable to cope with beginning to work through her grief and polarities. Without Gestalt Therapy, and especially its experiential approaches which allow clients to discover their own truths, Cheryl might not have taken the medications which are giving her the ability to work through her grief and polarities. Gestalt Therapy got her to psychiatry; psychiatry got her to Gestalt Therapy. And the therapeutic combination is bringing her closer to that "perfect combination of yin and yang."

DEBBIE: THE BUTTERFLY AND THE ELEPHANT

When I met Debbie in March 1994, I met an angry, demanding, intelligent, serious, and distrustful 39 year old, single mother. During other early sessions, I met a happy, easy-going, playful warm and friendly young woman. I accepted them both as Debbie, assuming that the happy presentation reflected her increasing comfort with me. Later, Debbie and I realized that these two presentations were two of her alternate personalities, "Holly," and "Missy" the latter being one of "the kids." If I had been blind, as were the men in the story, The Blind Men and the Elephant, I would have believed that I had met two different people. But I could see, and what I saw was one very complicated woman.

My feelings towards Debbie were as multiple as was she. Sometimes during our sessions, I felt heavy, and other days, I felt light. Nevertheless, she intrigued the gestaltist in me. She presented a classic picture of a retroflector[6], or as I prefer to call it, a primary resistance of retroflection. While at

---

6   By a primary resistance of retroflection, I am referring to Ralph Hefferline and Paul Goodman's idea of the retroflector as described by them in *Gestalt*

times she was angry or happy, most of the time she was emotionally flat with an impassive face, dead voice, and very still, slightly over-weight body. Her anger would escape retroflection in the form of masked, witty barbs and demands. She had many physical complaints: migraine, tension and "those" headaches[7], neck and back pain, and many more. She retroflected her aggression: she abused LSD for ten years; seriously attempted suicide at Christmas 1990; drank excessive amounts of coffee and over-ate inducing significant gastrointestinal discomfort, and an ulcer at one point; and she compulsively cleaned inducing profound exhaustion.

Gradually I discovered another form of retroflection: "forgetting herself," or dissociation. As my Physician Therapist made the diagnoses of Posttraumatic Stress Disorder (PTSD)[8] and Dissociative Identity Disorder (DID)[9], formerly called Multiple Personality Disorder, my gestaltist, diagnosing retroflection, had an approach to working with Debbie's physical complaints, compulsions, and eventually her traumas and dissociative states.

Initially I worked mainly as a Physician Therapist, taking her psychiatric history. I discovered other therapists had diagnosed her with PTSD, Bipolar II Disorder, Bulimia Nervosa[10] and Drug Abuse, the latter thankfully in remission for ten years. She had been the victim of childhood emotional and physical abuse at the hands of her mother, childhood sexual abuse at the hands of her grandfather, brother and possibly her father, and rape by a trusted friend when she was twenty-four years old. Debbie was

---

Therapy, Chapter XV, and developed by JoAnne Greenham.

7   At this point, Debbie was not fully aware that "those" headaches signaled dissociation.

8   The description of Posttraumatic Stress Disorder can be found in the *DSM IV* on page 424.

9   Dissociative Identity Disorder, or Multiple Personality Disorder, can be found in the *DSM IV* on page 484. Technically speaking, because Debbie's alters do not have full-blown personalities and have some awareness of each other, Debbie is classified as Dissociative Disorder Not Otherwise Specified which can be found on page 490.

10   The description of Bulimia Nervosa can be found in the *DSM IV* on page 545.

reticent about these issues, and I still know very few concrete details of what she experienced.

While she had four psychiatric diagnoses, she also had some medical problems. She smoked and consequently suffered from Chronic Bronchitis, had frequent migraines, and was recovering from ankle surgery for an accidental fracture. When I met Debbie, she was on seven different medications.

Furthermore, her current social situation was not healthy. Fracturing her ankle forced her to quit her college program in Human Services. Due to numerous problems, she was unable to work and was on Social Assistance. Her eighteen year old daughter, Joan, was living with her and "driving her crazy." Because of her own troubled history of rapes, "slashing" herself, and crime, Joan had mood swings which she dumped on Debbie. And Debbie was alone: she had broken-up with her long term alcoholic boyfriend, Bill, she had only one of her thirteen siblings living in Toronto, the rest living in Nova Scotia; she had a mother, also in Nova Scotia, who had disowned her when she was sixteen, and she had an alcoholic father who never contacted her.

As a Gestalt Therapist and Physician Therapist I felt confused, overwhelmed and challenged by Debbie. As a Gestalt Therapist, I suspected that as much as her story was complex, it had to be simple, or at least simpler: the other side of the polarity had to be true. And as a Physician Therapist, I set out to find this simpler answer. I used every relevant psychiatric investigative tool I could find to make a more parsimonious diagnosis[11].

Debbie and I spent our first year together making the diagnosis while we got to know each other by working on her headaches and social problems. Her physical examination, done by her family physician, and her lab work, did not reveal any abnormalities, eliminating any undetected "organic" conditions. Her charts from her previous therapists showed numerous diagnoses, and a very "complicated" and "challenging" picture. I referred her to the Clarke Institute of Psychiatry which suggested that the Prozac was

---

11   Parsimony, in the medical world, is the principle by which one attempts to bring all of the data together under one explanation, or diagnosis, if at all possible.

inducing mood swings. I took her off of the Prozac, and her mood continued to swing.

The Clarke Institute also suggested that she was a Borderline Personality[12], a "complicated" and "challenging" diagnosis with which to work. I had suspected this too, and was concerned that I was working with someone with problems demanding skills well beyond my abilities. At the same time, I was getting to know Debbie and appreciate how she suffered.

In the first few months, Debbie showed me how she suffered, leading me to suspect she had DID. One day she came in complaining of "losing time." One moment she had one of "those" headaches, and felt tired, and the next moment, she had no headaches and was alert. In the meantime, forty minutes had gone by during which she had made supper and seemed "not herself," according to her daughter who had witnessed the event. Debbie had no recollection of making supper, yet it was there before her, ready to eat. She had "forgotten herself."

The Physician Therapist went into action. Wondering about Temporal Lobe Epilepsy, I ordered an electroencephalogram (EEG). It was negative. Wondering about DID, I consulted Dr. D., a psychiatrist specializing in DID and PTSD. At her suggestion, I had Debbie complete the DES and DDIS questionnaires for dissociation[13]. They strongly suggested DID.

But I didn't believe that Debbie had DID. I didn't believe because I had never seen, let alone made, the diagnosis of DID. Surely the numerous psychiatrists before me would have caught this. (Later I learned that making many erroneous diagnoses, and needing a long time to make the diagnosis of DID, is very common when a therapist is dealing with someone with DID.)

---

12   The description of Borderline Personality Disorder, a highly controversial and sometimes derogatory diagnosis, and can be found in the *DSM IV* on page 650.

13   The DES (Dissociative Experiences Scale) and DDIS (Dissociative Disorders Interview Schedule) questionnaires are valid and reliable tools for diagnosing DID. See Burstein and Putnam: "Development, Reliability and Validity and Dissociation Scales."

While I doubted, Debbie continued to provide evidence of DID. She told me of an angry, negative woman's voice that she experienced on her left shoulder; and of a happy, playful little girl that she felt on her left thigh. Either one would "come out," without her control, and take over her personality. Her daughter, Joan, and boyfriend Bill to whom she had returned, both knew these "people," and would say, "Where's Debbie?" Over time I came to know them too as "Holly" and "Missy," the two people I had met in our first few sessions.

While the Physician Therapist doubted, the Gestalt Therapist accepted "Holly" and "Missy" as disowned parts. In the fourth month, Debbie did chair work with a child (? "Missy" or one of the "the Kids") and an angry woman (? "Holly") appeared in the opposite chair. Debbie felt extremely anxious, so I took off my Gestalt Therapy hat and put on my Physician Therapist hat, and guided her through a relaxation exercise to diminish her anxiety, and close the session.

In the next session, Debbie did chair work with a parent (? "Holly") and a child (? "Missy"). She realized that the child, despite the parent's reassurances, didn't trust the parent to defend her.

The parent lived up to her responsibility. In the next session, Debbie, or was it "Holly," came in angry, agitated and demanding "more processing" of chair work. At this early point, Gestalt Therapy was inducing anxiety, likely necessary, but Debbie, and I, weren't ready for it. The Gestalt Therapist backed off, and the Physician Therapist heard her complaints as recurrent depression and placed her on a new antidepressant, Fluvoxamine.

Despite the medication, over the next few months Debbie complained of increasing depression, anxiety, flashbacks, and nightmares as more and more of her alters made their presence known. She told me of a "flash" of each of her "selves" in a multi-paned window, all with dirty, tired faces, wearing army helmets, and saying. "We want to be seen." The Gestaltist treated the "flash" as a projection, and asked Debbie to try on each projection. She did and felt pleased with herself. In a subsequent joint session with her daughter, Joan, I saw a child. Joan, who by now was supportive of Debbie, confirmed that "Missy" was present. Debbie/"Missy" giggled, delighting at being seen.

Following this Debbie discontinued her Lithium and experienced no change in her mood. She and I started to put aside the diagnosis of Bipolar II.

During this first year, I worked psychotherapeutically with Debbie as a Gestaltist while I gathered evidence as a Physician Therapist. Debbie did numerous Gestalt exercises to work on her disowned and retroflected parts and polarities. She found these exercise's helpful. "Here and now I am aware of …" gave her a way to ground herself when overwhelmed by flashbacks and nightmares. Visualizations calmed her. And empty chair work, dream work, drawings and journaling invited her to reveal her alters to herself and me.

My Physician Therapist found the exercises helpful too as they provided me with more evidence for DID, and a framework for believing in, and understanding, dissociation. I don't know if I could have ever worked with Debbie if I hadn't been a Gestaltist because as a Physician Therapist, with no experience with DID, I had trouble believing that dissociation was a real phenomenon. By seeing Debbie as a retroflector, I began to see dissociation as an extreme form of retroflection. I began to accept the mounting psychiatric evidence before me: the diagnostic questionnaires, normal lab results (consistent with DID), corroborating reports of Joan, ineffectiveness and irrelevance of medications, and the multifaceted human being before me.

But a year after I first met her, I doubted the diagnosis again when Debbie came in describing a "vision." She had had one of "those" headaches and been unable to sleep when she "saw" a "Native seventeen year old male." For forty-five minutes, she had a telepathic conversation with him, and afterwards her headache was gone and she felt a "weight off her shoulders." Debbie believed this was more evidence of dissociation, but also questioned, "Is it possible that I make this up to get attention?" I wondered the same, repeating lab work, and the EEG. Again they were normal. Reviewing her chart, I saw glaring evidence of DID. I referred her to Dr. D, the psychiatrist, to reassure myself.

Dr. D confirmed that Debbie "has features of DID and PTSD, both frequent sequelae of childhood sexual, physical and emotional abuse and neglect." She found nothing to suggest malingering. She suggested that

Debbie and I continue working as we were, using Gestalt exercises to gently explore her experiences and alters, "with grounding and safety taking precedence." Dr. D also suggested that Debbie and I continue to understand dissociation along a continuum of experiences.

As a Physician Therapist and Gestalt Therapist, I felt vindicated. As a Physician Therapist, I stopped fretting, and loosened the reins on myself as a Gestalt Therapist. For the next two months, I forgot Dr. D's caution and plunged in too deeply and quickly. Protecting her alters — which she was starting to appreciate as creative adjustments to her traumas — Debbie resisted working with me. As I did with Cheryl, I stayed with Debbie's resistance and followed her lead. At her request, I reviewed Gestalt awareness exercises to promote grounding; visualizations to cope with anxiety and insomnia. She found these helpful.

Repeatedly I suggested that she "put me in the chair" to facilitate her sense of being "response-able" to cope with her problems. The Gestaltist recognized that the Physician Therapist's diagnosis of DID and PTSD, in making her "not responsible" for her problems through the act of labeling, could dis-empower her. Debbie's frequent requests for me to "fix" her confirmed this. Now Debbie spontaneously puts her own therapist in the chair when she is with me, and on her own at home. She feels positive that she is solving her own problems.

But initially Debbie resisted being "response-able," and accepting her diagnoses of DID and PTSD. For example, she asked for various psychiatric treatments. Ensuring that they were safe, I prescribed them. In an orderly manner (for example, conducting "n of one studies")[14], Debbie tried "light" therapy (for Seasonal Affective Disorder), and retried Fluvoxamine and

---

14   An "n of one study" is an experimental method, conducted on only one patient, usually to determine the effectiveness of a treatment for that patient. Typically it follows the following format: introduce the treatment for a given number of days or weeks, while measuring specific outcome measures; remove the treatment for the same length of time, while taking the same measures; reintroduce the treatment for at least the same length of time, while again taking the same measures; and stop or continue the treatment depending on

Lithium. None of them made a difference, and she stopped each of them in turn.

Continuing to resist her diagnosis, Debbie frequently requested help with her troubling headaches. Again I stayed with her resistance, hoping that following her lead would strengthen her sense of safety with me and herself. Through this work, Debbie and I discovered she has three kinds of headaches and how to deal with them. She has tension headaches which she can "cure" by going into them, exaggerating them and venting her anger. She has "those" headaches which signal the emergence of an alter, and which dissolve when she pays attention and lets the alter speak. This is done with chair work, journaling and visualization. And she has true migraine head-aches induced by the other two kinds of headaches, changes in the baromet-ric pressure, and Fiorinal abuse. Drastically reducing her Fiorinal use from thirty to four per month, and reducing her caffeine and nicotine intake has diminished all of her headaches. Debbie still has headaches, but they are fewer, less severe, shorter and not out of her control.

By staying with her resistance — preferring to address physical pain, headaches, rather than emotional pain, trauma and dissociation — Debbie, my Gestaltist and Physician Therapist were all satisfied. We all worked through her headaches to get to her traumas and dissociation.

In a similar way, by working on her day to day problems with family and friends, Debbie and I got to her trauma and dissociation. By doing empty chair work, and other Gestalt exercises concerning her family and friends, Debbie became more comfortable with them, herself, me, and with working experientially. By the end of 1995, she started to let her alters "speak" and give their opinion of her friends and family. This has naturally lead her to working directly on her trauma which is the precipitant of her DID.

---

the results. In Debbie's case we did not reintroduce the Lithium because we were both convinced of its ineffectiveness.

At the same time, however, Debbie's anxiety, flashbacks, "chaos" or "noise in the head"[15], nightmares and insomnia worsened. These symptoms, like Cheryl's, were blocking her work on her issues. This time when Debbie started the antidepressant, Paroxetine, she and I were both clear as to its purpose: anxiolytic and sedative to attenuate, not numb, her PTSD symptoms so she could face her traumas and alters.

Paroxetine has been helpful: it has allowed Debbie to stay longer with her feelings, flashbacks and interpersonal conflicts. She can see them through in the office, and more importantly, out of the office.

Discovering that her twenty year old daughter, Joan, was pregnant led Debbie into grieving her own pregnancy with Joan when she was twenty years old. Using empty chair work, and projection exercises, Debbie felt some of her pain caused by her abusive mother. For the first time, she expressed some sadness, hurt and betrayal as she recounted how her mother had shamed her by turning her head and walking to the other side of the street when she saw pregnant Debbie coming.

In January, 1996, I moved out of my office in a psychiatric clinic into a homey office at The Gestalt Institute of Toronto[16]. My physical, professional move paralleled (? partly precipitated) Debbie's move towards working directly on her PTSD and DID, and her move towards regarding herself, and working as, a Gestalt Therapy client, rather than a psychiatric patient. At the end of February 1996, Debbie asked to work directly on her DID and PTSD. She also agreed to seeing a psychiatric nurse at home to deal with her vocational and social issues, and so free-up her time with me to focus on her PTSD and DID.

---

15   When several, or all, of Debbie's alters were "talking in her head", she experienced "chaos", or "noise in the head". This is not an auditory hallucination; it is an extreme form of what we all experience when we have mixed feelings about something.

16   Since then, the building that housed the Gestalt Institute of Toronto has been sold, and I have moved again into my own solo practice. Somehow this symbolizes how I have gone from being a Physician Therapist to a Gestalt Therapist to a Physician Gestalt Therapist.

At the end of May 1996, Debbie took her first decisive step towards working on her trauma and dissociation. Up until this point, she had only hinted of her trauma in very vague terms. Staying with her distance and resistance to owning her story, I suggested that she write it, in the present tense and the third person, and then read it to me while looking away. She did so, and told a detailed story of how Zack, a trusted friend, had raped her when she was twenty-four years old. Instead of being emotionally flat, or expressing obtuse anger ("Holly") or silent, frozen fear ("the kids"), she cried gently, feeling the complicated feelings of hurt and betrayal.

Given that she had never before worked directly on a trauma, I was not surprised that she was angry with herself when she came into the next session: her entire system of self-preservation was under fire. I suggested she direct her anger outward, in fantasy, at her daughter Joan, Joan's boyfriend, and her own boyfriend, Bill. Having done this she realized, "I'm afraid of seeing reality" meaning her traumas. Verbalizing that placed her into reality and she became "chaotic." But this time, instead of asking to be "fixed," she went into the bodily sensations of her chaos, and then used chair work to let her alters speak. She realized, when she "saw the kids" sitting in a group beside me, that they were scared. And she also realized that angry "Holly" had been protecting them all along. Since then, Debbie has been able to feel hurt, as opposed to raw anger, and she has been able to be more appreciative of her parts especially "Holly" whom she had despised.

Debbie is by no means an integrated person. And she is on her way. Here are some of her recent comments about herself.

Headaches:
"Blocking excitement gives me anxiety and a headache."
"I do them (headaches) to me."

Interpersonal conflicts:
"Bill and Joan are not always the bad guys: I have a responsibility. But I know I'm not able to say 50-50."
"By dealing with conflicts now, I am letting go of the past."

PTSD:

"When I take responsibility out there, my feelings are neither bad nor good. They are what I feel, and they are real. So hear me."

DID:

"Holly's a resistor to better mental health, and she protects me and the kids from people Who aren't safe."
"Sometimes I feel very proud of my parts and what they've done for me. (I'm trying to not say 'they.')"
"Sometimes what they feel, I feel now."
"Nobody's alienated, everybody's waiting if they're needed."
"They'll always be a part of me."

Psychiatry:

"Investigations (Beck Depression Inventory[17], DES, DDIS, and 'n of one studies') are helpful to see where I am — I'm still like that."
"Seeing Dr. D was heavy and helpful. It was maddening and made me think."

Gestalt Therapy:

"Here and now is almost ingrained in me now."
"Learned by breathing how to stay with a memory for a bit longer without too much fear."
"Chair work is so hard but so good. The physical movement itself releases and opens parts of me."
"By doing the 'chair,' I can see my 'people' better and now there is much less noise and chaos within."

---

17   The Beck Depression Inventory, developed by Aaron Beck, is a valid and reliable diagnostic questionnaire for measuring someone's level of depression. See: Beck, A. T. Cognitive Therapy and the Emotional Disorders. New York, International Universities Press, 1976.

Therapy Overall:

"Never any major expectations. It's a slow but sure process of awareness."

"Awareness means less chaos."

Recently when Debbie told me she loves butterflies and elephants, and has pictures and figurines of them throughout her apartment, I thought, "How appropriate." The metamorphosing butterfly, and the story The Blind Men and the Elephant came to my mind. This is Debbie's story: She is becoming herself as she is beginning to own her different parts, to which she was once blind, and experience them all as parts of the same person, Debbie.

Of course, Debbie's story is not finished: she is just beginning to own her parts and deal with her traumas. Psychiatry and Gestalt Therapy will continue to provide the forums for her work. Psychiatry will provide the diagnostic focus, and medicinal treatments. Gestalt Therapy will provide the therapeutic, experiential tools to bring out her alters, and to bring out her traumas from the "there and then" into the "here and now" to allow healing and integration.

PSYCHIATRY AND GESTALT THERAPY: BEGINNING TO OWN PARTS

Cheryl's and Debbie's stories clearly illustrate how psychiatry and Gestalt Therapy can be blended to meet the needs of the patient/client. At times psychiatry was the figure for therapy, and Gestalt Therapy receded into the background; at other times Gestalt Therapy was the figure for therapy, and psychiatry receded into the background. Whether figure or ground, they were both always present informing Cheryl's and Debbie's processes towards healing and integration.

In terms of my integration as a Physician Therapist and Gestalt Therapist, I oscillate less between these two seeming polarities. At times I am more of a Physician Therapist, and at other times I am more of a Gestalt Therapist. And more and more, I am a blend of the two: I am a Physician Gestalt Therapist.

Whether or not you are a physician, you are profoundly influenced by the psychiatric world. In the interest of serving better your clients, I challenge you, Gestalt Therapists, to incorporate some psychiatric considerations and methods into your work. And in the interest of serving better your patients, I challenge you, physicians, and others working in the medical model, to incorporate Gestalt Therapy into your work.

REFERENCES

American Psychiatric Association (1994) *Diagnostic and statistical manual of mental disorders. 4th ed.* Washington, DC: American Psychiatric Association.

Perls, F., Hefferline, R., & Goodman, P. (1980) *Gestalt therapy.* New York: Bantam Books.

◊

Part II

Work with couples, children
and their families, groups,
and organizations

8
NO CHILD IS AN ISLAND

Felicia Carroll

◆◆◆

HISTORICAL BACKGROUND

During a conversation with Janet Lederman in 1979, I mentioned that someone should write a book about Gestalt Therapy with children. Such a book existed: *Windows to Our Children: A Gestalt Approach to Children and Adolescents* by Violet Oaklander (1978). It is now a basic reference for child and adolescent therapists throughout the world.

In her writing (1978, 1982, 1992, 1993) she has emphasized theoretical principles and concepts such as organismic self-regulation, contact and boundary disturbances, awareness, and experimentation. The Oaklander Model uses play therapy and the projective possibilities of clay, stories, sandtrays, drawings, and puppets. These provide the child with natural and enjoyable avenues to relate to the therapist, to come to know herself, to express her internal and external conflicts, to experiment within the therapy milieu with new options for her behaviors, to complete unfinished situations, and to integrate all aspects of the child's self. In this case presentation and discussion, I will develop theoretical issues that Oaklander has not treated extensively in her previous works, namely field theory and the process of integration. I hope to contribute to the theoretical understanding of her model by focusing my analysis and discussion of the following case presentation on a fuller articulation of the theoretical concepts emerging out of field theory and the dynamics of integration.

THE CASE: PRESENTING PROBLEMS
AND BACKGROUND INFORMATION

Jonelle, a nine year old girl, came into my office holding her mother's hand, with her stepfather following. She did not look at me as she entered and spoke reticently when I introduced myself. She sat in a chair across from her parents who sat on a small couch. She looked separate and alone as she seated herself in the chair. Her long black hair, olive skin, and dark eyes reminded me her mother had told me that Jonelle's father is Hispanic and presently lives in the northern part of the state. (Her mother and stepfather are Caucasian.) Although Jonelle visited her father on some holidays and for part of summer vacations, he was not actively involved in her life. He had also remarried, but was again divorced.

I usually see parents and a child together for the first session. There are many things that I want to observe as I come to know the child in her family. For instance, what happens now that I am a part of the situation? How does she relate to me? How do they relate to one another with me in the setting of my office? These initial contacts are important in establishing the basic foundation for my relationship with the child and her family, one based on openness and trust. I want her to hear what her parents' concerns have been, and anything else that they choose to tell me. I find it interesting what parents tell me in these first sessions; how they formulate the problem. And most importantly, from the beginning, I want Jonelle to know that I will tell her whatever I know about her and her life. In addition to learning from the parents, I want to hear from her as much possible in telling me about herself and the purpose in their coming to see me.

Jonelle was living with her mother, Mrs. Roberts, her stepfather, Mr. Roberts, and two step-siblings, aged three and one. Her mother had arranged the appointment after her daughter's school counselor had suggested that Jonelle might benefit from therapy. In fact, the headmaster of the private grammar school had warned Mrs. Roberts that Jonelle might not be allowed to return the following school year if Jonelle did not give up her defiant behavior. Mrs. Roberts had explained that Jonelle had been a "problem" since she was in preschool. This behavior was a problem at home as well as at school.

When her mother used the word "defiant" in describing Jonelle, I asked Jonelle if she knew what the word meant. She shook her head, shrugged but did not look up. I asked her mother to say in different words what she meant. Her mother described Jonelle as not doing what was expected or asked of her. That she got angry, talked back, and sometimes seemed to deliberately do what she had been told not to do. Her behavior seemed at times to be intentionally irritating and provocative of her teachers, her siblings, her friends, and her parents. I asked Jonelle if she knew what her mother was talking about. She nodded yes. Her mother said that Jonelle often did not want to be with the family on family outings. She did not seem to like her stepfather. Jonelle agreed that she and her stepfather, Mr. Roberts, argued a lot. Mainly, Jonelle said, she tried to stay away from him. Mr. Roberts said that he thought the problem was that Mrs. Roberts was too lenient with Jonelle; that she let her get away with everything and was inconsistent with her discipline. He admitted that he was not very involved with Jonelle, that her mother took care of most of her needs. He said that he was too busy with work and his other children to do much more.

Mrs. Roberts added that Jonelle had been a difficult child for some time. She told of instances in preschool when Jonelle would cause other children to cry or disrupt group activities in school. Jonelle blurted out, "You- always say that!" Tears welled up in her eyes and she fought back crying by tightening her face and looking away. Quietly I asked, "What does your mother always say?" "She always believes what others say; she takes their side. She believes that there is something wrong with me." Mrs. Roberts did not respond to Jonelle. She added, speaking to me, "That's another part of the problem. She doesn't see what she does to cause the problem. It's always someone else's fault."

During this session, Mrs. Roberts said her first marriage had ended in divorce when Jonelle was four, due to differences in values and her husband's infidelities. The divorce was precipitated by Jonelle's telling her mother that her father had taken her to visit a woman whom Mrs. Roberts recognized as a girlfriend.

Even though Jonelle did well academically, she was frequently on detention for being talkative, argumentative, and disrespectful to her teachers.

I was feeling overwhelmed with the issues and I could only imagine that Jonelle was ready to bolt out of the room. So I asked her to tell me about other things. She was quiet, withdrawn, mainly nodding or shrugging. She held in a lot, offered meager responses to my inquiries about her friends, favorite subjects at school, foods she enjoyed, etc. When I asked her if she ever had bad dreams she responded "Yes." Her mother added that Jonelle often woke up from nightmares and had trouble going back to sleep.

Asking Jonelle these questions not only involved her, but also was the beginning of a more direct relationship between us. My responses, I hoped, would convey my interest in her and her point of view; more importantly, that I knew she had a point of view. I could get an idea about her sense of self and her ability to talk about herself and her experiences. Her parents occasionally gave their views regarding some of the questions but basically this was an interaction between Jonelle and me.

As I talked with her, Jonelle became more involved. She looked up from the floor and began to look around my office which is equipped with a sand tray, toys, crayons, markers, puppets, dolls, shelves of games, musical instruments and numerous other items usually of interest to children.

I described to the family something of my way of working and explained that the first three or four sessions would be a time for me to come to understand more fully what was happening within their home and at school and that I wanted to spend a few sessions with Jonelle in order for us to get to know each other better. I assured them that at the end of these sessions I would meet with them all again and that we would then discuss a plan of treatment that would include family sessions as well as individual sessions with Jonelle.

Was it all right for me to talk with the school counselor? They agreed. I also said that I would want to talk with Jonelle's father. Mrs. Roberts so much as wished me luck, saying that his work schedule made him difficult to reach, and that he usually stayed uninvolved. Jonelle said nothing and looked away.

As we began to close, I asked Jonelle if she would be agreeable to staying with me for a few more minutes while her parents completed some forms in the waiting room. She stayed and we talked about the various items in the therapy room. She was particularly interested in my games. She recognized some, like Candyland, that she had played before when she was younger. She was curious about the sandtray and toys, and I showed her some pictures of sandtray scenes other children had done. She told me that she liked to draw and I explained that kids could draw whatever they wanted and that sometimes I might ask her to draw something. "Like what?" she asked. "Like an imaginary place or a picture of your family." "Which family?" she asked and turned to pick a musical instrument.

Already, Jonelle was letting me know of some of her distress. "Jonelle, I'd like to know more about how you experience your life, your family. I'd like to understand more how you feel about what your parents and you have told me today. These toys and games can help us do that — it can be fun and interesting. Would you be willing to come so that I can do that?" Jonelle looked at me, smiled, and said simply, "Sure."

INITIAL IMPRESSIONS AND PREDICTIONS

My initial impression of Jonelle was that she was lonely and alienated in every area of her life, i.e. family, school and friends. She had withdrawn and constricted herself. She held in much emotion by tightening her facial and shoulder muscles, and avoiding eye contact, e.g. throughout the first session she never looked directly at anyone. As the session closed I was encouraged as she showed interest in me and the materials in my office. I expected her to refuse to come again and was pleasantly surprised when she cheerfully agreed to return.

During the subsequent four sessions, I was reminded that our understanding of a child's behavior has to begin with a sense of the situation as a whole; that all of the factors in a child's life are coexisting and mutually interdependent. I had begun a relationship with Jonelle that would require me to relate not only with her internal life, but with most of the elements within her environment.

I began to get a better understanding of how Jonelle experienced her life and organized her behaviors. She was caught in a powerful struggle with her mother. She had conflicting views of herself and felt that she was the cause of so much difficulty in her family. This was poignantly represented in a sandtray scene she created during our second session. I had suggested that she portray, with her selection of toys, how she experienced her life. In the sandtray she arranged in one comer a hospital scene with parents and a baby. In one comer she arranged family figures identified as her mother, stepfather and step-siblings; and in another, her father with her aunt, uncle, and cousins. This is how I learned of the extended family of which her father is a part. Next, Jonelle carefully arranged about six spiders around the scene and then placed a single evergreen tree in the middle of the tray.

Through this sandtray scene, Jonelle told me about being born and then her parents getting a divorce. She did not remember much about her father's girlfriend, but she knew that when she told her mother about her that she did not see much of her father for a long time. She expressed much fondness for her aunt, uncle, and cousins. She usually stays with them when she visits her father. She stated that she did not like her stepfather because he never talks to her, even "when I'm standing right there, he'll tell my mother what to say to me." I asked her about the spiders in the scene. "Those are the bad things that have happened to me, like my parents getting a divorce, and my grandmother dying. I liked her a lot." She was quiet. "Even though your grandmother is now dead, she's still important to you." "Yeah." "Maybe you could select a figure to be her and put her in your scene." Jonelle selected a gray-haired, dark-skinned figure. "Was she your Dad's mom?" "Yes" Jonelle replied. It was then that she mentioned that she didn't have a figure for herself other than the baby. She chose another dark-skinned child figure and placed it next to her grandmother. "You liked your grandmother very much." "Yes," then she was quiet again. The session was almost over, but I wanted to know more about the tree. "This tree is all the people who have believed in me." Tears welled up; her face tightened. I was moved and astounded with the meaning she had given to the symbol. "Was your grandmother one of those people?" Jonelle only nodded. Then she added, "I wish that my mother could believe in me. She has always thought that there is something wrong with me. She's always sending me to therapists." "Do you ever feel that way, Jonelle, like there is something wrong with you?" Jonelle's tears broke through. She cried. "It's always been that way."

This session supported my first impressions of Jonelle and gave me more understanding of her struggle to be affirmed and accepted by her mother. I also got a clearer sense of her separation from all the members of her families. Her family had organized itself in a way that was creating unhappiness for its members. They appeared to be struggling to find a new balance, but kept coming up with the same difficulties.

Over the next few weeks, I talked with the headmaster of the school who said that Jonelle was basically a good kid, but that he thought she was deeply disturbed. She was a difficult child whom most of her teachers did not know how to handle. He wanted me to tell him how to "reach" Jonelle, and to get her to confide in him. I felt very uncomfortable with the conversation and realized that here, too, was someone who was blaming Jonelle for the existence of an interpersonal problem that included more than herself. This became clearer when he commented that maybe Jonelle would do better if she lived with her father. "She might be happier," he said, "being with her own kind."

Her father was pleasant and passive. He did not seem to want to be involved in her therapy. He blamed Jonelle's mother by saying that she was too lenient and was not consistent with her. He explained that his work schedule would not allow him to travel to attend therapy sessions. Jonelle did not give him any problems when she was with him. When I asked how he accounted for the difference, he answered that when he said something, Jonelle knew he meant it.

Jonelle had great enthusiasm for horseback riding. She took riding lessons at a local stable and had a particular horse to which she was attached. She also liked her instructor, a woman who took a special interest in her and recognized her capabilities. Jonelle liked all aspects of the riding experience, including grooming and care of the gear. She frequently opened her sessions by telling about her competitions. In that part of her life, Jonelle felt strong and recognized. In fact, she would rather be at the stables than at home.

Through these initial sessions, I learned that Jonelle had developed many strategies to cope with her estrangement from her parents. She disowned her need for her family and deflected their efforts to care for her. To minimize her belief that there was something wrong deep within herself, she constricted her body, desensitizing herself to the pain of being blamed, criticized, and rejected. Her defiance and oppositional behavior — her creative adjustment to this difficult situation — seemed to be her way of expressing not only her anger, but also her confusion and grief. She had lost her family early in life and she was alienated within the new relationships. At home and at school she had little support to learn about and enjoy her Hispanic roots and culture. Jonelle was alone within her family — an aloneness within which she isolated herself.

THEORETICAL APPLICATION: FIELD THEORY

Whenever I begin therapy with a child and her family, as a Gestalt therapist, I assume that the child, the parents, the family as a whole, are motivated by an internal tendency toward meaning, balance, growth, understanding (Burley, 1990). By the time the situation has come to the point when a family calls a therapist, the child has become the clearest figure around the issues at hand. One way or another, someone has decided that the child is the problem. The implicit charge to the therapist (and to the child) is often some version of "fix this child before I go nuts," or "help her before she ruins her life — or ours."

No child is an island. Children are intricately dependent on the resources within the field for their existence. This dependency is clearer to us when the child is in infancy. Her physical and psychological health and survival depend on her physiological, such as breathing, and social, such as being cuddled, interactions with her environment. Through her continuous interchanges within her world, the young child mentally shapes and constructs the order, the meaning of her life.

According to phenomenology and field theory, two of the four theoretical pillars of Gestalt Therapy (Van de Riet, 1993), the field is "a totality of mutually influencing forces that together form a unified interactive whole" (Yontef, 1993, p. 279). In Gestalt Therapy, a child and the circumstances which are bringing her into treatment are viewed by the therapist as problem(s) occurring within the organization of the field which has multideterminants. "In psychology," Yontef (1993) continues, "a field is used to emphasize the complex totality of inter-dependent influences within which an organization functions, the constellation of interdependent factors that account for a psychological event" (p. 297). A fundamental tenet of Gestalt Therapy is that behavior is a function of the field of which it is a part. In order to understand the behavior or the symptoms, the child therapist must begin with the situation as a whole and not exclude any part of it. There are many people who interact with a child: family members, school personnel, legal authorities, friends, parents of friends. Each individual and/or group is a significant part of the child's field which must be considered in the therapy.

The evolution and the dynamics within the current situation out of which the behavior is occurring is not what a family recognizes. In Gestalt terms it is not figure. These factors are part of the ever-present undifferentiated ground. What is experienced as figure is the distress organized around the child. Occasionally, parents, even children, will point to events in the past (such as divorce, hospitalization, abuse) as a way of explaining the present circumstances. This information is useful, but the Gestalt therapist must contain the press toward premature understanding (gestalten). Clarkson (1993) reminds us: "Understanding of human behavior needs to begin with a sense of the situation or field as a whole and only then proceed to differentiation of the component parts" (p. 42).

As a Gestalt therapist I am aware that I enter into the complexity of the current situation, adding to that complexity. My presence alone becomes a part of the dynamics and every person attributes his own meaning to my participation. In fact, an immediate shift occurs within the family or within the thinking-feeling-doing of its members depending on whether or not I'm perceived as a help or a hindrance to the situation. I am also aware of tension within myself as I hold the energy of the inertia of the system and its urge for change. I restrain my own tendencies to impose, and hold off the expectations of parents for me to say, "Here's how I see it" and "Here's-what-you-need-to-do."

I believe that the way the child is behaving reflects her effort at healthful growth within a given set of environmental influences. Clarkson (1993) reminds the reader that Perls (1951) suggested that the concept of neurosis should be replaced by the term "growth disorder":

> From the Gestalt perspective, organismic ill-health occurs when the person becomes over-controlled, anxious, or unable to engage and construct meaning in his life ... Thus, the individual's ability to grow through contact and assimilation of novel elements in his environment is disrupted and becomes fixed in outdated patterns of behavior (p. 68).

This perspective was helpful in thinking about the torment which Jonelle and her family were experiencing. It was becoming clear in the initial family sessions, that there were multifaceted, interrelated, fixed patterns of interacting that were interrupting their development of healthy functioning, as individuals and as a family.

My purpose as a therapist was to participate with them in discovering those dynamics which were interrupting their healthful growth as a family and to increase their mutual support for experimenting with other options.

As Jonelle, her family and I worked to form different and clear gestalten or meaningful understandings of their interactions and the difficulties those perceptions were creating, other solutions or options emerged. As we began their sessions, I knew there were many possibilities for this child and her family.

THE MIDDLE PHASE

In the therapy that followed, I combined individual work with Jonelle with family therapy and parent consultation. I stayed in regular contact with her father, involving him long distance. I organized an approach which would involve me with Jonelle in order to rediscover together her path toward creative living.

My purpose was to develop Jonelle's potential for meaningful contact with her parents, teachers, and friends. I recognized her need to learn constructive ways to express her emotions, especially anger. I hoped to assist her family in making a more satisfying adjustment to the changes brought on by the divorce and remarriages. I attempted to explore with them the perspectives held by the family which seemed to keep them disconnected and strangers. Ideally, they could attempt new ways of relating.

Throughout her therapy, I hoped to help Jonelle form a strong sense of herself and self-support (Oaklander, 1982) so that she would be able to examine the many negative beliefs that she had about herself and to incorporate acceptance and nurturance.

The family sessions with Jonelle, her mother, stepfather, and myself took place every other week. I met weekly in individual sessions with Jonelle (which I will discuss in the next section). I asked the headmaster of the school to observe her on a regular basis and to notice if there were any patterns to the disruptions at school. For instance, how often does she cause problems, in any particular class or activity, what time of day or week. I thought that this action would open up his thinking to consider that the disruption might be interactional rather than attributed to Jonelle alone. Also, by systematically observing Jonelle, he might begin to notice her strengths as well as focusing on the negative acting-out.

Jonelle's father was difficult to reach and initially seemingly disinterested. He continued to blame Mrs. Roberts. He became more involved as I showed an interest in him and his relationship with Jonelle. He expressed his appreciation for my calls at one point saying that he'd never had much information about Jonelle. She received her first birthday card from him during this course of therapy. He was included in a family session late in the therapy via a telephone conference call.

Throughout the early sessions with Jonelle and her parents, the relationship between Jonelle and her stepfather disturbed me. In my individual sessions with Jonelle I asked her directly, and watched for any indications of abuse. There were none. The "second shoe fell," however, in a family session in which Jonelle was bitterly confronting her stepfather for ignoring her, not talking to her, always going through her mother. It was becoming clearer that Jonelle experienced a lot of rage at her stepfather.

In one crucial session Jonelle sat rigid, tears washing her face in absolute frustration. I softly asked her what she was doing. "I can't talk to them. They don't want to hear. They just side against me." "What do you want, Jonelle?" I asked. While crying and probably constricting her chest and throat to hold back anger, she mouthed and whispered to her mother: "You know what I want, and you promised me." Her mother understood. Chagrined, she haltingly told us that, yes, she had confided to Jonelle at one time that she was going to divorce Jonelle's stepfather. She had decided against it after she discovered she was pregnant with their second child and the relationship had become more tolerable. Mr. Roberts said nothing. Jonelle's mother turned to Jonelle and told her that she was not going to divorce him and that they all had to work this out as a family.

Jonelle was furious with her mother's declaration and turned toward her stepfather. She began to berate him, saying he was just another child in the family. Mr. Roberts turned red, tightened his jaw and began to express his fury at her. Immediately, Jonelle's mother interrupted. She explained to Jonelle that her husband's lack of involvement with her had to do with an agreement she made with him when she married him. Jonelle listened intently as her mother spoke to her. "I thought marrying him was the best thing for both of us. I had very little. He was good to me, but he said that he didn't like kids. I was working all the time or dating Sam (Mr. Roberts). The problems I was having with you were constantly demanding my attention. And so, I agreed that he would never have to have anything to do with you, Jonelle. That he'd be my husband and not your father."

Jonelle gasped and looked at her mother in disbelief. Mr. Roberts spoke up. To me he explained, "I never wanted children and yet I agreed to marry her mother as long as she assumed all responsibility for Jonelle. Now I just don't like how Jonelle treats her mother. She's disrespectful, causes her to worry. Doesn't do what she is told. Hangs out with the wrong types of kids. We disagree about what to do so I think it's best that I do nothing, say nothing; I get angry and just leave the room."

Jonelle looked at her mother, then expressed her sense of betrayal, "You agreed to marry him. I'm not wanted here?!" "No!" her mother responded. "I love you. I want you here with me."

I felt Jonelle's pain about this decision that had shut her out; it had set in motion a constellation of dynamics, which had left her feeling alone, unwanted, enraged with frustration, and ultimately believing that she was wrong and to blame. I also felt the dilemma of her mother as well as compassion for both of these parents who slowly appeared to recognize the impact of their agreement on each other, Jonelle, and their family.

Even though so much pain was felt in that session and in the weeks following, making this contract explicit shifted the interactions just enough that a major change began to take place. Nothing dramatic nor miraculous, just more talking, less blaming. Jonelle began talking about going to live with her father. When we explored this further she said that she liked being with his family and she liked her cousins. Her father did not encourage this arrangement. Jonelle began to reconsider this move as her mother repeatedly reassured her that she didn't want her to go; that she belonged with this family. Her stepfather supported her mother. In fact, he directly told Jonelle "This is your home" and that he wanted her with her brother and sister. He just had a hard time with how she treated her mother.

In one later session, Jonelle supported her stepfather by telling her mother that for ten years she'd "been doing it all wrong ... You never mean what you say. If you ground me I can always count on you to change your mind. I get to do what I want anyway."

I was impressed by Jonelle's clear statement to her mother and supported this self-expression. I joked, "Well, Patricia, what more do you need? When do you get the message that Jonelle wants you to be her mother and not a wimp?" "Yeah!" exclaimed Jonelle. We all laughed.

In a subsequent session, I asked Jonelle's parents to read a book about limit-setting. With Jonelle present, we worked on their being more consistent with their expectations and rules with all the children. Over these weeks Jonelle became more involved with friends and her younger siblings. She became a little closer to her stepfather, (they began to enjoy watching sports together on television) and their arguments decreased.

PROCESS OF INTEGRATION:
GESTALT THERAPY THEORY APPLIED

Insurance forms. Diagnosis needed. As I reviewed my notes from the first few sessions with Jonelle and her family, I knew that DSM-III-R-313.81 (1990) described her well. She met all the criteria.

> Oppositional Disorder, 313.81, entails persistent opposition to authority figures for a period of six months or more, characterized by a behavioral pattern of disobedient, negativistic, and provocative behaviors, particularly toward parents and teachers. Continually confrontive behavior is exhibited, even when it is destructive to the best interest or well-being of the patient. Such an individual rarely views the problem as originating within himself and his passive resistance to external authority often causes more discomfort for those around him than for him. The disorder interferes with social relationships and often results in academic failure and other school problems. Typically arising in late childhood or early adolescence, onset usually coincides with increased difficulties in relations with the family and use of illegal substances. The course is described as chronic, lasting for several years; it often continues in adulthood as a Passive-Aggressive Personality Disorder (p. 87–88).

Not a hopeful prognosis, but otherwise this described her to a T! Yet it didn't help me to understand or know the whole situation: Jonelle (the organism) within the family (the environment). The insurance company would be satisfied, but the complete picture was not in that text. My understanding of Jonelle was slowly emerging both in family sessions and in her individual sessions.

As we began to know each other better, she revealed more of herself to me through drawings, sandtray scenes, games about emotions, and conversations about her feelings toward members of her family, friends, and teachers. But what stood out most prominently for me was the anger that she felt toward herself and that she was angry at almost everyone in her life.

As more of her history unfolded in the family sessions, her strong needs for love emerged clearly: to be held (physically and emotionally), to belong and be accepted for herself. Yet, they remained unexpressed by her and unrecognized by others. These needs were overlaid by her strong feelings of shame and blame. The faulty beliefs about herself, negative introjects, were reinforced continuously by her own thinking. "Something is wrong with me. Something is wrong with me." Along with this introject were other mental constructs about how she was to be in the world. Her daily behaviors seemed to be directed to prove this belief about some flaw within herself. Any contradictory experience of herself was denied repeatedly.

In addition to believing these introjects about herself, she projected these self-attacking ideas onto her mother and teachers who had actually provoked these projections. "They think that there is something wrong with me." Jonelle had constructed this explanation — meaningful to her — as she experienced her early childhood. Her understanding of the obvious and subtle effects of her parents separating (her father leaving her distracted and frustrated mother, her rejecting stepfather) was indeed ego-centric, yet developmentally determined. She concluded from these experiences that she was at fault, that it was something within herself. At nine and ten she was suffering, caught in the crossfire of her needs for acceptance, dueling with her beliefs about herself that were self-attacking and rejecting: "I need my mother and family to love me. I don't get it because there's something wrong with me." Jonelle's ideas about how she was supposed to be in the world led to her attacking others externally (projecting) and to attacking herself internally (retroflecting).

After building trust between us, Jonelle once cried in despair, "I don't know why I do the things I do!" This revelation opened a window for Jonelle and me through which we could increase our awareness Of her inner life and to understand more of the connection between her thoughts, feelings, and behaviors.

For many weeks we involved ourselves in strengthening her self-support and expanding her knowledge of her emotional life as I describe in the pages that follow. (Oaklander, 1979, 1982, 1992, 1993).

Gradually, in small steps, Jonelle began to gain a stronger sense of her self: she developed a clearer differentiation of the "me" — and — "not-me" (contact boundary). And yet, although Jonelle was feeling stronger about herself — more familiar with her emotions, her interests, her intellect, and her Hispanic roots — the negative beliefs about herself persisted within her.

To move on to more satisfying experiences, she needed to examine and integrate the negative introjects. In order to do this she needed to fully experience herself in a stronger and healthier manner as she had been demonstrating in the family sessions through her nascent abilities to support, express, and affirm herself.

The Oaklander Model stresses the need for a child to learn through the assistance of the therapist to use her capacity for self support in order for integration and growth to take place. If, in work with children, the core beliefs, introjects, are not explored they continue to fester and erode strengths gained through, otherwise, good therapeutic efforts. Thus the child is left with important work unfinished which "at some level still clamors for attention" (Clarkson, p. 71). These beliefs about the self, positive and negative, remain the sources of dis-ease throughout the individual's life.

Clarkson, again:

> The accumulation of unfinished business is instrumental in the development of growth disturbance. As long as the person remains in touch with the original need, there is a still a possibility of it being resolved quite naturally sometime in the future. (p. 67)

The self-nurturing process as presented by Oaklander is a way in which the therapist can bring a child back in touch with the original need(s) and to connect them with her present functioning.

Most, if not all, of the activities which the child and therapist share are supports for integration. The work usually occurs at the concrete level of experience and cognition and does not involve abstract insights and owning of responsibility which one might work toward in Gestalt Therapy with adults.

Oaklander (1978) observes:

> I find that some children, especially young ones, do not necessarily need to verbalize their discoveries, insights, and awareness of the what and how of their behaviors. Often it seems that is enough to bring out into the open the behaviors or blocked feelings that have interfered with their emotional growth process. Then they can become integrated, responsible, happy human beings,

better able to cope with the many frustrations of growing up in their worlds. They can begin to relate more positively with their peers and with the adults in their lives. They can begin to experience a feeling of calmness, joy, and self-worth (p. 194).

Even though new experiences of self and other are integrated throughout the therapeutic work, for the child to be free of the burden of the unfinished situation within herself a more direct process of examining the core introjects and assimilating a new experience with the self must take place. This process is not magical nor intuitive and needs deliberate interventions. Oaklander clearly identifies the movements in this work of integration which can be understood like those in a symphony or a dance rather than linear steps. She calls it "self-nurturing" work.

Through this process the child acknowledges and expresses the anger toward the self, self-hatred or self-rejection. These global feelings are focused toward a specific part of the self that is not liked. To further differentiate the figure of the unliked, rejected part of the self, the child is encouraged to concretize the image in drawings, with clay or puppets, etc; to give life to that part in the therapy session. Since they want the child to like and accept herself, some therapists tend to do what kindness — misplaced — would dictate, saying, "That's not so bad" or some other reassuring comments about the negative image. This only tends to inhibit the child's expression of the feelings she had directed toward herself.

What must happen at this point is for the child to be what she is (Beisser, 1970) which is angry, rejecting toward the despicable part. The retroflected emotional energy must become an explicit expression: "I hate you." "You get me into trouble." "Because of you, nobody loves me."

As the emotional energy is spent, the child is often open to learning something about this part of herself. In most cases, the introjects have originated during a much earlier stage in the child's life out of efforts to meet an unmet need, erroneous beliefs about herself held by someone else, or attempts to protect herself from some harm: simply the best she could do under given circumstances. The therapist gently suggests another construct, another meaning for the "bad" part of the child.

In time, the child is ready to experience the polarity of her self-rejection — self-acceptance. Again, this process needs to be concretized through an image such as a fairy godmother, a nurturing friend, or a part of herself that can accept, even like or admire, the unwanted part.

Usually, as this occurs, the child discovers some purpose for this disowned part — how these behaviors have been needed by her in some way, or were unavoidable. Finally, the child can own these behaviors, attitudes, characteristics in herself and express her acceptance of what was so unwanted (Yontef, 1993). As the child becomes self-accepting, not trying to change or be something different, change occurs.

Jonelle drew the despicable, hated part of herself as a grotesque, hairy spider with fangs. She called it "The Flaw." She also portrayed this part in clay and puppets (I have a black spider in my puppet collection). Over a few sessions we came to know her view of this part of herself very well.

In a session using puppets, Jonelle spoke as the spider and told of how "The Flaw" got Jonelle into trouble. I asked Jonelle to express to "The Flaw" how she felt towards her. She took the puppet off her hand and slammed it to the floor. "I hate you! I wish you were dead!" She repeatedly banged it against the floor. Then she was quiet and looked at me. She was not frightened by her emotional outburst.

I began to talk to Jonelle about the "The Flaw." I described to her a little girl "… who wanted very much to be loved and cared for by her Mom and Dad. But they argued all the time. Then one day her Dad left. Her Mom was scared and alone. The little girl was confused. She did her best to understand what and why all these things were happening. But because she was so little, it was not possible for her to figure everything out. So, she did what all kids do. She decided that these things were happening because she was bad. Many other things happened to her in preschool which made her feel bad about herself. Then her Mom remarried, but her stepfather didn't seem to like her, and her Dad was far away and she didn't see him much."

As I talked very quietly, Jonelle began to cry softly. I went on with my story. "The little girl kept trying to understand and kept coming up with the same answer, 'I'm bad. Something is wrong with me.'" Jonelle was quiet. She seemed to be at peace with herself. She held the spider. Then she put it back into the basket with the other puppets.

The next session she came in and retrieved the spider. She put it on her hand and turned to me. "It was not my fault," she said simply. Without asking what she meant, I asked Jonelle to select another puppet that could understand the Flaw. I suggested a fairy godmother puppet. She put on the puppet and looked at me. "Jonelle, have Fairy Godmother tell The Flaw what was not it's fault." Fairy Godmother said, "Flaw, it is not your fault they didn't want you. You were just a little kid and they were grown-ups."

I was touched deeply by Jonelle's simple insight, her way of seeing her life in a new way. I felt my tenderness toward her, as I asked Jonelle to have Fairy Godmother say to Flaw, "Flaw, even though you cause lots of problems, I understand you and I love you." Jonelle repeated my words, looked at me and smiled. I removed the Fairy Godmother puppet from her hand. "Jonelle, can you say that to the Flaw?" With feeling she did. Jonelle took off the spider puppet and stroked it for a while. The process of integration requires the child to move from the projection of the disowned (the puppets) to the owning self. Therefore, I removed the puppets one at a time and asked Jonelle if she could speak to herself. She had developed enough self-support to be able to do this. Self-nurturing requires daily practice to replace the strong negative experience of self. So, I asked her if she would talk to The Flaw inside of her each day and tell that younger part of herself "even though you do things that are difficult for me to understand, I like you" (language of self-acceptance rather the self-rejection). Jonelle and I practiced saying this a few times, and she agreed to say it to herself each night before going to bed. Then I asked her if there was anyone in her life today whom she thought liked her even with the "The Flaw." With no hesitation she talked enthusiastically about her horseback-riding instructor. The rest of the session was spent talking about her riding lessons, her trainer, the horses.

After these sessions, Jonelle began to be more open to talking about, and experimenting with, direct ways of expressing her anger. She became more involved in horseback riding and won competitions. In time, the energy that had been used in opposing and irritating others was being utilized in more lively and spontaneous interactions with her family and friends.

> As the patient's experience of himself increases, he becomes more self-support-ive and better able to make good contact with others. As he casts aside more and more of his neurotic techniques of manipulation, the therapist needs to frustrate him less and less arid is more and more able to help him towards sat-isfaction. As was said earlier, self-support is very different from self-sufficiency. When the patient is discharged from therapy he will not lose his need for other people. On the contrary, he will for the first time derive real satisfaction from his contact with them. (Perls, 1980, p. 115)

ENDING PHASE

Jonelle was eleven years old when our work began to close. She had come for weekly sessions for a little over a year with breaks for holiday and summer vacations. Over this time she developed into an enjoyable, preadolescent. Her interaction in the family sessions became more contactful and graceful. She became an integral part of the family by being a big sister to her younger siblings. In their sessions, the family laughed more and blamed less and less.

Jonelle continued to look forward to her visits with her father and her cousins. Her experiences of her Hispanic identity became clear during a family session when her parents, including her father (via a telephone conference call) discussed the selection of a summer camp program for her. Jonelle had perused the brochures for different camps. She told her parents that she would only go to a camp that had kids from various ethnic backgrounds. "I will feel more myself there than in an all-white camp," she explained. Her parents also decided to have her change schools. Jonelle was glad to attend a local, culturally diverse public middle school.

For the first time, Jonelle derived satisfaction from her contact with others in her family and at school. She had psychological room and energy to form her identity, "I-ness," and to enjoy her self. She had found a path that was hers. The family members had found a way of living together that allowed them to develop a comfortable process of conflict resolutions and support.

One of the pleasures of working with children and their families is that I become like a great aunt — a special member of their extended families. Closure is not goodbye. Children and parents frequently come in for follow-up sessions, to talk out a problem, work through another milestone. Children, themselves, request later sessions, usually to work on something that is troubling them, or sometimes just to say hello, or to touch base with a remembered toy.

I believe that Jonelle's therapy was a successful course of treatment, and that her prognosis is excellent (the DSM-III-R not withstanding). I anticipate and look forward to continuing as a part of the field of Jonelle's existence which serves to foster her on-going development and the fulfillment of her self.

REFERENCES

Beisser, A. (1970) The paradoxical theory of change. In Fagan, J. and Sheperd, I. L. (Eds.) *Gestalt therapy now*. New York: Science and Behavior Books.

Burley, T. (1990) A phenomenological theory of personality. Unpublished paper.

Clarkson, P., Mckewn, J. (1993) *Fritz Perls*. Newbury Park, CA: SAGE Publications.

Hyener, R. (1990) The I-Thou relationship and gestalt therapy. *Gestalt journal 13(1)*, 41–54.

Jacobs, L. (1989) Dialogue in gestalt theory and therapy. *Gestalt journal, 12(1)*, 25–67.

Lederman, J. (1969) *Anger in the rocking chair*. New York: Viking Press.

Oaklander, V. (1993) From meek to bold: A casee study of gestalt play therapy. In Kottman, T., Schaefer, C. (Eds.) *Play therapy in action*. Northvale, NJ: Jason Aronson.

Oaklander V. (1993) Gestalt work with children: working with anger and introjects. In Nevis, E.C. (Ed.) *Gestalt therapy: perspectives and applications.* New York: Gardner Press.

Oaklander, V. (1982) The relationship of gestalt therapy to children. *Gestalt journal, 5(1),* 67–74.

Oaklander, V. (1978) *Windows to our children: A gestalt therapy approach to children and adolescents.* Moab, Utah: Real People Press.

Perls, F., Hefferline, R., & Goodman, P. (1951) *Gestalt therapy.* New York: Julian Press.

Perls, F. (1980) *The gestalt approach and eye witness to therapy.* Palo Alto, CA: Science and Behavior Books.

Rapaport, J., Ismond, D. (1984) *DSM III: Training guide for Diagnosis of childhood disorders.* New York: Brunner/Mazel.

Van de Riet, V. (1993) Lecture at Gestalt Therapy Institute of Los Angeles.

Yontef, G. (1993) *Awareness, dialogue, and process: Essays on gestalt therapy.* Highland, New York: Gestalt Journal Press.

◊

9

QUATERNARY: FAMILY THERAPY WITH FOUR GENERATIONS

Ruth Lampert

❖❖❖

FOREWORD

In the thick of therapy, theoretical constructs are, as they should be, in the background. During the course of my work with this fascinating and difficult family, I found even more than the usual need for consultative support, whether face to face, phone to phone, or eye to page. Some of the concepts which emerged from that support are periodically indicated in italics. Many voices are blended in this "voice of the consultant in my head," especially those of Bud Feder and Ruth Ronall, Gary Yontef, Miriam and Irv Polster, John O. Stevens, Claudio Narajo, Liv Estrup, and Arnold Beisser.

THE CASE

Fifty-six year old Delila was a strikingly elegant woman. Her appearance suggested a quiet, well-bred manner with softly modulated voice and speech. This was not the case.

"You know how it is with second marriages well this is my third and I don't know why I married Stan well I guess I do it was because of my daughter Bette who is really almost the real reason I am here."

This, and much more, was delivered in a brassy staccato broken by frequent short bursts of nervous laughter. I wondered as I listened whether and when I should interrupt. When she got to "my daughter always was *gorgeous* and to tell you the truth I never knew how to handle her so I mostly just let her alone and I never have interfered with anything she does except that now I just can't sit by and see her mistreat that poor girl Nikki who if you ask me wouldn't be half bad-looking if she would fix her hair a little, but of course she'll never be beautiful like her mother —."

I wedged in with, "Was it concern for your granddaughter Nikki that prompted your call to me?"

Her voice slowed a little.

"Yes. Bette got your name from a friend of hers and suggested I see you for marriage counseling. I decided to use the chance to get some help for Nikki although God knows I could use help with my marriage. Actually sometime I'd like to talk to you about my mother too, I just can't keep driving all the way down there to take her to her doctor's appointments, but who else is going to do it if I don't ?" *Verbosity is one of the many ways to deflect, to avoid contact; it can become addictive.*

I told her that if Bette called I would be happy to set up an appointment; meanwhile, her own marriage issues sounded pressing. Delila agreed, saying "Stan probably won't come in though, he thinks he's perfect and everything is my fault."

In the next few sessions Delila proved agile in darting from descriptions of how the people in her life took advantage of her to denial that she was being taken advantage of. For example, she cancelled her third appointment a few days before the deadline for filing income tax returns, saying she needed the time to work on "all these returns."

"All these returns" turned out to be hers and Stan's ("I've *begged* him to get an accountant to do it, but he refuses, and of course I guess he's right, it only takes me a couple of hours and we never do anything at night except watch T.V. anyway") and a co-worker's who simply couldn't figure out the forms ("I feel so sorry for the poor little thing, she just sits and answers the phone all day, she only makes $6.00 an hour, that boss of ours is even meaner to her than to me") and her mother's "she doesn't trust anyone except me to do it right, and really it's not that hard to do."

"And your daughter Bette?" I asked. "When do you do hers?"

"Oh no," she replied, "Bette never asks for help from anyone."

"I wonder where she gets that ..."

For the first time Delila paused a long time before responding, looked directly at me, and quietly said.

"Maybe she's like me and thinks she doesn't deserve help?"

"Maybe," I answered, feeling my heart lift with the hopefulness contact brings.

However ... useful interventions, exercises, experiments, all eluded me. When I interrupted her monologue/litany, she switched to another topic; when I asked for clarification she assured me she was getting to that in a minute; and so on and so forth. I put my trust in the trusting relationship we were establishing, reminding myself that the root meaning of the word therapy is "to wait."

Include yourself in her field through respectful listening. Establish contact at the only boundary possible with this client at this time, supporting her resistance.

She talked about her early life in a small New England town, with an alcoholic father who beat her mother and her until she was old enough to escape, taking Mom with her. Her eight year first marriage was to another abusive alcoholic: this time she escaped to California with their baby daughter, Bette, and Mom.

"I still hadn't learned, and got married again, to another son-of-a-bitch, but this time I got smart sooner and left after six months. Now I'm married to Stan, who doesn't drink, doesn't hit me, but does what I think you call emotional abuse."

At the fourth session she said she had persuaded Stan to come in with her. "I told him you weren't like what he probably thought therapists were like. I told him you paid attention and made a person feel what they said was important."

"Thank you," I replied. It was good to hear. *By making contact figural, we are released from the concept that many interactions in therapy are distortions in the present out of the past. Consider what is and is not valid in the here and now.*

Naturally I expected Stan to be quiet, withdrawn, obsessive-compulsive. Wrong again.

Big, bluff, and hearty, he did most of the talking at the first conjoint session, while Delila sat quietly and demurely as he explained to me what Delila's problems were:

"I don't know if she told you, but her first two husbands really abused her something awful, besides what happened with her father. Is it O.K. if I talk about this honey?"

"Say anything you want, darling" she replied, adding sweetly, "you always do."

"Tell me about *you*, Stan." I suggested/invited/directed.

"Yes sweetheart," came the poisonously sweet voice of Delila, "tell her about your last two wives and how they and your children left you and you never hear from any of them. You see …" she said turning that sugary smile in my direction, "… I'm not the only one who has problems although that's what he'd like you to think."

The hearty salesman's smile left Stan's now purpling face, and he shouted, "Jesus Christ, you are something else, I thought you wanted me to come here to help you!"

I heard myself saying silently to myself, "You goofed, seeing them conjointly after seeing her one-on-one. You're in for it now."

I also re-heard Delila's "you make a person feel that what they say is important." Stan needed respectful attention too. I suspected part of the trouble was not with what he said, but the way he said it — in what I termed New York volume, very different from New England restraint. *Put yourself as fully as possible, without judgement or interpretation, into the experience of the other. That's a prime characteristic of the essential element of dialogue.*

I pursued this a bit, reframing Stan's bellow into a statement of frustration at being misunderstood, and conjecturing that Stan's way of expressing feelings might make Delila think he was a lot angrier than he really was, and in fact, sometimes what she heard as anger might be worry.

Another point of contact as the purple left Stan's face and he said, "Bingo! You got it! Where I come from, if you got something on your mind you just say it!"

"Where I come from," Delila answered, "people speak in a considerate tone of voice."

"Yeah, and you never know what they really think."

Words used for reasons other than direct communication are another way to deflect, to isolate oneself from contact with others, to reduce awareness of one's own experience.

The way was paved for some classic communication exercises such as changing "but" to "and," speaking in "telegrams," giving voice to gestures and substituting words for body language, and reframing questions as statements. The increase in understanding of how their different backgrounds and personality styles impacted interactions was followed by awareness of some similarities they had not recognized, such as each of them being terrified of the prospect of becoming "a third time loser" in marriage.

From fear of failure per se they moved to the fear of loss and abandonment.

Stan: "I married my first wife because she was pregnant, and I felt guilty when she left; I married my second wife because I hated living alone but ended up alone again; I married you because there is just something about you that makes my heart lift, and losing that would be Godawful."

Delila: "I've always gotten along on my own and I could again, but life without you would be like having only black and white T.V. after getting used to color. I guess I need you more than I want to admit; I'd rather be the one who is needed."

Ruth: "You're saying your lives are richer and fuller with each other than without. That's promising."

Then eleven-year-old Nikki ran away from home, showing up two days later at the apartment of Delila's mother, Nanny Ellen. Nikki, who had been her Grandma Delila's ticket of admission to therapy, now came in with her mom, the beautiful Bette.

Bette looked very much like Delila but she didn't sound like her. She opened the interview by saying in crisply perfect enunciation:

"I wish to express my recognition of your professional excellence. Since entering treatment with you the level of compatibility between my mother and her husband has markedly increased."

Good grief! What next with this family?

Next was Nikki, whose thin little pinch-featured face was spotted with zits and whose nails were bitten almost to the quick. There was, however, quite a sparkle in her eyes and a pride in her bearing as she chose to sit in the chair furthest from her mother. In answer to my question about what she hoped would happen by coming to see me, she responded.

"I want to live with Nanny Ellen. Can you make that happen?"

"If I can't, would you settle for you and your Mom getting along better?"

"Why bother? I already get along with Nanny Ellen. And with Grandma Delila and Stan. It's just my mom who can't stand me."

I thought I heard a little desperation in Bette's "I personally would welcome increased rapport between us. I do try. I am non-plussed by her attitude. She cares nothing for her appearance, or for our lovely home. She does not utilize any of the advantages with which I provide her including a fine private school."

"What about Dad? Is he in the picture?"

At the mention of her father Nikki got up and walked over to the sandtray and began examining the objects. Bette gestured as though to say, "See what I mean about her?" and I gestured back "That's O.K., leave her be." *Contact interruptions may be useful or harmful depending on context and field; here you have a nice example of how deflection can be a healthy response.*

Bette's voice dipped a degree further into chill. "My ex-husband chose to distance himself from all responsibilities, believing that to be the prerogative of artists, which he considers himself to be."

Nikki agreed to return the following week to "fool around with these paints and clay and stuff you've got." Three individual sessions revealed a youngster who coped valiantly with the pain of abandonment, using her considerable artistic talent both to bolster her low sense of self-worth and to keep hope alive. She had a dim memory of her father, drawing him as tall and thin, with long blonde hair in a pony-tail. She said she suspected he had left because of a mysterious ailment, possibly amnesia.

A favorite fantasy was that he would come to her opening at the County Art Museum where, seeing her artistic style so similar to his own, he would recognize her as the daughter he had left long ago. She concluded with:

"Course that's all bullshit, but it's better than nothing right?" *Interrupt the introject in the service of awareness!*

"You bet it is," I replied. "Actually I think it's more imagination than bullshit, and imagination gets you further than bullshit. What does Nanny Ellen think about your dreams of becoming an artist?"

"She thinks I should become a lawyer, but she'll go along with whatever I want. She says the reason she is still alive is because she wants to go to my graduation from law school, or, if I insist, art school!"

"She sounds like quite a woman. I'd sure like to meet her."

That was the overt reason for my requesting a family session including child, mother, grandmother, and step-grandfather, and great-grandmother. My covert agenda was to demonstrate in vivo to Nikki how many people there were who cared about her, since it seemed unlikely she would ever receive warm, loving affection from her mother. I wanted to avert the familiar pattern of a child desperately and vainly trying to coax warmth from an emotionally distant parent. It is a familiar syndrome: lonely middle-aged clients, locked into the belief that the only mothering that counts is that which comes from the actual mother, shutting out the nurturance that is available. Nikki already had a loving relationship with her great-grandmother; Delila and Stan, with a longer life-expectancy, had expressed affection and concern. Perhaps "improved rapport" with Mom could happen too, but first on my agenda was to spotlight the love that was already there. *Help her scan the environment and introject an image of an extended family.*

My office was crowded that first family meeting, and was to become more so, though I didn't know it at the time.

Nanny Ellen arrived with Bette and Nikki. At 87 her beauty was fragile and weathered but still elegant. She sat in the room's only straight-back wooden chair, commenting "Those couches look tempting, but I've been fooled before; once down I may not be able to get up and Nikki here would have to help me, which she is good at doing, bless her."

"Bless *you* Nanny Ellen," I thought. It was hard to imagine this forthright, forthcoming woman having ever been a "victim" of abuse; the word "survivor" seemed made for her. She quickly dispelled the notion of overdependence on Delila, as she demonstrated a nice grasp of free services available to senior citizens, including taxi voucher systems, ("Why Delia thinks I can't get to the doctor on my own is a mystery to me") income tax preparation ("Delila doesn't trust them to do it properly, as if my estate were so complicated!") and counseling ("They won't see the whole family though, and it's the rest of this family who needs it, so here I am, at whatever you charge which is probably plenty.")

"You're pretty peppery, aren't you?" I responded. "I think I'll take some lessons from you, I'd hate to become one of those boring sweet old ladies."

"You're not exactly a spring chicken now," she returned, creating an I-Thou relationship on the spot.

She remained the star of this and many sessions, with a talent for speaking her mind so artlessly and directly that the sting was more stimulating than painful. Even Bette warmed to her scolding about "it's time you stopped organizing your closet and paid more mind to that nice young man Carl who doesn't seem to care that you are such a fussbudget about everything. I'd be real happy to stay with Nikki while you go out and enjoy yourselves."

For her part, Nikki was mostly silent until I suggested that everyone say something they wished to change, and something they especially liked, about their family.

The broader the range of possible responses, the greater the possibility of creative solutions. Nikki burst forth with, "I wish I could change how my Mom treats me, I don't want to live with her, I'd like to change my looks and be grown-up and able to have my own apartment and have a lot of money and a car and a boyfriend. What I like is that Nanny Ellen and Grandma Delila are cool, and that Grandpa Stan lets me help him with his computer stuff."

Bette wanted, predictably, for Nikki to more responsible and neat and so forth; she liked that Delila and she had lunch together twice a month.

Delila's wish for change was that everyone would get along together; she too liked the lunches with Bette, and liked Nikki's coming over to visit her and Stan.

Stan wanted to change the way Delila would get sarcastic; he liked the way Nikki helped him with his business records.

Nanny Ellen wished Bette would get married again and have a regular family; she liked that no one bugged her to move to a nursing home as did the families of most of her remaining friends. *The Paradoxical Theory of Change in family work promotes each members awareness of his/her basic way of being; however, certain behavioral adaption may make it easier and more fulfilling to live in the world, and the family, as it is.*

We agreed to meet in family session every other week, with Stan and Delila continuing their work on a weekly basis and Nikki seeing me individually every other week with regular parent contact with Bette. Nanny Ellen said, "Looks like this family will be paying your rent for a while. Well, it's better than more divorcing and running away."

Joining this family on their divergent and convergent paths was often unsettling for me. I felt miles away from the well-planned and structured approaches of some current schools of family therapy, and self-doubts frequently assailed me. *Remember that inclusion — putting oneself into the other's experience with neither judgement nor confluence — is the highest form of validation.*

Self-examination, as well as professional consultation, was crucial to my staying on the course of commitment to the process, to facilitating awareness and growth, to illuminating choices and midwifing healing.

It seemed to be working. Delila and Stan's relationship was becoming more fulfilling to both; Nikki did not move in with Nanny Ellen, but she spent weekends with her, and worked for pay at Grandpa Stan's two afternoons a week; Nanny Ellen maintained her important role in family sessions, sharing reminiscences of both Delila's and Bette's girlhood, which was bonding to the three other female members and fascinating to the one male.

Then, just in time to avert any complacency on my part, Bette called to say that she was pregnant, Carl wanted her to marry him and have the baby, she didn't want to do either, and could they make an appointment to "explore, in an atmosphere of objectivity and reason, our differing stances."

I learned that Carl and Bette worked in the same computer software company, she as the office manager, he as an outside salesman. He had a boyish enthusiasm that went well with his freckles and shock of blond hair. His position was very simple:

"I'm 29 years old. I've dated a million women, fell in love with Bette the first day I saw her in the office. She thinks that because she's 10 years older than me I'll get tired of her, but that's a bunch of bunk. That baby she's carrying is mine too and I want it. Nikki and I can learn to get along.

What's the problem? *Consider shame, the handmaiden of a sense of inferiority, which often accompanies unrealistically high standards of competency.*

With the chink in her fortress now revealed, I said, "Bette, do you think you can let Carl know, without any words, how frightened you are of his someday leaving you?"

As though we had rehearsed it, she curled up into a fetal position, put her thumb in her mouth, and looked at him with sorrowing eyes.

During six more conjoint sessions her fears of entrapment/abandonment and his legitimate concerns of being a step-father were explored.

She agreed to let Carl move in, to have the baby, and consider marriage if "one year from the date of birth we find our family relationship sufficiently harmonious to formalize it with marriage."

They announced these plans at the following family session, which now included Carl. He and Nanny Ellen agreed they would prefer marriage to precede parenthood but saw Bette's point of view; Stan and Delila thought the "kids" were smart to not rush into marriage; Nikki rolled her eyes heavenward in the classic adolescent expression of giving up on adults, and said, "I won't have to share my room with the baby, will I?"

There had been subtle changes in Nikki's appearance over the months as her thin scrawniness evolved into a gamine delicacy, not unlike Nanny Ellen's. In an individual session, she commented on the new living arrangements: "Carl is a dweeb, but Mom is so busy trying to whip him into some kind of shape she is staying off my back."

Bette found two occasions during family sessions to express appreciation and praise for Nikki: 1) "I realize my standards of housekeeping are probably too exacting. I want you to know I appreciate your doing the dishes last night even though at the time my only comment was that the job isn't done until the sink is bleached. Thank you." 2) "I think having a pregnant mother may present some social difficulties for a girl your age. You seem to be handling it rather gracefully."

On both occasions Nikki flushed and responded: "No big problem." . *Progress. Flushing is embarrassment expressed in body language. Be careful not to interpret; rather, observe and utilize.*

Fourteen months after the first phone call from Delila, we had our "stopping place." Delila and Stan's marriage was still full of problems, but they now saw these problems as difficulties to either be worked through or lived with, rather than as propulsions to flee. Nikki's awareness of how much her extended family cared for her, plus her social skills with peers and her artistic talent, eased the pain of her mother's emotional distance. For her part, Bette conscientiously worked onlooking for points of contact with this daughter with whom she had never really bonded. Her work was cognitive, and she was not motivated to explore deep feelings.

She did recognize that her holding Carl at arm's length was a protective maneuver, and she was willing to risk letting him closer. Nanny Ellen, in sharing her reminiscences of the past, was doing what the elderly need to do for themselves at the late stage of their life journey, while providing connecting lore-links to the family saga.

Baby Joshua was present at this final full-family session, and Grandpa Stan observed, "I've gone from being the only man in the family to being one of three. Terrific stuff, this family therapy."

It *is* terrific stuff.

If I could re-do it all in this case, I would have a co-therapist during the family sessions. What did I miss that someone else would have caught, as five and eventually seven family members interacted? Did I really need to put so much pressure on myself?

Another thing I would change is that time and money would be of little consideration (I would say "*no* consideration" but have learned that some cost serves the process well) so that more in-depth, long-term work could have been done on individual bases.

What I liked was that in fact so much was accomplished in a relatively short time within the realities of this family's resources. The pervasive fear of abandonment that ran through the system was not fully allayed but was, with the support of awareness, manageable.

Of special personal gain to me (besides all those fees Nanny Ellen mentioned) was the broadening of my own experiences, and my deeper understanding and appreciation of the forces that move families and thus individuals — including mine and me.

I continued to work with different configurations of this family from time to time.

Stan and Delila periodically come in for a couple of sessions when strain and pain threaten to overshadow the gain of their married life.

After extending the decision deadline to two years, Bette and Carl did marry. In a recent phone message she told me "I realize I have unfinished emotional business. When Joshua starts pre-kindergarten I will address myself to individual therapy. Nikki and I still have our troubles but she is quite loving with Joshua, who is, and I say this objectively, remarkably lovable. He adores her. Her art is going well and she has many friends." *Deflection by intellectualization continues to defuse her intense emotions. Honor her need for the defense; support her awareness.*

Nikki sent me the following note last year on a Christmas card:

"Nanny Ellen died and I think my heart will break. Mom says if I want to see you I can make an appointment."

She did, and we laughed and cried together as we remembered Nanny Ellen. "I want to be like her when I grow up," Nikki said.

"So do I," I answered.

◊

10
THREE COUPLES TRANSFORMED

Anne Teachworth

◆╬◆

"What is transferred is not father-mother-child relationships, but what is transferred are certain fixed behavior patterns which at the time when they were acquired, were acquired not as resistance but as assistance for something. It's part of the development and then it becomes automatic. This implies a fixed gestalt of which one is not consciously aware. What we do in Gestalt Therapy is to de-automatize these fixed gestalten and thus make the patient aware of them as sources of energy which form a new basis of activity."
— *Laura Perls, Gestalt Voices, (1978)*
"A Trialogue between Laura Perls, Richard Kitzler and Mark E. Stern."

INTRODUCTION

Prior to this case study, my assumption was that most couples' difficulties stemmed from their unfinished business with their parents. I now believe that a couple's difficulties reflect the unfinished business from their parents' relationships. Troubled couples usually have similarly troubled parental sets, and "Introjected Couple" patterns become more apparent when an interactional history is taken before couple sessions begin.

The systematic approach applied here with Laura and Mike is based on written genealogical inquiries by which we first examined the three major

185

relationship patterns in each client's family-of-origin and, with amazing accuracy, located the repetitious unfinished business in each interactional pair.

The three Introjected Interactional Patterns (IIPs) we explored were: Mother-Child (M/C IIP), Father-Child (F/C IIP), and the never explored Mother-Father (M/F IIP). Each IIP represented a pair of assimilated beliefs, expectations, attitudes, cues, and responses which long ago had formed fixed gestalten. Introjected in childhood along with their two relationship role models, the previous generation's negative M/F IIPs were unconsciously being projected on the screen of Laura and Mike's marriage.

BACKGROUND

This was the second time Laura and Mike had come to me for couple therapy. Seven years ago, unfinished parent-child (M/C & F/C IIPs) business was foreground in my therapeutic work with them and every couple. Typically, each partner began with individual work on unmet childhood needs to prevent any unrealistic expectations from being projected onto his or her mate.

In the joint sessions which followed the individual work, Laura and Mike's couple issues were treated as if they had originated in this marriage, rather than having been inherited from their parents' relationships. Since their parents' interactions (M/F IIPs) were not explored seven years ago, those introjected impasses were never resolved. This case study will describe the results achieved in therapy the second time around by using a three chair approach which reenacts, resolves and reassimilates these family-of-origin relationship patterns.

Seven years ago, when Laura and Mike had first come in for counseling, Mike was having an affair and planning to leave Laura for "the other woman." His mother had recently died and Mike had gotten involved with Vicki shortly after. In individual sessions, we had begun with Mike's deflected grief and anger over his mother's recent death. "Ma always walked out on me in the middle of an argument," Mike had said then. "This time she stayed gone." Laura had been acting out her introjected mother's rules, (M/F IIP), working hard to avoid being abandoned by her husband. As a child, Laura had sought the approval of a mother she detested (M/C IIP), while longing for more attention from an absent father who was having an affair with her beloved choir teacher (F/C IIP). In addition to dealing with her parent-child issues in individual sessions, Laura joined a women's codependency group, dealt with her confluence and increased her self-esteem.

Through individual and couple sessions, Mike contacted his anger and sadness at his mother for leaving him (M/C IIP), and stopped projecting her argumentativeness onto Laura. Mike gradually began communicating his angry feelings to his wife, and instead of leaving Laura, left Vicki. The crisis seemed resolved.

But here they were again … with one big difference. Now it was Laura who wanted to leave. "I want out" she insisted on the phone when she, not Mike as before, called to make the appointment. I assumed she meant … out of the marriage. Later I was to find it was … "out of the house."

FIRST SESSION

Enter Laura and Mike. An attractive couple in their early fifties, they'd met in the Peace Corps and married twenty-five years ago in the Middle East. Now parents of a sixteen year old daughter, Jackie, they both have Ph.Ds, are accomplished teachers and have each authored several books on foreign travel.

"Get her to stop judging me," Mike opened as they sat down in my office. "She's so critical. My mother was just like that."

"He doesn't appreciate anything I do for him … and 'Bertha' here is the one who judges, not me," Laura said, calling him by his mother's name.

Change this, change that, let me count the ways! Like most couples who come into counseling, Laura and Mike knew exactly what their mates should do to improve the relationship.

"I give up. That's just what my Mother would do when she couldn't get her way. I don't know what to do with Laura when she says that," Mike sighed.

"That's the problem. He doesn't want to do anything with me." Laura's eyes filled with tears. She shook her finger at her mate. "He wants me to do everything for him. Baby him like his mother did."

I noticed their deflections as they talked to me about each other, but not to each other. Projections from parent-child unfinished business caused this couple's problems the first time. Or was that really the first time? Had lack of direct and caring communication also been the issue for their parents? I began to pay closer attention to the similarities between generations. What introjections were hiding here?

"Laura's always complaining that I don't do enough around the house. Whining and complaining is exactly what she doesn't like about her own mother," Mike continued. "Those two still can't talk nice to each other."

"Mike accuses me of being like his mother and my mother both." Laura said. "I'm tired of hearing it. He better stop comparing me to them or I am going to leave."

We've all heard those fighting words before. Couples have been arguing about parental influence for generations. Some things don't ever change, I thought … particularly familial patterns. Perhaps there was more truth than fiction in their accusations. A genealogical inquiry might clearly show not only why both their mothers were involved in this argument, but why their fathers weren't and how their parents still haunted this marriage.

GENEALOGICAL INQUIRY

I suggested Laura and Mike complete a family relationship history, as follows: 1) From your viewpoint as a child 0-12 years old, list ten personality traits and behaviors of your mother and your father as adults, and yourself as a child. 2) Describe the feelings and interactions between each of these pairs when you were a young child (0–12 yrs. of age): 1) Mother-Child, 2) Father-Child, 3) Mother-Father. 3) Indicate by a plus or minus sign whether each interaction was positive or negative in your opinion. 4) Place a check mark by your favorite parent.

GENEALOGICAL RESULTS

Laura's Description Of Her Parents
Mother: dour, slow, hardworking, no fun, no pleasure, caretaking, steady, dependable, capable, giving to others, religious, narrow-minded, alone, serious.

Father: alone, not interested in helping, intelligent, talented, liberal-minded, admired by others, no show of affection, silent, had friends at church.

Parents' relationship: disastrous, no talking, no sharing, no working together, no affection, no companionship, tension, stress, no nurturing, he had an affair, no show of appreciation for each other.

Mike's Description Of His Parents
Mother: friendly to others, church going, pigheaded, acquiescent, judgmental, controlling, dogged, talkative, alone on inside, liked herself, procrastinator

Father: hardworking, very quiet, old, alone, steady, quietly opinion-ated, judgmental of me, caretaking, certain, responsible, unaccomplished, protective

Parents' relationship: She was sweet, gentle, understanding, caring, appreciative, and defended him (not me). She was proud of him (not me). He was steady, responsible, caretaking and serious. He worked all the time, at home and away., Babied her. He knew she would always be there for him. She wanted more time with him.

Laura's Description Of Herself As A Child
Insecure, unsatisfied, perceptive, sensitive, shy, capable, bright, wanting acceptance, proud. I knew my mother would care for me and I found secu-

rity in her. She never praised, was usually critical, especially of me. Said I was like my father. My father treated me like his buddy, his son, until puberty, then distanced thereafter. I found it hard to talk to him. He had nothing to say to me, nor I to him.

Mike's Description Of Himself As A Child

My mother was always reprimanding me, fussing at and judging me when my father wasn't home. We'd argue. I'd do the opposite of whatever she wanted me to do. My father was loving toward me, but mostly judgmental of me because of what Ma told him. He babied me, was overly protective of, disappointed in and unforthcoming with me. I always wanted to be around him, but when I was, he wouldn't talk. Other people would tell me how much they liked him and how much he loved me and talked about me to them, but he never told me himself.

Assessment

I had expected Laura and Mike would each be similar to one of their own parents, but was surprised when I found out which parent it was. The genealogy indicated that Laura and Mike had each identified with mother. It was also obvious that they had projected their fathers onto each other. But what was most revealing was the similarity between both sets of parents. (Notice the reoccurring parental traits of hardworking, serious/no fun, dour/narrow-minded/pigheaded, religious/church-going, quietly opinionated/judgmental, caretaking/protective/babied, quiet/silent, responsible/dependable, and particularly the repetitions of alone, which appeared for all four parents.)

Also obvious in both Introjected Parental Couples was a matching pattern of polarities: procrastinator/responsible, quiet or silent/talkative, narrow-minded/liberal-minded, hardworking/social, unaccomplished/admired by others, serious at home/friendly to others, application/no show of appreciation.

Both mothers wanted their husbands to spend more time with them. Both fathers were quiet at home and not close to their children. Both spent a lot of time away. Both mothers were critical of their children. Both parents were a set of opposites, one introvert and one extrovert, as were Laura and Mike.

A familiar familial echo was emerging. It was not a coincidence that the same interactional difficulties that existed in their parents' relationships were surfacing here. Actually, their problems had been around longer than they thought. Both Introjected Parental Couples (M/F IIPs) were unconsciously interfering in Laura and Mike's relationship.

This time however, having studied the genealogical inquiry, I knew from the beginning exactly what Laura's and Mike's negative couple introjections and projections were, in which family-of-origin pair they had originated, and which family members needed to be role-played. Most of their parent-child IIPs had been resolved in the original sessions. Their unresolved relationship issues were parent-parent problems (M/F IIPs).

GENEALOGICAL EVALUATION

Although Mike and Laura came into therapy with their differences in the foreground, several M/F IIP similarities surfaced as we discussed their parents. Laura's serious mother and Mike's serious father did all the work around the house and were caretaking of their more friendly, social mate. Laura's silent father felt ignored by his hardworking wife, who, as he said, "would rather can peaches than be with me." Laura's hardworking mother complained to get her husband to help around the house. He would go and help out at church where he was admired.

Mike's hardworking, very quiet father did not complain. He kept busy at home and had several jobs away. "He worked. Ma played." (M/F IIP) Therefore, with his friendly, churchgoing mother as his role model, Mike would play as she did and project that Laura would work all the time as his "responsible" father had. Mike's mother appreciated his father, but felt ignored by him. Mike described both his mother and father as judgmental of him. Because he had introjected this trait from both parents, he was disappointed in himself (F/C IIP) and judgmental of his daughter, too

(M/C IIP). His parents were not judgemental of each other, so he (like his mother) would not be judgmental of his mate either (M/F IIP). The trouble was that Mike was reacting to Laura as if she were quietly judging him like he thought his father had in childhood. We had missed that F/C projection seven years ago.

Laura's role model mother was "judgmental" of both Laura and her father, leading to Laura's introjection of that trait in herself (M/C IIP) and her expression of it with both her daughter and Mike (M/C & M/F IIPs). Neither Laura nor Mike received verbal appreciation from their parents. Judgement, lack of praise and lack of affection emerged as an overall matching Introjected Interactional Pattern here. I reminded them "A compliment a day keeps the therapist away."

TREATMENT

As each session began, I purposely diverted Laura and Mike away from their current argument and attended instead to the husband-wife relationships (M/F IIPs) they had observed as children. We focused not on the unmet childhood needs of the unhappy couple who walked into my office, but on the unmet relationship needs of the two unhappy couples who floated in with them ... the ghosts of their parents.

Working in joint sessions, Laura and Mike brought their parents into the here and now for counselling. Three chairs were set up, two for each set of parents and one for the child who had observed them as a couple. Rather than having them role-play their parent-child relationships as I had before, I instructed them "Role-play your parents' relationship, alternately taking each part. Interact once as they did, and then once as you wished they had." I encouraged them to stop waiting for their parents to change, and instead, set up this experiment so they could "create a memory" inside themselves of their parents having been different with each other.

The genealogical inquiry acted as a map through the roadblocks and detours of each interactional pair and provided a checklist for pinpointing the unfinished business that we needed to role-play and resolve. I referred to both histories during their joint sessions and showed it to them as the IIP impasses surfaced. Increasingly aware of these patterns, Laura and Mike eagerly participated in "de-automatizing the fixed gestalten" which had been the foundation of their marriage.

Using the genogram, I explained to Laura and Mike that in childhood they had each introjected one parent's interactional behavior pattern as a model, and as adults had been attracted to a partner who could fill the role of the projected parent (mate model), thus recreating the familiar Introjected Parental Couple (M/F IIP). Since interactional identification is personality- bound, not gender-bound, either one of their parents could have been the introjected model. Neither Laura nor Mike had chosen to be like their mothers. Their fathers were their favorites. Each had wanted to be like him. Father, however, appeared to be the projected mate model for them both. I didn't expect they would be happy to hear the findings.

They weren't. Neither Laura nor Mike recognized their mother as their role model. So I asked them which of their own parents their mate was most like. Reluctantly, both said father's traits were actually more like their partner's than their own. Looking at the genealogical inquiries, their mate model projections were easily obvious to both Laura and Mike, while their introjected models were not. Both had identified with their mothers, but were still unaware of it.

Through role play, it would become apparent to each of them that their disliked mothers were their models. Recognizing this would be the first piece of work.

I gave them each a homework assignment as the first session ended: "List times in your relationship, when you, not your partner, exhibited each personality or behavior trait you attributed to your mother in the genogram. Do not discuss this with your partner. Bring the written list with you to the next session."

Mike did not have his homework at the next session (as I had expected). He projected his mother onto me and ignored my instructions (M/C IIP). He had told us on the inquiry that he had usually done the opposite of what his mother wanted him to do. We discussed his transferential behavior with regard to me.

Laura complied with my instructions perfectly (M/C IIP) and brought in her completed homework. Referring to the genogram, she recognized several situations when she had behaved with Mike exactly as her mother had with her father. She commented that at first, she had written only negative traits for her mother, but remembered some of her mother's positive traits and added them to her list.

Laura cried as she remembered that her mother never appreciated her helping her (M/C IIP) and noted that she, Laura, now felt that same way when Mike didn't appreciate her helping him. "My mother felt unappreciated by her husband, too," Laura noted, beginning to connect her feelings with her mother's (M/F IIP). "My mother always put my father first, just as I do with Mike. I don't want to act like her. I don't even like her," Laura said, still resenting the mother she had anxiously tried to please.

According to Mike, his father and mother had a good relationship. "My father did everything for my mother," Mike said. "And she loved him for it." Of the six IIPs listed on the two genealogies, only Mike's parents' relationship (M/F IIP) was marked plus. All the other IIPs were minus. Using experiments, we would have to restructure one negative IIP at a time starting with verbal appreciation.

EXPERIMENT

Laura and Mike alternately role-played both sets of parents, directly complimenting and appreciating each other. We added an extra chair so each one as "child" could also learn to receive compliments (M/C & F/C IIPs). These corrective emotional experiences enabled them to assimilate new positive introjects and provided Laura and Mike with permission to directly express appreciation to both partner and daughter.

When Laura sat in for Mike's father, she quickly identified with his constant need to be doing things for everyone. Then her mother, as role-played by Laura, spoke up in Mike's father's defense. "That is how he and I love people, by taking care of things for them." Excitedly, Laura told Mike, "I think I understand not only you and your father's relationship better now, but also yours and mine. It's strange, you've accused me of being like your mother, but I really am more of a loner like your Dad … and my mother! I'd stay home alone like her and do the housework, although the thought of being left alone was scary to me. I didn't know what to do if you didn't come back. I thought I'd jump off the bridge if you left me. Now I can enjoy being alone. I finally like myself. I'm 50 years old, and after 25 years of marriage, it almost seems like my original contract with you is over."

Mike looked shocked. "Laura, I don't want you to leave me and I don't want to leave you. Just stop making that damn housework more important than me. I want us to spend fun time together. I want us to be spiritual together. I still want us to go to church with Jackie as a family."

Laura stiffened. "Well, we were going to church together, but you got more involved at church without checking with me. You never told me you were becoming a deacon; I had to find that out from someone else."

After checking the genealogy, I concluded that Laura's resistance to Mike's getting more involved at church was more closely related to her father's getting involved with the choir director (M/F IIP) than to Mike's affair seven years ago. Laura had introjected her mother's reaction to the experience of her father's abandonment and expected Mike to also have an affair with a woman at church. I asked Laura to tell me about her mother's feelings.

"Everyone at church knew about the affair except Momma. After she found out, she told Daddy she was leaving him. We never went back to that church. She said we were moving to another town, and Daddy wasn't. At the last minute, he came with us. I don't know if she ever forgave him for it. I never even got to tell Maxine goodbye. I've felt betrayed by her all my life. I thought she was the one adult who liked me for me, but maybe she really liked me for my daddy."

LINDA'S LETTER

Using three chairs, Laura role-played her mother and father resolving their crisis. Mike as Laura's father asked Laura's mother to forgive him. Laura role-played her twelve year old self watching the new process. For homework, Laura's "child" wrote a letter to Maxine.

Summer 1954

Dear Maxine,

You told me I was special to you. I always acted like all the other kids and called you Ms. Wilson. I thought you loved me more, and we just had to hide it from the other kids so no one would tease me about being the teacher's pet.

At church I'd sit in the front pew with you. You'd sit beside me when you weren't paying the piano. Nobody else had such shiny fingernails — certainly not my mother. You were much more glamorous than my mother.

Now my mother won't let me go to church anymore. I felt hurt and humiliated and betrayed.

I was with my mother the other day when she came after church to see you. I was supposed to stay outside, but I hid in the hallway and heard my mother slap you and call you "slut." I had never heard that word before but I knew it was bad and dirty.

My mother has been crying a lot. We're moving. I don't want to leave my friends. It's because of you and my dad. I hope I never see you again. I hate you.

Next, two chairs — Laura as "child," and Maxine. Laura cried as she role-played herself at twelve years of age reading the letter to Maxine. As Maxine, she responded with genuine love and caring. Laura forgave her.

During the therapy sessions seven years ago, Laura had become aware of how abandoned she felt when she was twelve years old and her father wanted to leave home for Maxine (F/C IIP). Before his death, Laura had expressed this feeling to him, and forgiven him, so this time her Father-Child interaction was not role-played. She had forgiven her father. It was her mother who had never forgiven him for wanting to leave (M/F IIP).

Mike said he wanted Laura and himself to do things together but also to do a lot separately. Interestingly enough, that was exactly the relationship both parental sets had and neither of their mothers liked (M/F IIPs). Mike's mother (and Laura's mother) complained that her husband was gone too much doing things for other people and didn't spend enough time with her. Mike wanted to have more fun time together with his mate. Laura played alone, like his mother and Laura's father had, and Laura worked alone like her mother and Mike's father had. The Introjected Parental Couples were becoming obvious.

What emerged here was another identical Introjected Interactional Pattern that Mike and Laura both brought to their relationship. Namely, that one parent would be over-responsible and the other under-responsible. These were the polarities in Mike's parents' relationship, Laura's parents' relationship, and Mike and Laura's own relationship. Generation after generation. One like this parent and one like that parent.

EXPERIMENT: Role-play both hardworking over-responsible parents talking to each other: Laura as Mike's father, and Mike as Laura's mother; then Mike as his father and Laura as her mother; finally, the more social ones Mike as his mother and Laura as her father; then Laura as Mike's mother, Mike as Laura's father. Purpose — to establish contact and create bonds between similar introjected parts.

Laura proudly announced she didn't do the homework which I had assigned her at the end of last session, namely, to make a list of all the chores around the house that she wanted Mike to do. Since this was the first time Laura had not done what she was "supposed" to do, I considered it progress. Her M/C projection onto me as her mother had dissolved, and her betrayal by Maxine was forgiven and had become a completed Gestalt. She felt confident I liked her for herself.

But the M/F Introjected Interactional Pattern with Mike was still in place. Laura wanted Mike to clean the gutters, before they could take time off to play. "I can't do that all by myself. The leaves are falling so fast. He needs to keep up with them."

GOING TO THE FAIR: I asked Laura to close her eyes and search for early memories that paralleled that situation with the gutters. Laura remembered the time her mother stayed home alone to can the ripe peaches while she and her father went to the fair. Laura had felt guilty about going out with Dad instead of helping her mother at home (F/C & M/C IIPs).

We role-played using three chairs. As her mother, Laura said "I'm barely keeping up with the peaches now, they're falling off the trees so fast. If I go to the fair, they'll start rotting on the ground." As her father, Laura was unable to come up with a solution. Mike sat in for him and proposed they all go to the fair and then come home and catch up with the peaches together as a family. The child Laura loved the new idea, but couldn't even imagine mother actually going. Laura had become aware of the origin of her fixed pattern of rejecting positive suggestions (M/F IIP).

To help Laura assimilate the new introject with less difficulty, I asked Laura to be her "child" and write a story about going to the fair with both parents. She brought the story into the next session. After role-playing "OUR FAMILY GOES TO THE FAIR," Laura commented, "Mother, for once, seemed to be enjoying herself. We'll have to do more things as a family, too." She smiled.

It was no coincidence that Laura and Mike had gotten stuck in the same places their parents had. Their Mother-Father Introjected Interactional Patterns limited them to the same ineffective options their parents had chosen. Session after session, Laura and Mike role-played their parents and their partner's parents. By sitting in for each other's projected parent, they integrated the new solution into their own interactional repertoire at this point with little or no resistance from either spouse.

We rechecked the genealogy. Laura's projection of her father onto Mike was now evident. Since her social father was her favorite parent (F/C IIP), but her hardworking disliked mother was her role model (M/F IIP) in relationships, Laura could see why her self-image was low. She liked her mate more than herself. So had her mother and Mike's father. Mike had followed much the same pattern, resenting his internalized mother while wanting more attention from his quiet, hardworking father whom Laura had always represented to him.

Mike gasped, realizing how much Laura's interactions with him reminded him of the way his father babied his mother (M/F IIP). "You treat me like I'm unable to take care of myself," he told Laura (F/C IIP). "My father did that to me, too. Don't baby me. I want to be more responsible. Let me share some of the workload."

Although increasingly aware now of his projections, Mike was not yet ready to own his introjection of the negative aspects of his mother, as well as her positive M/F interactional behaviors. For weeks, he had procrastinated doing his homework assignment, i.e., to list similar examples in his own behavior.

I made a point of not reminding him. Each time Mike made an excuse for not doing it, I simply thanked him for telling me. I was aware of his attempts to engage me in an argument so he could leave angrily (M/C IIP) or project that I was disappointed in him (F/C IIP).

THE COUPLE'S OBSERVATIONS

Since they were both writers, I asked them instead to write their own progress reports.

Mike's: Laura and I have reached a clearing of sorts in our relationship. I have come to understand my wife in a new way. For the first time in our twenty-five years of marriage, I listened so intently as she spoke about herself to Anne that I know the kind of interior changes she needs to make in order to be who she wants to be in the world. I want to help her to become that person.

I can see more forcefully than ever before that no matter what I may say about others, be it Laura or Anne, I am only projecting my own internal experiences. As I study my interactional history, I can recognize how often in my mind Laura was my father, not my mother (F/C IIP). Anne isn't my mother and shouldn't have to wait for homework assignments which I have agreed to. I tried to disappoint Anne, Laura, and myself the same way I disappointed my father who wanted me to be responsible.

Laura's: I now understand how my program for relating to Mike was formed at a very early age. I felt such a relief when Anne explained how familiar/familial pairs and patterns were learned from childhood and were carried into adulthood. Finally there was a reason, an explanation, for my feeling that Mike was continuously reacting to me as if I were someone else. I knew the things he would say about me were not me.

I am well aware that I was much more relieved to hear the rationale for Mike's responses to me, than to hear one for mine to him. Maybe it is because I had been aware for some time of Mike and my father's shared characteristics: silence, lack of communication, repressed acted-out anger, procrastination, and unwillingness to take responsibility for routine jobs. My father was my favorite parent and I was always more aware of him. I never got enough time with him. My mother didn't either. He was always going somewhere without us.

I was less willing to become aware of how much, in times of stress, I reacted to Mike as my mother did to my father. I still want to resist that she is my role model, and that my low self-esteem reflects both her lack of self-esteem and my lack of esteem for her. I am eager to continue working on my likeness to her.

When I asked Mike to "take back" that he ever loved Vicki and wanted to marry her, I could feel a layer in my chest lifting. I had to hear it several times, in a particular tone of voice, before my body could take in what he said. I know Mike's role-playing my father saying "I take back that I ever loved Maxine," to my mother first opened me up to the possibility to even asking Mike to "take it back too." After he did, I felt a lightness in my chest that I hadn't felt since before Vicki was in our lives.

The session before, my homework had been to call my mother to take back all the things I'd said over the years that must have hurt her. My resistance was enormous. I agreed with Anne it was only fair to do with Mom what I was asking Mike to do with me.

My mother's reaction surprised me. I realize it was the first time I'd ever talked to her as a human being and not as "Mother." I was astonished she could respond with substance and grace.

I now hold in myself an appreciation of her as a human being. She exists in a space all her own in the world, not one I am trying to get away from either. This week I received a card from her thanking me again for my caring call and telling me how much my words meant to her. This change in my sense of my mother comes as a surprise to me. I never would have thought it possible.

MIKE'S LETTER

Mike came in to the next session with the homework he had consistently avoided. "Excuse my procrastination. I have been a little pigheaded about this," he said, readily admitting to two traits he had listed for his mother. "Laura and I argued last week and I got so mad I left the house. Then I remembered Ma did that too when she couldn't win any other way. I came back." Mike put his mother in the empty chair and read her this letter.

Dear Ma:

*I don't know how to start talking to you. My feelings are in my throat. Feelings of confusion, anger and sadness, love and hate …
you and I usually found something to argue about instead of talk, while Dad and I were quiet around each other. I wanted to tell him how you fussed at me all the time for nothing, but you were so agreeable with him, he'd tell me I needed to understand "all the pain you'd gone through to have me." So I married someone who for the first ten years of our life didn't want children, and I felt I'd be causing her pain if I wanted just one child.*

To this very day, I do not know how to ask my wife for what I want. I automatically wait for her to do it for me, like you did. I'd argue with her like I did with you, Mom, or I'd sulk and rage internally against her, as if she were Pops. Like Dad, she missed me and sought contact when I'd withhold it. I'd criticize her, or threaten to leave. I can't change her, only me.

I have made a decision to deal with my judgements of you and Dad. I have, as Anne says, still some unfinished business to work on with my parents, and I will continue individually. Laura and I are becoming closer and closer in a way that has not before happened. I can actually choose to bypass my judgements of her. I am also being more accepting of myself and learning to show affection.

Your loving son, Mike

FINAL SESSION

A year passed before Laura and Mike came in to update me. "I just had to tell you this myself," Laura told me with a big smile. "My mother wants to come in to see me for Christmas. It's the strangest thing," she confided. "I'm looking forward to her visit. I'm not angry with her. Usually I'd be dreading her coming. But ever since you had me call Mom and 'take back' my hurtful words to her, she's been treating me wonderfully."

"Role-playing her and Dad first helped me want to forgive Mike. And ever since he told me he never loved Vicki, I've felt great. It was a real breakthrough for me to forgive him. Nobody in my family ever forgave anybody anything. I used to hold silent grudges, too. And Mike never would say caring things to me either. But he does now."

She looked at Mike lovingly, more openly affectionate than I'd ever seen her do. Gone from her face was that stem look that had marked her appearance. Usually reserved around her, Mike seemed more "on" with her than without, a striking reversal for a man who had "disappeared" around his wife. He was laughing and they were playing together.

"Jackie just got back from a summer in Germany," Mike said about their only daughter, now 17. "We raised her to be independent, but didn't realize she'd turn out to be so much like us. My parents had a fit when I left for the Middle East," Mike grinned. "I thought they were babying me and I had to get far away. Now Jackie's going away to college next year for the same reason. She says I baby her, and won't let her make her own decisions. Jackie is stubborn just like me and Ma and has a caretaker boyfriend who's just like Laura and Dad. Now, how did that happen, I wonder?"

CONCLUSION

By working on their parents' unfinished business, Laura and Mike were able to give up the Introjected Interactional Patterns (IIPs) which had been plaguing their relationship.

In only twelve sessions, working mainly on their introjections of their parents' relationships, Laura and Mike resolved their marital problems with considerably less difficulty then if they had dealt with their current relationship directly.

By role-playing their parents' relationship first, this couple was able to identify their negative introjected patterns, and restructure and integrate happier attitudes and behaviors into the "now" of their daily lives.

The changes over five months of therapy were dramatic. Laura and Mike stopped blaming each other, themselves and their parents, and were able to live their relationship their way ... instead of their parents' way.

REFERENCES

Smith, E. (1992). *Gestalt Voices*. Westport, CT: Ablex Publishing.

Rosenfeld, E. (1978). An oral history of Gestalt therapy: I. A conversation with Laura Perls. *Gestalt Journal, 1(1)*.

◊

11

TWO COUPLES WHO "COULDN'T"

Bud Feder[1]

◆◆◆

INTRODUCTION

As we gathered chapters for this books, we the editors realized that with one exception (Houston's) all the stories had "happy endings," that is, all of the contributors were writing about cases that could be termed successes. Now all of us working therapists know that we often have failures, too. We decided that our book should have at least one such. So here is such a case: a failure — or is it? After writing it and talking about it I'm not so sure anymore. Certainly, as you will read, at the end of the case we, the therapists, felt sad about how it ended. And our clients felt even worse. On the other hand … but I'm getting too far ahead of myself. The point is, what do you think? Is this case a success, a failure, or some other animal altogether?

Here is the structure of the chapter. It is a chronological session-by-session account of the interaction between two couples: one a married couple in great distress and the other two therapists accustomed to working together. First I'll say a little about each pair, including how we, the therapist couple, work. Then I will describe in varying detail each of the 14 sessions, interspersing at times information about the therapists' conversations between some of the sessions. Finally I will return to discuss the original question: was this case a failure?

----

1   My thanks to Linda DiTullio, my friend and co-therapist, for reviewing this report and contributing to it.

205

JUNE & ROB: As we discovered during our (relatively brief) contact over six months, this was Rob's second marriage, June's first. He is about ten years older than she and came into their relationship with two daughters, now ten and eight. They met at work, he a successful manager, she a young secretary. They are both extremely attractive physically, he a dark Italianate type, good-looking enough for Hollywood, and she a tall slim blonde of Polish extraction. When June first came to work for their company, she believed Rob to be a happily-married man. He smiled a lot and was very witty, the kind of humor one couldn't help laughing at even though it often was barbed — a Jackie Mason type of humor. He let her know one day, though, that this marriage was in deep shit (they both are very enamored of scatological language). First they spent time together talking, mostly about his problems, then having fun and then sex, which was great. In fact, it was all great. They had a lot of fun together in those days (now, forget it). After Rob's divorce was finalized, they soon lived together and soon married. So far, still fun. June did not enjoy secretarial work; she loved flowers. With Rob's help and support she bought a little flower shop in a small town a few miles from their residence which was a two-family house which they also bought. No more fun.

LINDA & BUD: Linda and I were close friends long before we worked together as co-therapists. We met when each was single and quickly became good friends. We supported each other in her and my relationship struggles. For example, she agreed to Bud's then girlfriend living with us (by this time we had leased a house together); and I helped her deal with men, culminating in being the ring-bearer at her wedding. By the time we met June & Rob we had been close for fifteen years, and had shared many good times and bad times, fun times and sad times together. We had been instrumental to each other in many ways personally and professionally, too many to enumerate here. We had a few fights, of course, but never any of a catastrophic nature. We had learned from each other and with each other, including how to resolve (or overlook) differences. One thing for sure — each knew the other was there in time of need.

HOW WE WORK: Naturally we don't work exactly the same with all couples we see together, but there are some basic aspects of our-working: first of all, we are a couple, too — not a married or romantic couple but definitely a caring couple. We make no effort to hide that we are close friends and care a great deal for each other. It comes through. We don't share an office. One must come to the other's office, often arriving when the client couple is in the waiting room. When the occupant therapist comes out of her/his consulting room the two of us greet naturally, usually with a hug or a kiss. And we often pay attention to the other's need and bring a snack or a gift. So we begin by being people, consciously modeling caring and providing a warm setting.

Another piece is that during sessions we often share our own experiences in relationships. We both have had our share of successes and failures in marriage, and many of the issues our clients struggle with we have struggled with too. We do this more often with clients, like Rob and June, who have great difficulty empathizing. Similarly we often express our feelings during sessions, again more so with clients who have trouble identifying and/or expressing certain feelings. It is our hope and intention in this way to help our clients on their difficult path by accompanying them in a personal way.

In addition, as is described, we use many familiar Gestalt approaches involving awareness, responsible language, direct contact and others. In short, we haven't invented anything — we just put our personal spin on it.

FIRST CONTACTS: The first few contacts were actually with me alone. The very first was a phone call from June, saying she wanted an appointment, that her marriage was in trouble and that her husband said 95% of the fault was hers (uh-oh; this is gonna be a tough one). We arranged to meet. As indicated above, June is an attractive woman physically: tall, slim, pretty. Soon however it was apparent that there was much amiss about her. In addition to being very upset and troubled — natural enough in view of her serious marital problems — June evidenced a great deal of constriction. This came across through her posture, very tight, making her look somehow small despite her height; and it came across through her contact style which had a small girl quality; and through her voice, not at all rich and mature. She cried a lot during this initial interview as she told me some of her story, mostly about her deteriorating relationship with Rob. She expressed, in her constricted way, a lot of pain about their frequent arguing, about Rob's avoiding her in recent months both generally and sexually, and about his oft-voiced statements about the demise of their marriage and the inevitability of their becoming divorced. She stated that he had frequently, in the heat of their fights, threatened to see a lawyer. As far as she knew, he had not done so — yet. Somewhere during the middle of this session she elaborated upon what she had said on the phone, that she was 95% responsible for their marital problems according to Rob and further that she was crazy like her mother and she needed a psychiatrist like her mother (Whose psychiatrist had referred her to me). When she told me this I made a face and grunted without verbal comment.

As the session was ending I spoke my piece: that I would not see her alone in an effort to save the marriage, that I didn't buy it was 95% her fault and that I'd only work with her on the marriage in conjunction with Rob; he had to come in too or else count me out. June was very upset by this: "He won't come, I know he won't; he says I need the help; he doesn't need any." I responded that if he wouldn't come in there was not hope for the marriage and urged her to go home and tell him what I said. This was a Thursday; we agreed she'd call me by Saturday to let me know the outcome. Saturday and no word. I figured I would hear no more. To my surprise on Monday I got a call from Rob saying he wanted to see me alone. I decided, well, I heard her side alone, it's only fair I hear his. We made an appointment for that very evening.

Rob arrived — the other end of the pole from June: physically very space-consuming though not a huge man. Very well-dressed and very socially articulate. There were not tears this time — there were jokes. None that I specifically remember, just little cute remarks about the decor and the circumstances. Despite myself I smiled. Like June, Rob was very detailed; like her he told me long stories about events in their relationship, all the details pointing towards June's deficiencies as a person: her obsessive cleanliness, her lying, her rigid jealous attitude towards his kids' mother, her foul mouth, her overdependence on her mother, her overdependence on him etc. When I asked him how he thought he had contributed to their problems the most he could come up with was that he had been too accommodating to June's whims in the earlier days of their marriage (more bad news - Rob doesn't look very hard at his contributions to the problems). Despite everything he expressed a wish to save the marriage. His first divorce, he told me, had been bitter and painful. He didn't want to go through that again. He accepted my idea that the three of us meet on the coming Saturday afternoon for a lengthy, perhaps double, session.

I was sure that this joint meeting would require a lot of time. I wasn't yet clear that this was a case I wanted Linda on — but I was moving in that direction. One of the reasons we work together is for support — when one of us gets a couple's case which leads to "Uh-oh, this one's gonna be tough and painful" we dial the other and say, in essence, "Help." I was beginning to get that feeling so before Saturday arrived I contacted Linda and told her about Rob & June and asked her if she would and could join me if they agreed. Obviously she said yes. I called Rob & June, explained the setup to them. They accepted it and we set up an open-ended session for the coming Saturday afternoon.

DOUBLE JOINT SESSION

They were some ways similar in their style during this two-hour meeting, in others different. Both were very detailed, recounting incidents at great length; both were very recriminating, generally blaming the other and look-ing at self rarely. They also had remarkably different recollections of the same event, coloring the event in question so the other looked bad and the narrator good. In the five days between my initial contact with June and my first meeting with Rob they had had a huge fight over money. It had been on a weekend, a Saturday night, an important detail because no judge was available until the next morning. In anger he had threatened to get his gun and kill June. She had immediately called the police who removed Rob to the municipal hoosegow, mugshot and fingerprinted him and held him until Sunday morning when a judge could be found since only a judge could release him on his own recognizance. So Rob had to spend the night in jail. In recounting this Rob repeatedly used words like humiliating, embarrassing, unbelievable, unforgivable; he insisted "nothing like this has ever happened to me or my family." When I probed his contribution to the event he could only come up with "it was a dumb thing to say" but then "how could she take me seriously?" He omitted to tell me (which came out later in joint session) that earlier in the evening he had kicked her in the ass as she was leaving a room — "kind of swiped at her with my foot" as he put it. I also recalled that in my session with June she had reported violence on Rob's part on their honeymoon, and a few other times since — acts like pulling her hair, kicking her in the butt, etc. Usually Rob had been drinking during these episodes. Obviously he was not computing this past into June's present behavior.

Where they differed was in their manner. June was more soft-spoken and often tearful; Rob shifted between vicious anger and sardonic humor. The tricky thing about his humor was that he was so good at it: even though the topic was painful it wasn't possible, at least for me, not to laugh at his jokes, his delivery and timing being so skillful. Of course, it was mostly gallows humor. The issues were: from June's point of view Rob was cold, distant, secretive about money, verbally abusive and disrespectful; from Rob's, June was attached at the hip to her parents parroting their old world views, had no sense of humor, was constantly worrying and if not was cleaning, was jealous of his kids and his exwife, had tricked and humiliated him in the police incident, etc. In short, he concluded with a smile, she's a dumb Polack.

Some other interesting aspects of this first joint session were these: at first both Rob and June directed their words towards me — by the end of the session Linda had intervened effectively (more about this later) and they were addressing her, too; both Linda and I asked frequently about feelings and about the meaning to them of events, such as "maybe it means a loss of face to you" (they were both barren in this kind of articulating); Linda asked them each to recall a good time together: Rob recalled a fun time at someone's wedding while June recalled a serious time when Rob was going through his divorce and leaned heavily on her. This was a major difference between them, fun v. serious. Their memories of their respective families of origin fit this pattern, too - June remembering hers as hard-working and serious and Rob his as fun-loving and actively playful.

CONFERENCE: In talking afterward we found that we both felt pretty drained, but also very interested in helping this appealing couple. We agreed that they manifested so much potential. We strongly wanted to help them climb out of the pit of despair which they had dug for themselves. We had let them do most of the talking, mainly seeking clarification at times and often reflecting on their pain and disappointment over the deterioration of their relationship. At this stage we felt some hope, especially since they left agreeing to work with us on a weekly basis.

SECOND JOINT SESSION: ABOUT HURT

Although the first session had taken place in my office, we arranged for the future ones to be in Linda's because of scheduling logistics. When I entered her waiting room Rob and June were already there. We had to wait a few minutes until Linda was free. During this time Rob asked me "Are your married?" I answered: had been married for a long time and now divorced for a long time.

In session their focus continued on anger and actions. No appreciation of hurt feelings, especially the other person's. We again brought in the language and experience of hurting, Linda particularly asking "What does that mean to you?" and "How does that feel?" Rob joked a lot but ultimately owned a knot in his stomach. June spoke of easily feeling embarrassed. We joined them by saying things like "I know what you mean" and "Sometimes I feel my pain there too."

Other things talked about in this session were families and feelings. June's parents argued and drank a lot and held grudges, with June as the mediator. In Rob's, anger surfaced at times but passed quickly (interestingly in our work together, June let go much more easily while Rob couldn't).

During the session Rob owned a macho stance: he doesn't ask for help or show hurt. Bud and Linda gave lessons at times, e.g. adult children of alcoholics feel cheated and that macho is a cover, everyone feels hurt at times. The most poignant moment in the session came when Rob spoke glibly about losing his kids through divorce - I shared my great pain on my separation from my son, then 10.

We learned they were not living together at this point, not since the jail incident. So for homework we suggested they go for dinner together at a restaurant and tell each other of times in their lives that they had felt hurt.

JOINT SESSION # 3: ANGER, THAT'S ALL

They had done their homework and learned a few things. Rob had spoken of being denied his rightful place on the varsity baseball team as high school senior, though he deserved it and he owned also that he must be a winner. June had spoken of shyness and pain as an adolescent. Nevertheless this session was most difficult; anger, anger, anger. We kept digging for other feelings but anger was all they owned. Finally we experimented with their expressing wants. This was also the homework.

CONFERENCE: Between sessions we went over together the protocols of autobiographical materials they had filled out at our request. These consisted of a package of forms which I had developed over the years: a page for father, for mother, for siblings, children and partners or spouses. Each page asked a few questions with a great deal of space for response. In addition there is a page requesting information on health, another a sociogram and another consists of a large circle with instructions to draw in it anything the client chooses (see figures following). In looking them over we noted Rob's evasiveness and superficiality — all his family relationships were "excellent" and he gave the minimum information. June's was more detached and reserved but much more complete (she also had more trouble following directions and had poor spelling — no doubt providing fodder for Rob to resort to his favored "dumb Polack" quips). Their drawings, as can be seen,

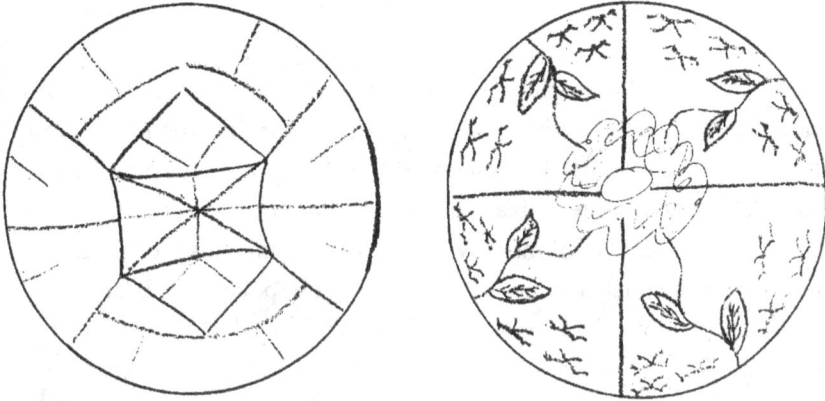

are contrasting: Rob's rather geometric and hard-angled (a spider's web?) and June's softer and more artistic (a clinging vine?). This all fit with impressions we'd been forming during our contacts so far and confirmed our belief that we had a tough job ahead of us, particularly with regard to engaging Rob but also in light of their different styles.

FOURTH JOINT SESSION — WIT AND ITS RELATION TO THE UNCONSCIOUS (S. FREUD)

June began by asking about having longer sessions (generally we were with them 50-60 minutes, as much as we could squeeze out). We told them we couldn't manage that at this time and suggested they work more from the bottom up rather than from the top down. Usually near the end of each session we all felt connected after a lot of hard work by Linda and me. I mean we repeatedly asked for feelings, bodily reactions and shared many of our own. June also told us that the longer we worked together the more she liked this process. We were helping her "get closer to her deeper feelings." Rob, on the other hand, said he was very embarrassed about seeing "shrinks" and said, in his typical hurtfully humorous way "Well, that's what I get for marrying a wacko." June didn't respond to his barb at this time so I supported her by saying "Wow, that really hurt, Rob. I feel hurt at your calling me a shrink but feel much more for June, calling her a wacko." Still silence from June.

But later he did it again and this time she reacted. June, in her serious way, remarked that sometimes she thought about writing Rob letters, since they dialogued so poorly. His response: "You can't spell." This time June reacted: "Your humor feels like pins in my heart." Rob blew this off with "You've got no sense of humor." When both Linda and I also reported to him that we often felt attacked by his humor, Rob spoke of his being afraid we were trying to make a robot out of him. We stressed that we wanted to help him get more not less out of his humor, that he had a great gift for wit and that we were challenging him to use it in other ways besides ballbusting. I don't think we got very far.

In efforts to connect more deeply, especially with Rob — since we felt that June was much more engaged and trusting — we did two other things this session: at one point, when it fit the contact, I talked of my own marriage, my own discomfort with and resistance to therapy and how hard it had been for me to come off what I termed the "King Shit" perch in my marital relationship. This arose when June, beginning to be more aware, said that she noticed she felt like a "Dummy" often and that she looked up to Rob as older and more experienced. In addition to this sharing, there was also the aspect of our purposely using earthy language (fuck and shit, etc) to pace and connect with Rob, since these words were so much a part of his vocabulary, and sometimes June's too.

And the body: Linda noticed Rob with arms across his chest after he said he was feeling that old knot again.

L: Is it under there?

R: What does it mean? Make it go away.

L: We have no formula — you tell us.

R: (more softly and without humor) It means "Don't try to change me."

L: (also softly) This session feels different. I feel more connected to you right now.

NEXT SESSION, LINDA AWAY: WIN—WIN

Their homework had been around fairness since each often complained that the other's act or opinion or attitude wasn't fair. They reported that this had been an unpleasant experience resulting in bickering and disagreement and neither had been able to appreciate the other's point of view. When we explored this some more at first we didn't get very far. Finally the notion that control and respect were the relevant issues emerged. At my request they played with discussing fairness again and it soon became apparent to me that they each had a hardened win-lose attitude. The concept of win-win was quite foreign to each. So we talked about that and about the other possibilities in conflict-resolution. I offered to teach them some approaches to experiment with. They agreed to try it on. I emphasized brain-storming and tuning in to the other. That all sounded good in the abstract. Dishearteningly, though, the topic of Rob's former wife came up and they immediately reverted to their fixed patterns of namecalling, judgementalness, rigidity, angry cursing (June) and sardonic humor (Rob). In the heat of the session everything we had talked about flew out the window. I pointed this out and said I could relate some to what they must be feeling because just listening I experienced bitterness and pain. I gave them a guide sheet for conflict-resolution for couples which I had prepared and recommended they play with it for homework. Not a happy session.

JOINT SESSION #5: SOUR FACES

They came in with sour faces: they had had another heavy-duty fight over money and hadn't done any conflict-resolution homework either, particularly during that fight. We focussed on their mutual mistrust based on past secrecy and betrayals. We reemphasized responsible language, vulnerability and feelings. We (Linda & I) both shared some experiences of vulnerability in our relationships. They left with sour faces.

CONFERENCE: This was a down time for us. We both talked of some feelings of helplessness and despair. Our initial hopefulness was a dim memory and now it was more a prayer than a hope. We wondered aloud if we could ever dent the rigid fixed Gestalten of these two people. We decided of course that we'd keep on trying. The next session, though, provided a (temporary) glimmer of the faded hope.

JOINT SESSION #6: CAN WE CONNECT?

Again fights over money and bank accounts, for three days running.

R: She lies.

L: He has no patience.

(Both of course true). We worked on getting each to look at her/his own contribution to their painful interactions. June was much more open to listening and experimenting. Rob continued to be very blaming and frustrated (impatient?) We asked him to notice this in the here-and-now and experiment with finding that interesting. But it seemed to be getting harder not easier to get any cooperation from him. I shared my own stubbornness and impatience in relationships and told him how hard it often was, and is, for me to let go of my stubbornness and impatience when relationships hit sour spots or phases. Rob listened with apparent interest.

JOINT SESSION # 7: THE DOWNWARD PATH

I began this session by acknowledging that I was in a very somber mood: as I was leaving my house to come to the session I saw my next door neighbor being wheeled into an ambulance, probably never to return. He had been suffering for years from throat cancer and in our last conversation he for the first time spoke to me despairingly. I also owned to having a bad cold. The session soon began to resolve around anger and nastiness and how Rob and June had each become so good at both. This segued into their fear of vulnerability. Linda worked with June's "bitchiness."

The session culminated in June crying over feeling put down and in Rob working on his knowing only either being a pussycat or a wiseass.

CONFERENCE: We weren't sure why but we were feeling very concerned that we were sliding backwards. They were feeling like the teflon couple, especially Rob but June, too. Nothing sticks.

JOINT SESSION # 8: HARD TO SOFT

June began the session expressing her yearning for a baby. Rob could only see that as a trap for child support. Neither could appreciate the other's complexity. Both frequently used the phrase "Yes, but you always …" or an equivalent. When they looked very glum as we pointed this out and their tit-for-tat styles, we tried to support them by remembering out loud similar difficulties in our own marriages. We felt some softening by the time we parted.

CONFERENCE: Really not so much a conference as a support group for therapists in trouble. We consoled ourselves with this fantasy: "if only we had them every day!"

JOINT SESSION # 9: THE UNFORGIVABLE BETRAYAL

Now it came out — why we were losing momentum. June began by stating it explicitly: "It feels like we are going backwards. All I hear from Rob is 'Fuck this' and 'Fuck that' and 'Fuck your parents.'"

Rob: I'll never forgive her for what she did to me, throwing me into jail, humiliating me, mugshots, handcuffs, fingerprints. Humiliating, embarrassing, degrading. I'd be an asshole to forgive her. I can never trust her again.

June defended herself, repeating Rob's threat to shoot her and Linda helped her put it in the ground of the violence in her family of origin. But neither showed any appreciation or acceptance of the other's feelings. I talked about how difficult it is sometimes to forgive and how I had held a hateful grudge for years for the woman who had betrayed me. Rob wanted to know more, wanted to know what had been the nature of the betrayal. I told him: multiple infidelities. Linda added that she knew about betrayal, too and shared some of her experience. The session ended on a quiet and sad note.

JOINT SESSION # 10: A TURNING POINT

Rob began: I feel like shit. I'm in limbo. I'm not sure she deserves me after what she did.

June reported feeling very upset and physically poor. And she looked it — drawn and downtrodden. I said that I felt we were on a plateau. Rob picked up on the metaphor and said he was afraid to go up the mountain (meaning decide for the relationship) and afraid to go down the mountain (to end the relationship). If he goes up June can't be trusted; "She'll revert to being a bitch." If he goes down he will have to endure again the "pits of divorce."

The session revolved around Rob's indecision and June's reaction. She reported "holding back"; so she was on a plateau too. I suggested she pay attention to her holding back, as homework (believing it's a pattern or a fixed Gestalt of great importance in all of her relationships, not just this one.) There wasn't much anger this session, more a grey-ness — the fog of despair coming in perhaps.

JOINT SESSION # 11: LAST SCENE BUT ONE

Rob was still on his plateau and had nothing new to add. Linda honed in on June's reaction and expressed great concern for her. She was very depressed and anxious and tearful and reported difficulty in taking care of herself, in eating, sleeping and working. She reported being shaky and very tense: Linda expressed fear that June couldn't take a lot more of this suspense and urged Rob to make a decision. He owned that he was stalling and that Linda was right. He had to "shit or get off the pot" soon. He couldn't do this much longer in fairness to everybody. No anger; an ominous calm.

CONFERENCE: We discussed Linda's spontaneous expression of concern for June's survival and her intervention in which she pressed Rob to make a move. I told her I not only supported her doing so, but I actually appreciated what she had done. In fact I felt remiss that I hadn't been more in touch with the need to do this. Perhaps I was constraining myself through some introject that a good Gestalt therapist lets it happen and doesn't press for action or movement. (I momentarily forgot one of Laura's greatest legacies to me: "Give as much support as necessary …"). At any rate we agreed we were both okay with her intervention and at the same time were anxious about what would follow.

JOINT SESSION # 12: THE END

They came in slowly and quietly. Without waiting to be asked, Rob said he was resolved to file for divorce but he wants to be "considerate." He wants there to be as little suffering as possible and he's willing to wait until after the Christmas holidays, for their families' welfare, too. June is bitter, sullen, sad and sulky. She is rigid bodily and tight in her speech. She is no longer a participant. He can do whatever he wants, what's the difference, the holidays are down the tubes anyway. She finally cries a little. She doesn't want his pity or sympathy. It's all or nothing, it's love or nothing. They become vituperative and we are bleak and helpless. We offer our concern and express our sadness. We suggest they consider individual therapy for support through the painful times ahead (but we never hear from them again except regarding insurance forms). Some hugs with June and handshakes with Rob and it's over. "This is the way the world ends … not with a bang but a whimper." (T.S. Eliot)

EPILOGUE

In the interest of this report and with curiosity as well as concern we each contacted one of the partners a few months later: I, Rob and Linda, June. In both instances the contact was unrewarding. Each responded to us tersely and cooly and each reported the divorce was going forward and that it was a drag and a hassle or words to that effect. Neither made any effort to connect.

DISCUSSION

> Perhaps this is what love is: the momentary or prolonged refusal to think of another person in terms of power. Like an enzyme which blocks momentarily a biological process, what we call love may inhibit the process of power negotiation — from which inhibition comes the illusion of equality so characteristic of lovers. (from Parallel Lives by Phyllis Rose, p.8)

These lovers had not the ability to move successfully past the "illusion of equality" "through the process of power negotiation" — certainly not unaided and, sadly, we were unable to effectively help them to do so. Some serious questions arose for me out of this experience:

-----

was our work deficient? is there some thing or things we missed that could have made a big difference in the outcome of this case?

-----

how come we couldn't help this couple to productively go through this process of power negotiation?

-----

was this case a "failure"? or can you call it a partial success that they learned something about communication, body awareness, feelings, their interpersonal styles? and most difficult of all, can we say that the outcome (i.e. divorce) was the best creative adjustment to this difficult situation that they could make, given their rigid fixed Gestalten? Or to put it another way, is this better for them then their remaining tormented on their plateau as they had been for the time we knew them and for quite a time before? We like to think the latter. What do you think?

REFERENCE

Rose, P. (1984) *Parallel lives: Five victorian marriages.* New York: Alfred A. Knopf.

◊

12

THE HEALING THROUGH RELATIONSHIP IN AN INTERACTIVE GESTALT GROUP

Jay Earley

◆◗◆

FOREWORD

Increasingly Gestalt Therapists are using approaches to group therapy that go beyond individual work in a group to focus on the interpersonal interactions or the group-as-a-whole (1–3)(4, Chapter 7). I believe that the important therapeutic potential in any group therapy situation is the interpersonal learning and healing which takes place in the interactions between the group members. Therefore my approach to Gestalt group work focuses on the feelings and the relationships between members.

I started developing this approach in 1978 when a group of therapists in California formed a group practice for the purpose of leading groups for our clients. We all had training in Gestalt and also in encounter groups, and therefore we combined these two modalities. After moving to Long Island in 1988 I continued developing the method on my own. I then began to offer training in leading Interactive Groups, which led to the formation of the Group Therapy Center of Long Island.

Interactive Gestalt Groups are designed to intensify and maximize the interpersonal contact and the work that emerges from this. I work with a group member individually only when he or she brings up an issue with the group in the here and now. Otherwise the work tends to be in pairs, as people explore their relationships with each other, expand their awareness, and experiment with new ways of relating. This approach embodies Gestalt

Therapy in its emphasis on contact, awareness, and experimentation, though it uses very little in the way of conventional Gestalt techniques.

The groups meet for two hours once a week. In addition, I hold weekend retreats for each group, usually twice a year, as a way of deepening the work and people's connections with each other. For any group member who is not in individual therapy with me, I require occasional individual consultations with me which are focused on enhancing the person's use of the group.

THE CASE

In this chapter I will describe the work of Sharon, from the time she started as one of the original members of her group, until now, a year and a half later. Sharon is a recovering alcoholic who has been sober for over a decade with the help of AA and much therapy. In that time she has worked through enough deep issues in therapy to get to the point where she is generally not in emotional pain and feels pretty satisfied with her life. She is a successful management consultant, has some close friends and an active social life when she wants it.

Her two major unresolved problems are other addictions and lack of intimacy. She is still struggling with an addiction to smoking and a tendency to work compulsively. She tends to keep people at a subtle distance in her life and stays away from a committed love relationship. Since her marriage ended many years ago, she hasn't allowed a man close enough to her to become a new love relationship. She thinks she may now be ready to tackle these problems.

Judgement As A Defense
We all want to be liked; we all want closeness with others. To express these desires directly to other people puts us in a vulnerable position. They might not reciprocate. They might even reject us or put us down. Therefore we develop various defenses against our own wanting and accompanying vulnerability. In an Interactive Group, people are encouraged to reach out

to connect with those group members they want contact with. They are encouraged to take the risk to make themselves vulnerable in a situation where we are dealing with people's real relationships with each other.

We also help people to become aware of their defenses against vulnerability and risk. If they defend by being nonchalant, it will be pointed out. If they defend by being judgmental and arrogant or by being distant and cold, they will probably get feedback about it. This gives people a chance to realize that they are defending against their needs and desires, and to try out different behavior.

When Sharon joined the group, she had a tendency to defend against her softness and openness. She didn't feel safe to show her desires for other people for fear of being rejected or shamed. Instead she adopted one of two attitudes. One was an internal stance of arrogance and judgement. "There's something wrong with you. I'm not sure I'll let you in." She was not aware of this and rarely expressed it, but it would leak out in little ways. It was a way for her to feel better about herself. The second attitude was a pretense of not desiring the other person. "I don't care. I don't need you." This was also not conscious or expressed, but it succeeded in keeping her away from people.

As the group developed, Sharon got feedback from time to time when her judgmental style would leak out. She is very aware and dedicated to growing, and she has an especially courageous way of acknowledging difficult things about herself in an undefensive way. So when she got this feedback, she was not only willing to acknowledge that she had been judgmental but also to explore what she was defending against. She would often discover that hidden underneath the judgement was a desire to make contact with the person.

For example, in one early group, Jill was telling the group about her anger and desire to pull away from a friend. When Sharon pushed Jill very hard not to do that, I encouraged Sharon to explore why she was doing this. She realized that she saw Jill as doing something similar in group, and she didn't want Jill to pull away from her. When she told Jill this, Jill took in the feedback, but then Jill also told Sharon that Sharon had told her in an aggressive manner that made Jill pull back.

Knowing that she feels good about Jill, Sharon was surprised to hear this, but she took it seriously and became interested in changing this way of relating. I then encouraged Sharon to show her positive feelings directly to Jill, and she was able to express some affection in a soft open way. This then enabled to the two of them to make warm contact.

Sharon also worked on her fear of confronting people. Before joining the group she tended to avoid bringing up difficulties with her friends, and then she would withdraw from them because the negative feelings festered. This was directly tied to her fear of vulnerability. As long as she was holding back negative feelings toward someone, it didn't make sense to reach out or be vulnerable. She felt justified in keeping people at a distance or even writing them off. She was also afraid of the people's reactions if she confronted them.

When she brought this up in group, I suggested that she work on confronting people in group directly, and this terrified her. She was afraid that they would be hurt, abandon her, or get angry at her. I encouraged her to get feedback from the group members about this, and only one person expressed fear of Sharon's confrontations. The rest of the group welcomed them.

After this, she began bringing out her negative feelings and to confront people, and in the process she learned more about how her judgements were a defense against wanting contact. This also got the judgements out in the open so that they didn't fester inside. Even in the cases where Sharon wasn't defending against her needs and felt genuinely annoyed at someone, if she didn't express the annoyance, there wasn't much chance for her to move past it and connect with the person. Sharon also found that when she did confront someone in a soft way, the person would often reveal the reason behind the behavior and would open to her and change. This then encouraged Sharon's own openness. Confrontation became a way of becoming closer to someone.

For example, Melissa joined the group about nine months after it started and Sharon didn't feel very receptive to her. Sharon describes it as follows: "I had an internal attitude of: I'm in the in-crowd and I've got something that you don't. You can't come in." I feel this way toward some people.

They have to prove that they appreciate me and let me know that. Once they do that, then I can trust them. I originally felt that way toward another woman in group, and Jay and I worked on it in a consultation, but she left the group before I was ready to do it. I was much too scared and couldn't have done it then.

"I was very scared to confront Melissa, especially because it was something that was part of her character and couldn't be changed. When I mentioned that in a consultation, Jay encouraged me to work on it with her because both of us could benefit from it. That gave me the idea that my response to someone could be appropriate and helpful to them. So he gave me the courage to do it."

Even though at first Sharon didn't say anything about her judgmental response, Melissa sensed it, and after a couple of months she questioned Sharon about it. This gave Sharon an opening to do the work. She acknowledged that she had a tendency to make people prove themselves before she would accept them, and that she was feeling that way toward Melissa. Melissa asked her why, and Sharon said it was because she didn't sense warmth from Melissa toward herself or toward other people in the group.

"This was very scary. If I would ever talk back or challenge my mother in any way she would be so wounded. She could dish it out but she couldn't take it. The guilt I would feel at hurting her the way I did! In the family, I had all this training that you can't disagree, or argue, or confront in any way. People get so hurt! I had already worked on that in individual therapy, so in the group I was ready to try it out and break old habits."

Melissa felt hurt by Sharon's statement, but she also acknowledged that she had a tendency to be guarded at first with people for fear of not being accepted. Melissa was feeling shaky about not being accepted in the group, and I encouraged her to explore this rather than defending herself. It was naturally very difficult for Melissa to make herself this vulnerable, but with encouragement and reassurance from me and from the group, she was able to do some very courageous work. As she explored this issue it led back to some deep pain about not being accepted in her family of origin, and Melissa opened herself and expressed the pain in a vulnerable, appealing way.

Sharon's attitude toward Melissa changed right in the moment. She melted and felt genuine caring and respect for her. She realized that Melissa had warmth, but that she had some blocks to accessing it and that she expressed it in a different way than Sharon. Thus because Sharon had confronted Melissa and Melissa had responded so well, she was able to see past Melissa's defenses and connect with her. They continued to work on this issue and other differences between them as the group progressed. In addition, because of this work Sharon saw the possibility of being more receptive to other new people whose style might be different from hers.

Desire And Vulnerability

In an Interactive Group we encourage people to be honest with each other about their responses, so if people reach out to them in group, they could get hurt. However, if they are strong enough to handle this, it can be an opportunity for growth. They can learn how to deal with the hurt. They can learn that it need not be devastating; it need not be proof that they are worthless.

What is more important, as people learn to reach out in a vulnerable way for contact, they are likely to be received positively. Vulnerability is very appealing, as is the direct expression of positive feelings. The more people learn to express themselves in such a healthy way, the more it is reinforced in group.

In an early group, as part of some work Harry was doing, I encouraged him to pick someone he wanted to connect with. He chose one woman and indicated a couple of others as alternate choices. Sharon was later able to tell Harry that she was hurt that she wasn't even on his list of second choices. Harry explained that he didn't choose her because he felt intimidated by her, that she was so sharp and perceptive that she would see right through him. I encouraged Sharon not to get caught up in responding to his explanation, but instead to say with her feeling of hurt. This allowed her to soften, and her previous front of appearing nonchalant disappeared. In an open and appealing way she let Harry know that she liked him and wanted him to like her, too, and that she felt hurt.

This had three effects. 1) She discovered that nothing terrible happened when she felt vulnerable and showed it. She didn't get rejected or ridiculed.

2) She also found that she was strong enough inside to tolerate the hurt feeling, and that she didn't feel bad about herself because of it. As she did this kind of work in group over time, she developed a sense of inner support so that she could be open and vulnerable without fear. 3) Harry began to appreciate Sharon's openness and softness (along with the earthiness and spontaneity that he had always liked in her). He was increasingly drawn to her. She was nicely rewarded for her vulnerability, and as time went on it became more and more her natural response.

"This interaction was a key, a turning point for me. I used to think that I was warm, but other people experienced me as hard. It was with Harry that I began the process of recognizing that I present an imposing or intimidating presence. I remembered people being afraid of me in my life, but I was surprised that was the way people saw me, because that wasn't what I felt inside. Inside I felt warm and open. It was a surprise to learn that my defenses were so hardened that people didn't see me. It was a real surprise that someone like Harry should be intimidated by me."

In one group, Sharon had made a comment about how "the universe moved" when Harry said something to another member. Then later she confessed that she had really meant that the universe had moved when he'd said something special to her. At another point she told him that she had a crush on him (but she wasn't coming on to him). She expressed these very vulnerable feelings in an open and contactful way, and Harry responded in kind. He was very moved by this reaching out and deep vulnerability on her part and grew very fond of her. As the group continued, Harry and Sharon developed a deep connection. Thus she continued to receive emotional support for her healthy behavior, and that made it possible for her to assimilate it, to make it her own at a deep level. There was no longer any chance of Harry ignoring Sharon. "I liked Harry very much and once he began to appreciate me more, it had a strong impact. His recognition of me liberated me."

Sharon also did some important work on reaching out to another man in the group, John. In one group he let us know that it was very hard for him to feel a desire to connect with people. He got scared and closed down and couldn't even feel that he wanted anything. Sharon then told him that she hoped at some point he would want to connect with her. He wanted to know why. Why anyone would want to work this out with him? She let him know, in a vulnerable way, that she really liked him and wanted to connect with him, and that she wanted him to want her in the same way.

In a subsequent group, when I was working with John on his fear of reaching out, I suggested he choose someone to work with, and he chose Sharon. We decided to try doing this work non-verbally, and when that came up, Sharon got quite scared. In exploring her fear, she realized that she was afraid that if she really opened up and liked him and became happy, she would be happier than he was. That would mean that he was more important to her than she was to him, and she would feel rejected and humiliated.

She decided to risk doing the non-verbal work, and I suggested that they sit next to each other and just notice their feelings. To her surprise, her fear seemed to leave, and she felt aliveness and energy in her body, though she had to work not to sexualize it. On the other hand, John got quite scared. With John closing down out of fear, it could have been a replay of Sharon's worst fears, namely that she was more involved than he. However she discovered to her delight that she didn't feel rejected or humiliated. She was able to stay with her good feelings and let him struggle with his fear and shame. He did some very important work on his own issues, and she experienced her strength and ability to stay open even when she didn't get exactly the response she wanted.

All of these changes transferred directly into Sharon's life outside group. She was able to confront people in her life as a way of clearing away obstacles to being closer. She has largely dropped her old defenses of subtle arrogance and withdrawal. She feels more comfortable with people and finds it easier to be open and to reach out. When someone doesn't respond to her overtures, she doesn't feel rejected or attacked, just disappointed. She feels that she is "clearing away the obstacles to feeling love and union with people."

Need And Commitment

People deal not only with their relationships with the other members of the group, but also with the group as a whole. One of the issues that comes up for many group members is how much they are committed to the group and how much it matters to them. This is often a reflection of how easy it is for them to commit to a love relationship and let people really matter to them in the their lives.

Through the group work described so far, Sharon progressed to the point where she was ready to deal with the deeper issue of how she hasn't allowed permanent, committed relationships in her life. It became apparent that even though Sharon could express desire in a vulnerable way, she didn't allow herself to need the group or the people in it. In one group Jill was talking about who she thought would miss her if she left the group, and she didn't include Sharon even though Sharon had expressed positive feelings toward her many times. When Sharon challenged her on this, Jill said that she didn't feel as connected to Sharon because Sharon didn't seem to need anything from her, that Sharon seemed independent and always able to assertively ask for what she wanted.

Sharon thought about Jill's feedback, and a couple of weeks later told us that she had come to the understanding that she uses her independence as a defense. She doesn't really let people close to her in deep ways, and she doesn't let them know when she needs them. Even though she is satisfied with her life in many ways, she is lonely, and she usually hides this from others and often even from herself. She talked about her loneliness and how it was affecting her currently and allowed herself to cry in a vulnerable way. She also shared her struggle to stop smoking and ease up on her workaholism, and she talked about the pain associated with that. This was very important work; she opened up to the group and let us in at a new level. The next week she told us how much she valued the acceptance she received in that group and how much it had helped her to be able to reach out to people in her life during the week.

For the next few months, however, Sharon's work seemed to retreat from this kind of depth. Then the group members challenged her on this, and she explored it. She realized that she was doing with the group what she tends to do in her life. She was subtly pulling back so as not to let the group members and group really matter to her. One way she was doing this was to avoid really needing things from people in the group.

As a result of this realization, she began to tell us about a major crisis in her life. Her sister had recently been diagnosed with cancer and was due for surgery. She is very close to her sister, and she shared with us the pain this brought up for her. After allowing her to cry deeply about this, I helped her to become aware of what she needed from us then. She realized she needed to be held, and Marla volunteered to hold her. Marla had been in the group for about six months at this time, and Sharon and Marla had been developing a warm relationship. Sharon moved over next to Marla, and Marla held her like a child and let Sharon cry very deeply. Sharon let herself relax fully into the situation and take in the love and nurturing she was receiving. Marla told Sharon how much she liked holding her, and they made a wonderful connection.

Thus Sharon took a very important step toward letting herself need from us. After this she began to share with the group more of the pain and difficulties she was experiencing in her life and to take in the caring and nurturing she received, from Marla and from all of us.

It is interesting to look at the development of Sharon's feelings towards the group as a whole, especially how much she allowed it to matter to her. She joined the group with the intention of not staying very long, just getting what she needed and leaving. After a few months she became connected to some of the people and realized how much she was getting from the work, so she decided to say indefinitely. However, she still wasn't that attached to the group. After about six months, when I first brought up the idea of doing a weekend retreat, she wasn't interested because she didn't want to give up "a precious weekend" of her time. This was really an avoidance of connecting with the people in the group. "In fact, I generally spent my weekends completely alone. Except when I have to be with people, I covet the time alone. I was clearly dismissing the weekend."

Harry told her that he felt hurt by this response, and this had an impact on her because of her connection with him. When the idea of a weekend came up again five months later, she was very enthusiastic. This was partly because of hearing about Harry's experience with weekends in another group of mine, and partly because of her deeper involvement with the group. The weekend couldn't be scheduled until four months after that, in the group's 15th month, so by then she had begun to do the work just described on allowing herself to need us at a deeper level.

It turned out that her sister's surgery was scheduled a week before the weekend retreat, and she felt the need to be there at the hospital for her sister as much as possible. However, she had allowed the group to become important to her, so she went to a great deal of trouble to come to the second half of the weekend. When she arrived, the group welcomed her with caring concern, and she shared with us all the fear and pain she was going through.

Then she took an even bigger step and told us directly how important we were to her. She was wide open and vulnerable in a wonderful way. She told us that it felt very shameful to her to need us so much and to let us know, but compared to facing the possibility of her sister's death it didn't seem like such a big deal, so she was willing to take the risk. "It was really very profound. Recognizing how sick she was and that she might die, I thought, 'So it's embarrassing and shameful that I need you. Who cares. I can handle that.' It was wonderful, a breakthrough."

Harry was so moved that he wanted to hold her, and she let him cradle her like a baby. Then the whole group gathered around her and touched her and nourished her. Once Sharon lets herself feel and express a need, she has a great capacity to receive fully what is given to her, so it was a very satisfying experience, for her and for all of us.

Sharon has continued to bring her pain and her needs to the group and to allow us to matter to her. She also has become able to tell people in her life about her needs and to let them care for her, especially around her sister's continuing battle with cancer. This will probably help her to develop the deeper friendships she wants.

Already Sharon has grown enormously in her 18 months in group and is seeing the effect in many ways in her life. She isn't yet ready to deal with her remaining addictions, and it's too soon yet to see what effect this work will have on her openness to a committed love relationship. I have confidence that as she continues her current work on need and intimacy, her friendships will deepen and eventually she will find a successful love relationship.

SUMMARY OF THE APPROACH

In many ways this approach to group work is similar to the interpersonal approach popularized by Irvin Yalom in his classic book on group psychotherapy (1985).

However, Yalom's leadership style is to sit back and make interpretations from time to time, while as Gestalt Therapist, I more actively direct the group toward interpersonal contact. I aim to minimize the usual discussion and advice-giving and talking about outside issues, and go right to the heart of the matter. I also direct members toward awareness of their emotional reactions in the here and now and toward experimenting with new behavior. Group members are encouraged to interact with me when they have feelings toward me, but otherwise I remain in the role of facilitator.

This method works by enabling group members to live out their interpersonal patterns directly in group. This gives them a chance to become aware of those patterns that are problematical for them and the feelings and motivations that underlie those patterns. They then have an opportunity to experiment with new behavior right in the moment. While trying some thing new, they learn from their own awareness and from feedback from the group. Group members are also encouraged to become aware of their successful patterns so they can validate and expand on them. These are long term groups which foster a deep level of intimacy, so members can enact and then work through primary character patterns from their families of origin.

There are four ways in which an Interactive Gestalt Group differs from the traditional hot seat group.

1) Real relationships. In a hot seat group, when members do interact, it is usually because the person working is doing an experiment where he or she is using the other group members as projection screens. In an Interactive Group, the emphasis is on the real relationships between members. Of course, people can't help using projection and transference with each other, but we start with people expressing their real feelings toward each other and deal with the defense mechanisms when they arise. The healing often comes from the real relationship as the person works through defenses and develops a meaningful connection in the present.

2) Peer dialogue. In traditional Gestalt work, the significant contact and dialogue happen between the client and therapist. In an Interactive Group, it also happens between group members. In fact, the primary contact is between group members, and people only work directly with the therapist when they have feelings toward the therapist specifically or when they have authority issues that cannot be worked on with anyone else. Dialogue with peers has a different quality from that with the therapist. A group member encounters real reactions from people who are not in a helping role and not primarily focused on his or her experience. There is a richness and challenge to this dialogue, and many important issues emerge which can't come up in the more protected situation of dialogue with a therapist. On the other hand, peer dialogue is admittedly harder to control, and you can't guarantee that the responses are always therapeutic.

3) Relationship with the Group. In an ongoing therapy group, each member has an important relationship with the group-as-a-whole as well as other members and the leader. In an Interactive Group, this is an important focus of work. This allows people to work on issues of acceptance, attention, inclusion/exclusion, belonging, autonomy, and commitment. It brings up many issues from the family of origin, and provides an opportunity for healing by creating a healthy family-like situation.

4) Intimacy. In a long-term Interactive Group, people eventually develop relationships that have meaning for them beyond the normal boundaries of the therapy group. I hold occasional weekend retreats for the group, and I encourage people to have relationships with each other outside of group (with the understanding that they bring pertinent issues into group). This extra level of involvement allows people to engage in and work through deep intimacy issues, and it also fosters transfer of learning from the group to a person's outside life.

REFERENCES

Feder, B. and Ronall, R. (1980) *Beyond the hot seat: Gestalt approaches to group.* New York: Brunner/Mazel.

Harman, R. (1984) Recent developments in gestalt group therapy. *International journal of group psychotherapy, 34(3),* 473–483.

Melnick, J. (1980) Gestalt group process therapy. *The gestalt journal, 3,* 86–96.

Zinker, J. (1977) *Creative process in gestalt therapy,* New York: Brunner / Mazel.

Yalom, I. (1995) *The theory and practice of group psychotherapy.* New York: Basic Books.

◊

13

AN EXTENDED GROUP EXPERIENCE

Jack Aylward[1]

❧

HISTORICAL BACKGROUND

In 1946 Kurt Lewin developed what was to be known as the "T-Group" at the National Training Laboratories in Bethel, Maine. Originally designed to train leaders to deal with community racial tensions, it evolved into a California-based hybrid group experience known in the early sixties as an encounter group. This format marked a shift from Lewin's original intention of human relations training to the arena of personal growth soon to be known as the "human potential movement." Two of the pioneers in the movement, Frederick Stoller, who was conducting groups with institutionalized adults and adolescents, and George Bach, who was experimenting with extended-time group therapy, began co-leading groups which were to become known as "marathons." Bach, (1971) described the marathon experience as "a practicum in intimate, authentic human interaction" (p. 132) and as "a transition from self-defensive alienation and exploitive 'gameplaying' to psychological intimacy" (p. 137). Later, this format was supported by ground rules excluding physical violence and stressing interpersonal honesty, and the primacy of experience over interpretation. The growing influence of Gestalt Therapy and the guru-like quality of Fritz Perls work-

---

1   ·The author wishes to thank Bud Feder for his helpful input, collaboration and ongoing friendship in preparing this chapter.

ing with individuals in group settings added the "hot seat" technique and a "here-and-now" centeredness to the armamentarium of marathon group leaders and facilitators. Gestalt therapist Erv Polster (1970) saw the marathon group experience as a way of placing a higher priority on the social nature of humans than is ordinarily possible in modem individualistically-oriented capitalistic society. By dealing directly with feelings of alienation and powerlessness produced by such a society, he hoped that the encounter or marathon experience could serve as a bridge between individual relationships, including those of a therapeutic nature, to the community at large.

Since these beginnings, the structure and process of marathon groups have received considerable attention and revision. Elizabeth Mintz (1972, 1994), a Gestalt therapist with a psychoanalytic background, has been a major contributor to the theory and practice of Gestalt marathons. Mintz views the group as the therapist, emphasizing the power to be found in a format in which interpersonal honesty and intense emotional exchange are supported by an evolving experiential energy primarily concentrated in the present moment. Of particular importance is her direct work with marathon group participants using Gestalt Therapy techniques throughout the group's developmental phases, beginning with the removal of "social masks" to experimenting with the preliminary expression of authentic feelings and then going on to deeper levels of feelings and mutuality. Mintz also includes bodywork in the group and sees the marathon as an important adjunct to, rather than a substitute for, ongoing individual or group therapy.

Others began experimenting with various formats and structures. Attention was given to the number of hours involved, member selection, optimal group size and the psychological effects of sleep deprivation (Stoller, 1972), as well as the role of therapist self-disclosure and participation (Egan, 1973). Verbatim transcripts of marathon groups were published as a means of tracing the growth of extended group experiences over time (Mann, 1970; Haigh, 1968). Disciples of various psychological orientations were experimenting vigorously with this therapeutic style as a means of providing a systematic approach to marathon group process and development. A major contribution to this quest was provided by Lieberman, et al. (1973) through their statistical analysis of outcome data from various forms of encounter and marathon groups and leadership styles. The overall conclusion was that while such groups did make a difference in personal growth and learning based on the response patterns of the participants, they could also be dangerous and counterproductive. In light of these findings they recommended that considerable attention be given to the selection of clients for such groups and facilitators were warned against an overly confrontative and provocative leadership style as a way of protecting the participants.

PRESENT BACKGROUND

Gestalt therapists have continued to be fascinated by this from of group work since it provides a suitable structural support for the experiential/experimental approach that has evolved from Gestalt Therapy theory. Additional focus has been given to an analysis of contact styles and boundary disturbance phenomena as they occur and interact throughout the stages of group development (Ronall, 1994; Mintz, 1986, 1994; Frew, 1986). What follows is an account of the experiences of marathon participants over a single weekend led by two Gestalt therapists (Bud Feder and myself). I will attempt to highlight such issues as participant selection, leadership styles, structural format, developmental phenomena and the dynamics that developed in the group relating to therapeutic issues for the participants before, during and after the group experience itself.

As a clinician, I believe the extended group experience (or marathon) offers a valuable extension to and an intensification of continuing individual and group therapeutic work. The most obvious element in this regard is the time frame. Weekly groups are usually limited from one to two hours. I have often noticed that the energy generated between and among group members is limited by the time available and cannot emerge as completely or develop as fully in that context. The extended time available in a marathon situation creates the support for deeper and broader emotional expression and interpersonal contact as well as greater opportunities for closure and assimilation. One difference from a T-group is that a marathon has less structure and fewer exercises. The nature of a marathon group is more organic, in that the dynamics develop from the specific experiences of clients and therapists. It provides a fertile ground on which issues evolve through the collective creative adjustments of the members. Fritz Perls would work in a similar manner in his demonstration groups, although unlike a marathon leader he often used the experience for teaching purposes and did not encourage much in the way of interpersonal contact between group members. This is not to say that anyone way of working with a group is better than another. The extended group experience is yet one more and, I feel important, addition to what could be called the evolving palette of Gestalt group formats.

The marathon provides me as a therapist with an opportunity to work more intensely and differently when I've felt stuck with a client. Marathons require an enormous amount of vigilance and uninterrupted attention, can be very tiring, and as such I usually work with a co-therapist. There are other advantages to this: my clients are seen and worked with from my co-therapist's perspective; this adds a dimension to the therapeutic situation and helps me gain a new perspective on whatever problem is figural at the time. When the work in the group session echoes back into individual therapy, I often experience myself becoming unstuck with whatever impasse I had reached with that client.

CO-THERAPIST

A good relationship between co-therapists is essential to a successful experience. I began co-leading marathons with a former partner of mine: our relationship was very special and very powerful — and this was evident in our work. The flow between us was natural, intuitive and in a way self-regulating. I never appreciated the importance of these parameters until he retired. I experimented in running marathons with other therapists only to be disappointed. It was then that I began to fully value the importance and complexity of the relationship between co-therapists. I don't mean confluence or even agreement on all levels. For example, Bud and I differ on certain theoretical issues. However, we are able to articulate our differences and accept them. We feel comfortable disagreeing and this contributes to our knowing each other better. There is no doubt in my mind that it is our strong personal relationship that makes our clinical work so fruitful. If we disagree while working, we may stop what is going on and discuss our differences in front of the group, sometimes even agreeing to disagree. This also lets the group see us as people who respect each other and who tolerate and appreciate differences. This in itself is growth-inducing not only to the group, but to us as well. Another element is how we play together, and how we feel toward each other. Recognizing this, we make it a point to spend time together an hour or so before the beginning of each group to exchange impressions and feelings about the group and about each other. In this way differences are recognized — and sometimes allowed with awareness, if not resolvable. This is primarily an intuitive process that can only be partially described. Another aspect is our emotional connection. Bud and I have a fond and mutually respectful relationship that is apparent in the group. We hear this in feedback from participants.

Over the past several years I have paid closer attention to the composition of the groups. First of all, we only accept people into the group who concurrently are in therapy with one of us or another therapist or give ample indication during the screening process of being able to integrate the experience on their own. Usually this is the case when they have had previous therapy. We exclude understructured clients, who we believe couldn't handle the pressure of an emotionally intense group experience. Before the group begins, we exchange information about each client, what our purpose is for including the person in the group. This degree of clinical responsibility is important to us as leaders.

As for the group process, a participant who chooses to work becomes the evolving figure in the field in which the group is background — not a static but a vibrant one which both supports and is affected by the individual work. An analogy is that of playing the guitar. Even though only one string is being struck or played, the others vibrate and resonate in reaction.

When a particular piece of work is brought to closure, it recedes into the background, allowing someone else's issue to become figural. Often, these issues are similar, accelerating the move from one person to the next and making group interaction a natural and self-regulating process. The possibilities are endless and they emerge organismically as the group progresses. What is figure at one moment can be one person, two persons or the entire group. While working with one person in the hot seat, the rest of the group is still involved as an active ground. Contact emerges and evolves naturally and spontaneously in the process of gestalt formation and destruction as a group finds its own rhythm and balance. This process is consistent with Gestalt Therapy's definition of self-functioning as one's contacts at any given moment through figure/ground formation within an organism/environmental field.

THE GROUP

The group described here was composed of ten people, four men and six women. Eight of the ten were currently in therapy with one of us; four of them had not been in an extended group experience before. The remaining two members had been in therapy with Bud some time ago, had prior marathon experience and wanted to use this format to work on specific issues they were confronting in their lives at that time.

To begin the group we do "rounds" wherein group members have a chance and are expected to briefly say who they are, what they're feeling and what they want from the weekend. We ask each person to tell us about past or present therapy, marathons, and outside connections between group members: who knows whom and how does it feel to be in this group together. We go over some of the ground rules — confidentiality, a prohibition against physical violence during the marathon. We also deal with "housekeeping matters" not only in terms of food and sleep, but encouraging community. A very important aspect of a marathon is the in-between time. Any significant interaction or experience can become "grist for the mill" and is expected to be brought back to the group. If it is not, this creates a disturbance. This degree of structuring is important especially for people who have not been on a marathon before. Explicit statements of what is expected provide the support to later confront the "safe emergency" that characterizes so much of gestalt work.

THE GROUP IN ACTION

Gail

The group soon becomes aware that Gail is presenting herself as intellectually aloof and distant. A group member comments on Gail's distance, saying she feels somewhat alienated from Gail and, underneath, afraid of what she imagines to be a lot of intellectual criticism. I set up an experiment that highlights this issue.

JA: Gail, I'm wondering if you would be available to do an experiment with the issue that has been raised in the group concerning what others perceive as your intellectual distancing.

Gail: Well, I personally don't see any particular urgency for me in that regard, but no, I have no objection to doing the experiment.

I then ask the group, leaders included, to form a "gossip circle" in the middle of the room, leaving Gail on the outside, observing and listening to us talk about how we have been experiencing her.

Joe: It really seems as if Gail doesn't want any part of this group. I wonder why she came. Anytime she brings an issue up of her own, it seems to be very intellectual, and I really can't get a grasp of what she is looking for.

Ann: Yeah, and every time I try to reach out to her or say something to her, I always get these intellectual reasons for this and for that and for why she thinks that way.

Joe: Yeah, it's like she doesn't want to share anything emotionally, just from the head, you know, like it was a debate rather than a group.

Pete: I've noticed myself being very quiet whenever she says anything in the group. She seems to be real bright and knows a lot, and sometimes that scares me. I get a feeling that if I ever really told her how I felt about her, she would just cut me up with a lot of intelligent words and phrases, letting me know how stupid I am for feeling like that.

Sue: I don't know if we're really being fair to Gail. I think underneath all of that intellectual bullshit she really is feeling something about what's going on this weekend. I notice when other people are working she is looking at them and really seems to be absorbed in what they're doing. It is only when she opens her mouth that she kind of ruins all that and goes back to a lot of intellectual stuff.

Ann: Yeah, that's right, I'm really tired of hearing about all the important people she knows and all of the important things she has done. I would rather just get to know her as a person, but I don't think there is too much hope of that.

At this point Gail is crying quietly outside the group. Bud asks her if she would consider joining the group and tell us what's going on with her. At first Gail shakes her head, and continues to cry very softly. At this point the group spontaneously expands with no direction from the leaders and includes Gail, yet allows enough physical space around her so as not to violate her boundary. The group remains quiet and attentive to her experience, allowing her as much space as she needs to expand on what she is feeling. After several minutes, her crying becomes louder, and Gail begins to tell the group how her intelligence has helped her survive some very difficult experiences in the past.

Gail: (continuing to cry and allowing herself to take tissues from another group member) You people just don't seem to understand that I had to be intelligent. I was the first one in my family to go to college, and it wasn't an easy ordeal. My father continually made fun of me, asking if I thought I was a "big shot" or something, being a woman and all that stuff. He would ridicule me about reading books. He said that book learning was for people who couldn't do anything. I remember saying to myself, "I'll show that bastard, I'm going to really be somebody, and that somebody is going to be more important and smarter than he could ever imagine himself to be!!!" So I went off to school, worked 30 hours a week to get myself through and did really well — Dean's List every semester. Unfortunately, my father died somewhere in my junior year of college, and I remember feeling "It's all over. I'll never be able to prove to him that I could do it — that I could really be successful and be somebody." And I'm really proud of what I've done. I do really like hobnobbing with the intelligentsia. They stimulate me, they reaffirm me, and I feel a real sense of power whenever I see my name in print on an article that I know is pretty damn good. And I am not going to apologize

to anybody, in this group or anywhere else, about what I have been able to
do for myself.

JA: What are you experiencing emotionally?

Gail: Just sadness.

JA: Just.

Gail: Okay, Okay, I feel sad.

JA: Would you be willing to give your sadness a voice and talk
to the group?

Gail: (after some moments of what seemed to be uncomfortable
silence) I am sad because despite all I have been able to do in my life, as
successful as I have been professionally, all my relationships have been disasters. Married men, cheating men, insincere men, alcoholics, all of them have
paraded into my life for brief moments and then disappeared. I don't want
to grow old alone like my mother had to. All of my hard work, and I can't
even find someone to share my life with.

The group is supportively silent. Linda puts an arm around Gail's
shoulders. The warmth in the group can be felt as if in the air. As projections
are explored and destructured and Gail experiments with a way of being that
contrasts with long-held convictions, a cohesive fabric of intimacy develops
between people.

This type of ice-breaking experience is common in the beginning phase
of marathons. The initial tentativeness with which individuals express emotion slowly gives way to a more open and fluid expression of feeling that
provides the group with some early emotional connection. As the cohesiveness grows, any defensiveness present becomes more figural commanding
the attention and concern of other group members. Certainly Gail's intellec-
tualism formed a polar dynamic to the growing closeness experienced by the
rest of the group. Through initial confrontation and experimentation, much
of her defensive wall crumbled away as she was able to experience the support of the group and to connect that moment with her world outside. The
paradox of her desire for long-term intimacy and her persona of intellectual
distance became immediately apparent.

At some point later in the marathon, Gail did some very poignant
empty chair work with her father, dealing with a lot of the unfinished busi-

ness that existed between them prior to his sudden death. More importantly, Gail's early risk and work in the group helped create a climate of safety for others to work on similar issues.

Bill

One of the members, encouraged by Gail's work, is ready to experiment next. Bill, a very withdrawn and passive man in his mid-thirties is a commercial artist, who works alone in his studio and, apart from his wife and his child, has very little meaningful social contact. He initially experienced the birth of his baby as alienating him from his wife on whom he depended for emotional nourishment and support. In individual therapy with me he had spoken of his difficulty in dealing with art agents, neighbors and family members. Despite his formidable artistic and musical talent, he had made no attempt to find friends in the musical or artistic communities of which he belonged. Ordinarily, this is not the type of armored client to whom I would suggest a marathon, at least not in the beginning of his therapy. However, because I felt that the two of us had a good relationship, I invited him to this weekend group. At first he resisted, protesting that he never would be able to open up in front of other people, especially in such intimate surroundings. I did not push but encouraged him, and he eventually decided to come, again letting me know how difficult this would be for him and asking me not to expect too much of him. This type of "catastrophic expectation" was typical of him. I remember that, indeed, I did not expect much work from him at this first marathon. I anticipated a lot of residual issues of fear and discomfort which would become figural in our subsequent individual sessions. However, I was pleasantly amazed at how Gail's work gave him the spark he needed to experiment with involvement and participation.

JA: (addressing Bill directly after watching his reactions to Gail's work) Bill, I would like to hear something about how you are feeling about the work you just saw.

Bill: Uh, uh, I don't know. I'm not even sure of what just happened or what I saw. I mean, not that I want to criticize what went on. I just am sitting here feeling a lot of shock inside about how she was able to just put it all out there and let herself just explode.

JA: Would there be a part of you that would like to do that?

Bill: Well, yeah, sure, but that doesn't mean I would do it. I mean, we've only been here for about four hours. I mean, basically we're all strangers. I don't know her, I don't know them, they don't know me. How do you know when it's right to do something like that?

JA: What are you feeling inside?

Bill: A lot of stuff. Some of it feels like electricity. Like, kind of like I am short circuiting. It just keeps coming up in flashes and then going away. Like fireworks.

JA: Is there any theme to your fireworks?

Bill: Well, it started when Linda went over to Gail and put her arm around her after she finished with the group. When I saw her touch Gail like that, that's when it all seemed to break loose inside me. But I couldn't even imagine myself doing anything like that, I mean like touching anybody or even being here in a group and having somebody touch me after saying all those things.

At this point the two women who are sitting next to Bill reach out and hold his hands. His jaw drops, his face reddens, and he becomes visibly anxious. As he talks, he begins to stutter, and no words came out.

JA: Rather than saying anything about what's going on right now Bill, I would ask you to just tune into what's going on inside of you and allow that to go wherever it wants to.

As Bill allows his experience to be the center of his attention, he spontaneously gradually starts to cry in a very agitated manner; wordlessly this goes on for several minutes. The women on either side of him move closer to him, embracing him. After some time he begins to speak quietly.

Bill: I can't believe what's going on here.

JA: Believe it.

Bill: I know, I know. I believe it, but I just can't imagine these people …

JA: What people?

Bill: Linda and Jean.

JA: Talk to them. Tell them.

Bill: (turns to Linda and Jean alternately) It's, it's real hard for me to believe that the two of you actually wanted to reach out and kind of let me know that you knew how hard this was for me to do. I mean, I hardly know either one of you, and you hardly know me, and there we were doing this kind of thing without anybody asking for it, without anybody telling you or me what to do … it's just amazing.

This particular experiment continues as Bud asks Bill to get feedback from Linda and Jean in terms of what was going on for them that led them to reach out to him. The feedback is valuable to Bill in that he often has no idea of how and why people relate to him. The experiment marks a very important turning-point for him as a group member. From that point on he is more active and vibrant. Bill's work, as described in our jargon, is referred to as "piggybacking." Clearly, Gail's issues around intimacy and aloofness triggered Bill's own problems around withdrawal and isolation. As the group develops, individuals emerge with their unique variations on familiar themes. As a result, the group becomes richer: more people directly involved with each other and the group experience deepened. It is important to note that Bill's work did not arise out of a pre-designed experiment or direct suggestion of the group leaders. Rather, it arose spontaneously from the unspoken sense of connection and healthy confluence that had grown in the whole group over time. Also as this process continues, the safe emergency provides support for rather novel, and at times even outrageous, experiments that could hardly ever occur in the context of traditional ongoing individual or group therapy. Norman's work on the last day of the marathon offers a good illustration.

Norman

The intimate emotional tone of the group at this point was very disturbing to Norman, a college student who had been in therapy with me for a few years and was on his second marathon. The work he did on his first extended group experience was appropriately cautious, in that he mostly observed and it was quite helpful to me in our subsequent individual sessions. Norman presents as a somewhat withdrawn and isolated young man who experiences a lot of pre-contact scare resulting from catastrophic expectations about ridicule and rejection from others who, he is sure, see him as inadequate and "not enough" for any type of relationship. His most prominent boundary disturbance is retroflection resulting in physical armor and phobic ruminations about his imagined ugliness, his pockmarks and his receding hair. While he expresses a strong desire for intimate contact with others, especially women, most of his energy is invested in predicting and evaluating the consequences of his behavior: always negative, of course. As is typical with this boundary disturbance, more of his pain is experienced in the resistance to the expression of feeling than in the affect itself.

As mentioned earlier, Norman, toward the end of the marathon, said he wanted to work. The leaders designed the following experiment for Norman; we asked him to tune into whatever physical sensations and emotions he was aware of at any given time, and without filtering or speculating about them, relate his ongoing awareness to the group.

Norman: I am aware of some discomfort in my back and shoulders. (pause) My legs and arms feel tense. (pause) My breathing is tight -like it's being held in.

JA: Are you aware of how you are holding things in?

Norman: Part of me feels like I want to cry.

JA: Want to?

Norman: (Begins to cry in a quiet manner.)

As Norman allow himself to cry, he begins rubbing his hands on his thighs in long deep strokes.

JA: Attend to your hands. What do you experience?

Norman: (Long pause — continues rubbing) It feels very soothing.

JA: Norman, what I would like you to do, if it's okay with you, is to allow this experience to continue in whatever way it is forming for you and begin to look around the group and focus in on people who may interest you for whatever reason and share your experiences with them. Try not to do this in a mechanical or rote way. Just allow your intuition to support you.

Norman: (Begins looking from person to person and focuses his attention on Bill.) You must really be identifying with what's happening to me. I imagine that you think that I must be pretty fucked up, not being able to even feel anything — even the slightest little thing. If we ever meet outside the group I bet you could imagine us sitting somewhere for hours without talking — each of us afraid to begin the conversation. (nervous laughter)

JA: I'm aware of how you seem to be more concerned with how Bill may react to you and how that seems more important to you than your own feelings. Let me suggest something. Look at Bill again and tell him what is going on for you and avoid speculating about what is going on for him.

Norman: Okay (looks over at Bill again — his eyes tear up and his jaw drops somewhat). I really feel alone and cut off. I mean really alone. (Begins to cry more audibly.) And I really don't want to stay here (rubs his hands on his thighs in a more rapid and agitated manner).

JA: Would you let your hands speak to Bill?

Norman: (Pause) I need to be comforted (begins to cry again). I mean a lot. I get so jealous even when I see a couple in school holding hands. I explode inside, I hurt so much!

As Norman continues to tell his experience, his voice becomes louder, his language more "I-centered" and his manner more energized. He gives himself more support for continuing emotional contact. Spontaneously, Bud picks up from my work with Norman and goes with it.

BF: Are you aware of your hands as you continue to speak with Bill?

Norman: Yeah, I am.

BF: What I'd like to suggest, if it's okay with the others, is to find someone in the group who, for whatever reason, you would like to know better and with his or her permission close your eyes and silently allow your hands to connect with and explore the other person's body. How does that sound to you, Norman?

Norman: Scary!

BF: Good. Take your scare with you and let it develop (long pause).

Norman: Okay. But I gotta tell you how scared I am.

BF: Fine. Now, would you be willing to find someone you would like to know better?

Norman takes his time visually scanning the group and settles on Rick, with whom he had some contact during one of the breaks. After getting Rick's permission to participate in this experiment they sit together in the center of the group. Norman closes his eyes and, at first tentatively, and then, with more vigor, begins to explore Rick's face, head, hands, and arms.

Norman: I feel weird doing this. I don't ever let myself get this close to a person. Something in my head says I shouldn't be doing this but my hands seem to have a mind of their own and really want to know what's out there. (He spends more time silently exploring Ricks' body.) I really feel every little part of him.

BF: I would suggest other people in the group find objects in the room for Norman to explore.

The group begins to place various objects in Norman's hands as he continues to relate his experiences with different textures, shapes and temperatures of the objects. At one point Bud puts a chair in front of Norman and sits in the chair and places Norman's hands on his torso. I then suggest to Norman that he tell Bud what he is feeling.

Norman: (fakes a while exploring Bud's body). You know, Bud, I only met you once before on our last marathon and I meant to tell you how much the work you did with me on that weekend meant to me. I mean, you really saw what I was feeling and respected the fact that I was scared and you seemed to be there for me without making any demands on me (pause). I am not used to that, especially from a man. I mean, my father left the family when I was young and I hardly ever see him and when I do, he still thinks I'm a "mama's boy" and is always critical of what I'm doing. I never felt any criticism from you and you seemed to care how I felt.

Shortly after this Norman, eyes still closed, makes a spontaneous request of the group.

Norman: I want to go out on the porch. (there is a back porch on the house which abuts on an ocean beach.) I want to keep my eyes closed and throw things at the ocean.

The group accommodates Norman, hands him tennis balls and other objects which he throws off the back porch and on to the beach. People then begin handing him fruit and Norman first squeezes each piece of fruit, letting the juices run down his hands and arms. He makes a variety of noises and continues to throw the fruit off the porch with greater and greater intensity, at times screaming to the group, "Give me more" or "Give me something harder." After about 20 minutes of this he opens his eyes, silently looks at the group members, thanks them and returns to the main room.

Norman: I feel cold.

With that one group member takes a blanket off one of the couches and covers Norman who is sitting. He allows himself to accept this comforting and for the rest of the afternoon seems to be able to interact with the group in a more spontaneous manner. As Norman supports himself in contacting others and allows himself to take up more space in the process by reporting what he's scared to do, the group provides him with the time and encouragement to explore the way he constricts himself and to enable him to expand and empower himself. It was as if we had arranged a series of mini-experiments on the theme of restricting and expanding.

ENDING

As the marathon draws to its ending, we make sure to provide closure: to give support to re-entry as a transition from the group to home. We reserve time for participants who require extra work, those who express fears about leaving and confronting on-going problematic life situations. Frequently, group members exchange phone numbers (and sometimes we encourage it) so as to create a support network after the group. With few exceptions, primarily involving potentially destructive acting-out, we do not object to group members meeting each other after the marathon ends.

At times we use the following experiment: the group forms a circle; a pillow is placed in the middle; a group member may leave the circle and sit on the pillow, indicating a willingness to accept appreciation without responding. In this way the person on the pillow can absorb and take in the reactions that others have had over the weekend. Silent assimilation is a valuable closure tool for a lot of people.

Another experiment runs as follows: after the initial round in the opening session, we ask participants to close their eyes for a few minutes and to become aware of how they feel about the other people. At the group's end we ask them to repeat the experiment and this time to be aware of any difference between their feelings now and at the beginning. They often report a shift from relative alienation to increased levels of intimacy. We remind them that when they leave the group and return to their daily routines they will meet people whom they will experience as "strangers" just as they did the group members at the beginning. The openness for the potential for intimacy can be taken back home and not left the in the group.

FOLLOW-UP ISSUES

The effect of marathon does not end with the marathon as is true with all effective therapeutic experiences. This can be measured by the kind of work people do in their follow-up individual sessions. Often, the group accelerates the one-to-one work. The group experience often adds a sense of urgency and possibility to work that had previously been avoided. It's like a knot that up to that point has been resistant to unraveling and now opens.

Bill is an example. The feedback he got at the end of the group was helpful to him in providing a transition from the group back into his usual life. While he was very excited and exhilarated at the end of the group, my hunch was that the contrast between that nurturing environment and his personal life-space would be problematic. Indeed, when Bill came for his next individual session, he was still excited by his experience in the group but was concluding that that sort of occurrence only happened in these special settings and was not really available in the world at large. This provided an opening to explore Bill's fixed and maladaptive view of the world.

CODA

To sum up, an extended group session offers unique opportunities for healing and personal growth: these include intensity of therapy; long stretches of therapy time; the support of evolving intimacy especially in a residential marathon; and experimentation and awareness not only during formal group session but also during breaks or in-between times. All in all I hope I have been able to transmit to the reader the special features and valves as well as the pitfalls, of the Gestalt Therapy marathon.

REFERENCES

Bach, G.R. (1971) The marathon group: Intensive practice of inmate inter-actions. In Siroka, R. W., Siroka, E. K., & Schloss, G. A. (Eds.) *Sensitivity training and group encounter: An introduction.* New York: Grosset and Dunlap.

Egan, G. (1973) *Face to face.* Monterey: Brooks/Cole.

Frew, J. (1986) The formation and patterns of occurrence of individual contact styles during the developmental phases of the gestalt group. *The gestalt journal, 9(1),* 55–70.

Haigh, G. (1968) The residential basic encounter group. In Otto, H.A. and Mann, J. (Eds.) *Ways of growth: Approaches to expanding awareness.* New York: Grossman Publishers.

Lieberman, M.A., Yalom, I.D., & Miles, M.B. (1973) *Encounter groups: First facts.* New York: Basic Books, Inc.

Mann, J. (1970) *Encounter: A weekend with intimate strangers.* New York: Grossman Publishers.

Mintz, E. E. (1972) *Marathon groups: Reality and symbol.* New York: Avon Books.

Mintz, E. E. (1994) The gestalt therapy marathon. In Feder, B., Ronall R. (Eds.) *Beyond the hot seat: Gestalt approaches to group.* Highland, NY: Gestalt Journal Press.

Polster, E. (1970) Encounter in community. In Burton, Arthur (Ed.) *Encounter.* San Francisco: Jossey-Bass.

Ronall, R. (1994) Intensive gestalt workshops: Experiences in community. In Feder, B., Ronall R. (Eds.) *Beyond the hot seat: Gestalt approaches to group.* Highland, NY: Gestalt Journal Press.

Stoller, G. H. (1972) Marathon groups: Toward a conceptual model. In Solomon, L. N., Berzon, B. (Eds.) *New perspectives on encounter groups.* San Francisco: Jossey-Bass.

◇

14

LIVING, LOVING, AND LAUGHTER
IN AN HIV/AIDS THERAPY GROUP

Perry Klepner

◆◆◆

FOREWORD

> "... when actuality is pressing, certain values oust other values, furnishing a
> hierarchy of what does in fact marshal brightness and vigor in its execution
> ... Sickness and somatic deficiencies and excesses rate high in the dominance
> hierarchy. So with environmental dangers. But so also do the need for love,
> someone to go out to, the avoidance of isolation and loneliness, and the need
> for self esteem. Also maintaining oneself and developing oneself: independence
> ... so that sometimes heroism and bearing witness dominate the fear of death."
> (Perls et al., p. 278)

It's April 1993, three months since an HIV-positive group I led for almost
six and one-half years has come to an end. These words inspire me as I am
moved by many powerful positive memories of courage, love, and laughter
in the face of the scourge of AIDS; also, by overwhelmingly sad memories
and feelings of loss remembering those who became ill and died and those
still living and fighting for their lives. I still feel their presence, see their faces
glowing with bright excitement, grim determination, fear, bravery, and love.
This chapter is intended to further our group's work — to contribute to
psychotherapy with HIV-positive people and people with AIDS.

BEGINNING PHASE

By the mid 1980's the AIDS epidemic was spreading throughout the United States and the world. I had been volunteering as a leader of HIV/AIDS care provider support groups for the Gay Men's Health Crisis (GMHC) in New York City and decided to organize a therapy group for HIV-positive men and those with fear of AIDS. I was responding to the pain and anxiety I saw in people seeking therapeutic help, as well as to my own feelings of loss and pain at watching beloved friends and colleagues succumb to AIDS. I wished to help individuals transcend this disease's potential to overwhelm health and joy in living.

As a Gestalt Therapist I have a distinct approach, values and concept of structure in organizing groups. I view the group as a whole to which each member makes a unique contribution. The whole — different from the sum of its parts — has the power to support its members with information, new ideas, and emotional nourishment, to help members focus on issues and concerns; and to mobilize members' capacities for experimentation, learning, and change (Kitzler, 1980, page 32).

The group began in October 1987 meeting once a week in a ninety minute session with six men either HIV-positive or untested and preoccupied by fears of HIV infection and progression. For example, Mark and Peter were anxious, hypochondriacal individuals whose presenting issue was preoccupation with HIV/AIDS including obsessive self-examination and an ever-present sense of doom. Three to four times monthly they would experience intense fear of AIDS for three to six days. Mark, thirty-three, was married and lived in Connecticut with his wife and two girls, ages five and seven. In addition to fear of AIDS, Mark was concerned with how to live a "normal" life and to keep his gay experience secret and non-disruptive of his work and family. Peter, thirty-five, was gay and lived alone on the Upper East Side of Manhattan. His presenting issues were anxiety due to AIDS and an inability to form a lasting love relationship, which he desperately desired.

The other members — Scott, Bill, Richard and Alan — had been diagnosed HIV-positive. Bill and Richard were Ph.D. candidates. Bill, thirty-seven, was executive director of a large state agency. He suffered intense depression and anxiety following a positive HIV test. He feared being unable to function socially and professionally, and a nervous breakdown. He also experienced himself as a fraud, i.e., of appearing intelligent and competent while really being stupid and incompetent. In addition, he was "closeted" about being gay and felt incapable of having a satisfying long-term love relationship. Instead he had contentious short-term relationships and brief affairs. Richard, thirty-one, was also experiencing severe anxiety after being diagnosed. His anxiety from AIDS exacerbated panic attacks which he had experienced over the prior eight years. He had been in psychoanalysis for these attacks for the past five years but had made no progress controlling them. Since his diagnosis six months earlier his panic attacks had become more severe and were now occurring at bridge crossings, theaters, and in tunnels. He had begun dating Bernie approximately three months prior to being tested and was afraid that Bernie who was HIV negative would break up with him. Alan, twenty-eight, got a positive HIV result at a time when he and his wife were considering having a baby. His last gay experience had been five years before during a period of sexual experimentation. Now he was suffering acute anxiety accompanied by morbid thoughts such as "my death is imminent" and "my life is over." Scott, forty-two, was anxious and angry over the threat that being HIV-positive posed both to himself and his lover, who was also HIV-positive. He also felt vulnerable to stress at work as a computer salesman and experienced disabling depressions and was on anti-depressant medication.

During the beginning phase members introduced themselves by talking about their histories, strengths, weaknesses, wishes, and personal character-istics and began to identify areas of concern and interest for their ongoing work in the group. This period lasted IS months as members tested and explored the group for safety, as a place to share, risk and learn and thereby get the emotional and informational support they needed.

I emphasized contact — being in touch, member's moment-to-moment here-and-now experience along with an experimental approach. These basic Gestalt Therapy principles were our modus operandi. Doing experiments utilizing concentrated awareness helps people to examine and learn by experiencing new behaviors under safe conditions. This encourages insight into interruptions to contact, i.e., unaware projecting, retroflecting, introjecting, and confluence; also it promotes identifying needed support and trying out new responses. Gestalt Therapy's emphasis on here-and-now awareness mobilizes high levels of interest, concern and excitement. In combination with an experimental approach producing affective responses along with insight into one's emotional experience, powerful forces for discovering and inventing creative adjustments — solutions in the form of new behaviors and attitudes — are energized. With action taken and new behaviors, people gain a sense of self-reliance, integrity, self-esteem, and hope.

I informed members I was interested in whatever thoughts and feelings they were having. If something was too uncomfortable to speak about directly, it could prove helpful to talk about their difficulty in discussing the matter, rather than addressing the issue itself. I pointed out that there were many difficult, powerful feelings involved with HIV/AIDS. Sometimes these feelings are clearly identified — foreground — even to the point of being overwhelming. At other times they emerge quietly in the course of talking about everyday events, or "just come up" as ideas or in dreams.

During the beginning phase, trust developed as members expressed their fears and difficulties living with HIV/AIDS. Members learned they could reveal their lives and/or feelings and ask others for advice or information without being judged negatively and with assurance that confidentiality would be maintained. Sharing built understanding, connection, and trust. An array of topics unfolded as the group members shared more and more of their experience with HIV/AIDS, their personal and professional lives and reactions within the group.

Negative thoughts and feelings arising within the group became a focus for discussion. These included fears of loss of confidentiality and respect, being judged and concerns that some members had special influence with me and others. The appropriateness of the group as a place for friendships, therapy, and support was discussed as members explored their concerns, desires, needs for limits/boundaries and their expectations of group therapy. I supported members' raising their concerns, giving their thoughts and feelings the fullest possible expression in order to investigate their experience, including positive, negative, and defensive feelings. Support of the aggressive expression of honest feelings and conflict, along with my non-defensive, non-blaming attitude, helped members identify clearly their strong emotions, listen to different viewpoints, and gain understanding, relatedness, and trust.

For instance, Peter, Bill, and Alan had heated discussions about relationships, love and sex: whether, how and at what speed to proceed with dating, revealing one's HIV status and having sex. In one interaction Peter sounding defensive and argumentative said, "I want to have sex — I don't want to be in confession box." Bill retorted angrily, "It's false and hurtful not to tell someone the truth about your status." Alan sounding frustrated and angry answered, "Stop being judgmental, Bill. Can't you see how scared Peter is of being rejected? I'm scared and you're scared, too." In a soft tone Bill replied, "Yes, I am. I'm sorry for sounding so angry, Peter." Then Peter responded more softly and sad, "And I'm sorry also. I really want to share the truth. I feel lousy not being up front but I feel so miserable about being positive. I've been rejected so much …"

The Go-Around

Members' ability to uncover issues laden with feelings and develop awareness was importantly affected by the structure of the group. Sessions began with a go-around in which each member expressed how he was feeling in the group right then and what if anything he wanted to work on that evening. At the end of each session there was a final go-around dealing with closing thoughts and feelings including unfinished business of that session.

The go-around was supportive in that it provided a creative and nurturing routine in which members could identify thoughts and feelings about themselves and learn about and understand each other. This contrasted with the unpredictable, unknowable nature of AIDS and the assaultive hysteria about AIDS of the society around them. It contributed a sense of respect and importance to each member and assured them that they would have an uninterrupted time and place to express themselves. It also oriented members to their "here-and-now," i.e., the dimension available for experience. In the course of time, the go-around changed and expanded to meet the group's evolving needs. At first a check-in and orientation, it later became an opportunity to review their week and the session. In this way the go-around contributed to members' learning to relate their concerns and interest in living to their capacities and opportunities. It thus developed perspective — elasticity of figure and ground, and enhanced meaningfulness and satisfaction in living. It also established a group norm of patience, honest disclosure and attentive nonjudgmental listening as a basis for their relationships — in the group and outside — and as a method for doing work in therapy.

Disclosure

Being "out of the closet" with respect to HIV/AIDS was an issue for all group members. Fears of social and professional isolation and rejection were prevalent. Members also struggled with their lifelong defensive adaptations of inhibiting personal disclosure. Many members had suffered shame and rejection for not "fitting in" and thought of themselves as being impaired and inadequate. They had learned to withhold (retroflect) their thoughts and feelings and to live secret lives. Identifying and talking about their feelings evoked anxiety, fears of rejection, and memories of past humiliations.

For instance, Alan had difficulty identifying and expressing his feelings and concerns and was frightened by anger and conflict. Unaware, Alan retroflected, interrupting contact. When members expressed strong emotions of anger and sadness he became quiet, withdrawn, unable to focus on his concerns, feel and think and tight in his chest. Then he felt inadequate and alienated. I supported him by asking him what he was experiencing and bringing his withdrawing to his attention. After recognizing this pattern and discussing it in group, he could relate it to his growing up experience of not being listened to by his family and to his withdrawing and withholding comments from them in order to avoid conflicts.

At one time or another all the members needed support and reassurance that their disclosures would not meet with rejection and judgment. However, unintended injuries did occur. These were discussed and were important opportunities for examining values, attitudes, and self-esteem.

Therapist's Task

My role as group leader was influenced by both my being a Gestalt Therapist and the particular needs and themes raised by HIV/AIDS. As a Gestalt group therapist I performed my usual functions — organizing, initiating, opening and closing go-arounds, doing one-to-one work, facilitating members' interactive work, leading guided fantasies, visualizations and other experiments with the group as a whole.

The quality and amount of my participation varied as I worked individually and with the group within the contact sequence: fore-contact, contact, final contact and post-contact, to promote learning and growth. In *forecontact*, feelings and ideas are vague and in a formative state. I was supportive by being less active — available with patience and attention to members' emerging thoughts and feelings. In contact, feelings, values, and attitudes are examined and reformulated. I facilitated by contributing new information (teacher-leader); sharing my own affective responses or thoughts (member-leader); and helping members promote awareness of their experience (therapist-leader). In the contact phase I was aware of members' ideas and excitement and provided support for their advancing analysis of the point under discussion. My therapist's task varied including also that of sympathetic listener, mediator, and facilitator.

I supported members' efforts to work through their fore-contact and contact experiences toward final contact, a spontaneous reformulation or integration of their experiences forming a "new Gestalt" — experienced as a coherent thought, perception, movement or satisfaction of a feeling and involving a sense of completion, clarity, and closure. Following final contact there is post-contact, during which a person assimilates learning. This last phase occurs without conscious awareness after the therapy session as the new learning is digested, becoming part of the person's repertoire as in personality or habits of everyday living. I was alert for lapses in memory or learning from preceding therapeutic work which might be due to a postcontact disturbance. This signaled the need for further therapeutic work.

In this process I was careful to limit my participation to that which was needed to sustain the work. Providing more support than necessary can foster dependency and insecurity. This is especially important with HIV/ AIDS which is unpredictable, insoluble, and potentially fatal and induces people to be more vulnerable to introjecting the views of "authorities." My leadership role became more background through the contact sequence as members gained confidence, self-support, and assumed their own leadership.

As a Gestalt Therapist I also aim to be a person "in contact" and frequently expressed my own anger, sadness and frustration in response to HIV/AIDS issues of loss, illness, and death. Expressing my feelings con- tributed to my effectiveness by demonstrating "healthy self-regulation" -the ability to organize experience freely so as to permit dominant needs to become known, expressed and resolved to the greatest extent possible. It also helped bring difficult feelings such as anger, sadness and fear to the group's attention. On one occasion, when members sat in silence following Bill's description of being rejected by a potential date, I responded by recalling my own experiences of rejection. This provided support by example and helped others discuss their experiences. Emphasizing contact and my being contactful also offers the potential of an I-Thou experience between myself and group members. This is a particularly empathic and intimate experi- ence, which can be especially powerful in conveying being understood and accepted — something people with AIDS (PWA's) keenly need.

In this group I also provided information about social/cultural/politi- cal influences that lead to hysteria and undermine self-esteem and individual expression. Gestalt Therapy as a unitary and holistic psychotherapy stresses the irreducible unity of the person in her/his cultural, social, political con- text. Indeed all aspects of the field are considered in appreciating a person's behavior and experience. In the case of HIV/AIDS there is stigma as well as preexisting social attitudes of homophobia, fear, denial of illness and death, and hostility toward minority groups which cause rejection and isolation. The holistic approach facilitates PWAs' understanding of their experience and thereby fosters self-confidence and respect.

At times I offered the group information and approaches to HIV/AIDS issues. For example, the negative effect of stress on the immune system, safe sex guidelines, the importance of investigating medical reports, and being educated and assertive about AIDS and health care matters such as exercise, nutrition, and vitamins. Being knowledgeable and facilitating discussions on these topics reflected the impact and complexity of HIV/AIDS issues and my being an available, caring resource.

While I had my own points of view, I worked for the broadest possible exchange of ideas and exploration of feelings and preferences. I conveyed the value that all feelings, thoughts, and behavior needed to be respected and understood if individual integrity and self-esteem were to be established and maintained. This reflects Gestalt Therapy's emphasis on self discovery and actualization and avoiding unaware introjection — i.e., the uncritical acceptance of values, ideas, attitudes that are not assimilated. Thus, "doing the right thing" was not always right for a person, e.g., taking AZT or going on an organic diet could be counter-productive if it was incompatible with a person's individual style or something he didn't really want to do.

This approach to being a group therapist valued my being a "co-equal" facilitator. I am not a therapist whose task is to adjust or change people to a prescribed or "appropriate" behavior. Group members are not ill and in need of correcting or fixing, an underlying assumption of interpretive or behavioristic therapies. Rather they are individuals with intelligence and courage engaged in a process of self-examination and actualization. I work with the belief and faith that people with the opportunity to assimilate new information about themselves and their environment will form new gestalten. That is, have clear ideas and take strong action to make corrective adjustments to enhance themselves to the greatest extent possible. This implies a "self" different than an internal unconscious psychic entity requiring fulfillment of past unmet needs. Rather, the "self" is a composite of sensory, intellectual, and physical capacities which cohere to creatively organize purposeful human experience and behavior. Thus, the client with a present concern requires new resources, i.e., ideas, attitudes and feelings, and trial and experiment to support growing into new experiences, insights, and behaviors. This is most efficiently achieved by a co-equal facilitator who conveys a sense of mutuality between the client and therapist as active participants in a common endeavor. In our HIV/AIDS group my being a co-equal facilitator minimized introjection and advanced members' sense of social connection, self value, creativity, wholeness and health.

Because of the uncertainty and lack of clarity of HIV/AIDS issues including its course, treatment, and outcomes, I was watchful for anxiety, hopelessness, and helplessness. In many instances, these are understandable and appropriate. Sometimes hopeless helpless feelings resulted from prior losses or experiences with which a member had felt unable to cope. I would work with members to identify and differentiate the present (the nexus of Gestalt Therapy) from the past, to bring to their awareness habitual responses — fixed gestalten — that don't adequately solve a current problem. With Peter and Mark, for example, I would be alert to their introjecting and retroflecting in fore-contact, a losing of ego-function — a person's capacity to be aware of and identify needs and preferences — that made them vulnerable to hysterical reactions. I would suggest they pay attention to their body experience and physical tightening until they could relax constricted muscularity, breathe, and feel. Then they would become aware of anger, sadness, fatigue, or anxiety confronting AIDS or other events in their lives. They each had experienced a great deal of guilt and shame about their homosexual urges resulting in important personality and id function disturbances. Mark thought being gay was abnormal; Peter wished he was straight. Both were ashamed to disclose their homosexuality to their families, inhibiting their capacity to experience and respond to their needs to be sexual, to love and be loved.

Toward the end of the first year the impact of HIV/AIDS on members' lives and therapeutic issues became more prominent in the group. For Bill, fear of relationships meant fear of exposing himself to what others might think of him. Since he thought he was a fraud, HIV/AIDS was final proof of this. Richard feared Bernie, his lover who was HIV negative, would leave him because of Bernie's intense fear of AIDS. Bernie would hesitate or withhold from touching or love-making with Richard for fear of infection. Richard felt rejected, inadequate and sexually frustrated. Alan saw himself as "the contagion." His interest in sex waned. His wife was sympathetic and not concerned with contracting HIV. She was not afraid of sex with a condom, but Alan was uncomfortable and adapted to his fear by losing interest in sex, avoiding it and reaching orgasm after withdrawing from her. Scott clarified his insecure and fearful feelings about leaving his job on an HIV physical disability and was evaluating alternative living sites, somewhere with a relaxed pace, and beautiful surroundings.

Middle Phase

During the middle phase people's feelings and concerns became clearer and evoked continuing and heightened interest. A working through process occurred that involved examination and deliberation of concerns. Additional information, insights, feelings, and new behaviors were explored. Members' self- and mutual understanding, trust, honesty, support and contact increased. This phase lasted for three years, from January 1988 through January 1991.

During this time a number of important changes occurred: the group became a clearly identified HIV/AIDS group; Peter and Mark, who had negative test results and suffered from severe fear of AIDS, left the group in November 1988 and July 1989, respectively. They came to recognize their hypochondria and other issues that needed to be pursued outside an HIV/AIDS group. Scott left the group in February 1990 to live in Hawaii with his lover as he had always wished. David joined the group in September 1988, Bruce in September 1990 and Ted in November 1990. Transitions were generally smooth, with new members becoming integrated into the group over a two-to-four month period.

Throughout this phase the group continually struggled with the impact of the cultural and social context. All members experienced intense fear of being identified by family, friends, business and professional associates as HIV-positive. Equally disturbing was the fear of an unfelt, uncontrollable and deadly spread of HIV within them. When Bill was diagnosed with AIDS he wrestled in a new and more urgent way with how and when to inform others of his AIDS status. The group discussed the pros and cons. This was obviously an urgent matter for everyone. Bill worked on his intense fear of misleading someone and being guilty of deceit. Over time, as Bill explored the emptiness and lack of love of his early life, he began to value himself as a human being, recognize his accomplishments and talk about discussing his HIV-positive status with men he was dating.

All the group members struggled with the question of whom to tell of their HIV-positive or AIDS status. The work on this seemed circular, with recurrent discussions that didn't achieve clear closure. I first thought that secrets created additional stress and members would be "better off" without them. In the course of the group I realized my view was simplistic. Secrets are functional. They serve to preserve connections with family, friends and business associates in a society that provides conditional acceptance and love and can be rejecting and destructive. Disclosure in the face of such danger is not easily undertaken and may not be possible or prudent in a neurotic society in the midst of a deadly epidemic.

Transcending AIDS

The middle phase was marked by an increasing group cohesiveness and identification. Members were accepted and respected by each other and shared common efforts, namely, dealing with and surviving 1) the emotional trauma and stress of HIV/AIDS; 2) a homophobic, illness — and death-denying environment that threatened members with being stigmatized, isolated and rejected; and 3) a need to improve their quality of life. Development of a mutually supportive trust, sense of belonging and purpose strengthened members in dealing with the diagnosis, stigma, and dread of AIDS. Members turned their attention increasingly to transcending the negative aspects of HIV/AIDS and discovering how to experience greater happiness, satisfaction and health — if not physical health, then emotional and spiritual health.

I was continually inspired by members' courage and perseverance. When Ted joined the group in November 1990 he was deeply depressed and was considering suicide. One day he brought in a book published by the Hemlock Society that discussed suicide as an option. The group supported his reading the book and acknowledged their own suicidal thoughts and the view that living or dying was the individual's right and choice. I suggested Ted and the group do an experiment: to fantasize being dead and become aware of how this feels, what this would be like. To ask themselves what feels attractive and not attractive about being dead? I proposed members consider what particular issues and concerns they would be free of and to allow themselves to be aware of what that would feel like. Some new perspectives and possibilities emerged out of this work.

Ted feared the terrible wasting syndrome and pain and suffering often associated with AIDS. I encouraged Ted's examination of alternatives -suicide as well as living. The group focused on his depression and also agreed with his right to make his own life-and-death decision. Ted was also supported by members' expressions of concern, their own experiences, frustrations and fears. This validated Ted, made him feel connected and gave him the opportunity to express feelings he found difficult to keep to himself or share with colleagues, family, and friends. From Ted's discussion of suicide, dying and death emerged group discussions of his dissatisfaction and how to improve the quality of his life. This included talking about his physical weakness, missing his deceased lover, his desire to travel, date, have sex and have an honest relationship with his family. During the next six months Ted traveled, spent more time with close friends, discussed how to reach out to his family and recovered from his depression.

This example points out the existential aspect of Gestalt Therapy: the emphasis on awareness of one's experience moment-to-moment, of what is — what exists. This is well-suited to dealing with the uncertainty of living with HIV/AIDS. It values the essence, focusing on existence in the present where life can be lived and de-emphasizes fears and concerns about the future. Ted's work also demonstrates the importance of contact — being in touch with one's self and with another. Contact enabled Ted to examine and explore his feelings and to bring new resources to bear on his problems. In contrast to the outside world, the group supported his experience while examining his feelings, nourished him and helped him assimilate his retroflected anger and loneliness. Ted's example also shows the contribution and necessity of aggression, conflict and suffering in the process of a person forming increasingly clearer and sharper ideas and feelings, in forming new gestalten and achieving changes in experience and behavior, namely, creative adjustments. Ted grieved the loss of his lover and his health. In grieving, his losses (absent figures of interest) were confronted, suffered and accepted and over time became part of the ground of his experience, i.e. a process of figure-ground adjustment. In this way he grew into a person living with a new reality in which he could breathe, feel and act more freely.

FACING HIV/AIDS — AND SUSTAINING HOPE

Facing HIV/AIDS issues posed a constant challenge to members' perseverance, courage, and positive outlook during the middle phase. HIV/AIDS concerns were never far from their consciousness and included a myriad of issues that defied clarity or solution. Some examples are: the question of "coming out" to family, friends, colleagues and lovers; stigma of the disease; rejection and acceptance; empowerment, entitlement, self-esteem; vulnerability, guilt and victimization. Also issues around sex, loving, being loved, loneliness and isolation. Furthermore, health care concerns such as choice of a doctor, frequency of doctors' visits, T cell counts, disease symptoms, test results, hospital care, home care and insurance. In addition it meant recognizing, celebrating and mourning anniversaries and milestones such as hospitalizations, opportunistic infections, birthdays, deaths, dates for going on disability, participating in treatment protocols and making lifestyle changes. How to have a feeling of well-being despite taking 50-100 pills a day, living in fear of "being found out," becoming ill, poor, forgotten and alone, losing one's mind to dementia or one's body to wasting syndrome. Facing AIDS included exploring more topics than I could count, had anticipated or imagined.

Dealing with HIV/AIDS issues and sustaining faith in one's capacity to survive was arduous. Although HIV/AIDS issues were both numbing and paralyzing, faith in living was achieved by authenticity, mutual care and support. When we discussed and examined HIV/AIDS issues this way, hopelessness and impotence could be transformed into a sense of possibility and power. AIDS was not inviolate. It could be understood and fought with hope and action.

LOVE AND LAUGHTER

Love and laughter were especially important. They gave members an especially motivating, strengthening and healing experience. As members shared, they came to appreciate each other and in many instances this transmuted to love. Loving and being loved are fundamentally sustaining and empowering and enabled members to experience self-worth and extend themselves outside the group to connect with others. In one group, Bill shared his self-deprecating thoughts and fears. Richard responded unequivocally, "I think you're terrific, Bill. I admire your perseverance and honesty. I care about you a lot. I love you."

In another instance Bruce informed his closest friend that he was HIV positive, the very first person outside the group to whom Bruce made this disclosure. Although his friend was accepting of this news, Bruce was depressed and afraid of rejection, seeing himself as "spoiled goods." He recalled his lifelong need for privacy, fearing that if others really knew him, they would think less of him. The group supported Bruce's disclosures by listening, expressing concern and sharing their own fears of rejection and needs for secrecy. They expressed their respect and love for Bruce. These expressions — especially love — were significant for Bruce. This provided a deep sense of connection and acceptance which they all needed. I suggested that Bruce be aware of his looking away as he spoke about members seeing him as "damaged." This unawares retroflecting interrupted his visual contact and supported him in filling the void with introjects such as: "I'm inadequate," and projections onto the group such as: "You don't like me." I suggested to Bruce that he make eye contact with each member. This experiment supported Bruce integrating his visual experience. As he did so, he experienced support, acceptance and love, and his eyes filled with tears. This made it easier for Bruce to endure his pain in disclosing, to become aware of unawares retroflecting and projecting and to begin to examine his self defeating introjects.

Laughter played a similarly vital role in the group. Most importantly, it helped release tension from fear, sadness, and loss. As such it strengthened members' capacity to risk being vulnerable, discuss difficult concerns and deal with the uncertainties and ups and downs of HIV/AIDS. In one instance, Alan recounted the surprise of the Italian customs agent who opened a large suitcase full with vitamins. Laughing at this helped members tolerate facing their fears of rejection and illness and enabled them to discuss Alan's anger, sadness and pain about his family, with whom he couldn't discuss HIV/AIDS.

The issues of depression, self-esteem, illness, death, dying, and healing also emerged in a group session we called The Last Laugh Comedy Hour. This session recognized the importance of humor in healing. The group did a go-around of jokes. Bruce related, "When I get really depressed I go gangbusters dressing up in the most outrageous costume I can find." Bill laughed affectionately as he recalled his ex-lover Karl who took secret delight in his rosy complexion which was due to medications he was taking. Ted confided with pride and good humor, "When my ladder became too heavy to carry, I cut it in half. Then it worked fine."

STRENGTHENING SELF-SUPPORT

At times I suggested the option that members see themselves as "fighters" against HIV/AIDS. They could "embrace life" by developing their capacity to say "Yes" to those things that made living exciting and worthwhile and say "No" to anything that undermined their emotional health. We practiced this in group and talked about ways to do this outside group.

In combating hopelessness, certain supportive attitudes were identified and became part of the group's culture. These included: 1) It is possible to live with AIDS. 2) A cure for AIDS is possible. 3) There is no blame for getting AIDS. 4) In order to love new people and things you must survive. 5) There is immense healing power in interest, excitement, and other positive feelings. 6) One can take actions to enhance health and improve one's immune function, e.g., diet, exercise, medical care and stress reduction.

It wasn't easy to discover how to strengthen self support, improve one's quality of life and physical health to transcend HIV/AIDS. Each member identified different ways of doing this. Alan would take meditative showers and give himself pampering treats such as massages. He also carried a picture of his family (his wife had been artificially inseminated and gave birth to a healthy baby girl in October 1989) and looked at it frequently throughout the day. Bill and Alan took 50-100 medication and vitamin pills a day. Bruce put himself on an exercise regimen and took mega doses of Vitamin C. Ted and David expanded their contact with friends and traveled to Europe, the Caribbean and Key West and also went to the theater and ballets. Richard and Bill got their Ph.D.'s, they changed jobs and Bill began to date.

ENDING PHASE

A sense of ending emerged during the group's fifth year; this phase lasted eighteen months. During this time many members' issues, concerns and struggles reached some resolution. In Gestalt Therapy, closure or final contact in therapeutic process is the culmination of preceding contact efforts and is marked by clarity, strength of feeling and sense of completeness in a new insight, feeling, or action.

During this phase members built on earlier group learning and assimilated changes in their lives. By the group's fifth year they had greater capacity to cope with HIV/AIDS and now confronted different challenges. For example, Richard no longer had panic attacks and had a close, stable relationship with Bernie. However, he now felt more in touch with angry dissatisfaction and the need to be more assertive with Bernie, his family and colleagues. While Alan now could talk about AIDS, enjoy sex and not feel doomed by AIDS, he was now aware of dissatisfaction with his inability to express his feelings and his lack of intimacy — with his family. In addition, during the ending phase members were confronted by earlier group issues: life and death, mourning, goodbyes and endings — some members could now face these issues with a sense of purpose and meaning.

LIFE AND DEATH

The group was increasingly able to broach the subjects of illness, death, and dying. It became less anxiety-provoking for them to discuss the meaning of life and death than to put it off. Members wanted to derive a significance in their lives that would sustain them in the face of the uncertainties of HIV/ AIDS. Although a philosophic perspective on life at age 30 or 40 is not easily attained, members had experiences both fearful and provocative which made mortality and the meaning of life figural, e.g. Bill had an episode of PCP (Pneumocystic Carinii Pneumonia), David had fevers and night sweats. Still, coming to terms with illness and death was difficult and the urgencies of day-to-day tasks and coping with threatened and actual physical illness, conditions, and prophylactic treatments often took precedence over philosophic discussions.

I presented the concept of a "healed death" during this phase, one in which a person has completed tasks most important to him and feels able to meet approaching death with some acceptance and readiness. Members who had opportunistic infections and symptoms of weakness or deterioration seemed ready to do this. Bruce, Richard and Alan, who were healthy, were not. They felt confused by the unknowability of death and were overwhelmed by this theme. Bill, David and Ted, though, struggled with the subject and each made peace with his friends and loved ones and to some extent, his family. Bill did a lot of work on death and mourning, meditating, praying, completing his will and in his words, "accepting what is."

DEATH AND MOURNING

In April 1991 David was hospitalized with severe headaches and fevers. He rapidly deteriorated, slipped into a coma and died three weeks later. He died as he had wished, without pain, confusion and fear. In the months prior to his death he had also completed two important tasks: he bought a home for Saul, his lover, and expressed his feelings of love to his parents.

With David's death the group took on an even more serious, compelling tone. While we all knew people who died of AIDS, death had not reached into the group before. Alan and Richard disclosed a fantasy they each had been secretly harboring: the group would protect them and other members from death. Without this magical hope they felt condemned to helplessness and hopelessness and were self admonishing: "What did we expect? This was inevitable!" The group's grieving for David seemed dulled and incomplete to me, a Gestalt that lacked clarity, strength and vigor; perhaps the suddenness of David's death had not allowed time to say good-bye. I expressed my own anger and sadness at David's loss, with the hope that this intervention would support members' expressing their own feelings. Nevertheless, the members seemed intent on discussing David's weakness and illness in the preceding month avoiding their own pain, fear, and rage about losing him. I felt dissatisfied with their work of grieving. In my judgment, they avoided this by focusing on their health concerns and needs for care and love.

Over the next six months, the group focus shifted to increased concern over emotional and physical health, healing issues and disclosing their being HIV positive to family members. Ted lost weight and grew physically weaker. In September he discussed his HIV status with one of his sisters, who was a nurse. This was the first time he had broached the topic with a family member. He felt relieved about having faced the truth of AIDS with her. It was confirming and nourishing to have this barrier between them removed. In October Alan informed his sister and brother-in-law of his HIV status. During this period, the group took a renewed interest in healing meditations and visualizations, vitamin therapy, diet, exercise, and medical protocols.

During January to May 1992, Ted's physical condition weakened despite his efforts to gain weight and to exercise. He discussed the possibility of death without fear. Since Howard had died three years before, Ted had not formed a new love relationship, and he missed the excitement and the joy he had with Howard. He reaffirmed, however, a strong desire to live with dignity and independence, without pain and suffering. During this period he tried to bring closure to what remained unfinished in his life.

In May, Ted was hospitalized with a collapsed lung due to PCP. The group, though surprised and fearful, was reassured by a prognosis of a two-to-three week recovery. But Ted's healing didn't go as expected. His lungs were too weak. The group felt impotent and resigned. Members held hands and did a healing meditation. Our prayers and love were with Ted. We experienced a sense of closure and completion for the moment — we had done what we could. With his health deteriorating rapidly Ted informed his family of his condition. His sisters flew to New York and were able to have a day speaking with him authentically, as he had always wished. Ted, out of pain, sank into a coma having said goodbye to his family. He died a few days later.

The members' fear that Ted would die had been confirmed. His death triggered fear for their own lives and for their having to bury their hopes and dreams of surviving AIDS. It was impossible to comprehend the death of so beautiful, gentle, and wonderful a person as Ted and to express fully the pain of losing him. As with David, members weren't able to say good-bye. Bruce expressed his need to see the positive aspects of Ted's brief and relatively painless illness and death. Alan was sad, afraid and he blamed Ted: "Why couldn't he do something for himself sooner?" Alan was also angry with Bruce for emphasizing only the positive and not sharing his pain and fear. Bill talked about his sadness and his worries about his health. He was possibly ill with K.S. (Kaposi's Sarcoma), he feared he would be the next to die. To facilitate closure with respect to Ted's death, I suggested the experiment of each member having a silent, personal fantasy of saying good-bye to Ted. Some members could do this; others were too sad.

I too was sad about Ted's death. I questioned my work. Had I been there enough for Ted? Had I been supportive, insightful and creative enough to facilitate the mourning process effectively in the group? Reminding myself that such doubts are inevitable given the insoluble problems posed by HIV/AIDS issues, I was able to support myself and go on with the work.

Three weeks thereafter Bill was hospitalized. Without having had time to mourn, much less recover from Ted's death, Bill's hospitalization was another shock which angered and further depressed the group. Alan and Richard were in pain worrying about Bill's health. They were missing him and did not want to come to group and feel his absence. Shortly thereafter,

Bruce announced he was leaving group to attend a creative writing course for four months. It was something he had always wanted to do. In response members struggled between their desire to support Bruce and wanting his participation in the group. The four remaining members, Alan, Richard, Dan, and Eric, (Dan and Eric joined the group in June 1992 and May 1993, respectively) agreed to resume group after the August break.

GOODBYES AND ENDINGS

At the first group session in September, Eric announced that he wanted to leave the group. He had joined the group in May for support and contact with HIV-positive men. At the last session in July he had been enthusiastic and committed to continuing group. He now argued he didn't like my office furniture, my fee and my policy of charging for missed sessions, and that I didn't provide clear direction and bring out enough emotion in the group. Exploration revealed that he had felt terrified when Alan said he had been in the group for five years. He thought it would take forever to achieve results from therapy and he felt trapped. Furthermore, he believed I should be doing more to help members face AIDS issues and feelings and thereby strengthen their immune function and fight depression. This examination did not give us a sense of completion and Eric was not swayed from his decision.

Discussion continued of actual and feared loss. Bill's condition and outlook varied from week to week. Members talked to him by phone. In addition, other pressing concerns became dominant. Alan's mother had a stroke that left her paralyzed and in a coma. In November, Dan contracted CMV (Cytomegalovirus) and Richard became depressed over Bill's weakening condition and over another close friend who had AIDS.

By early October it became clear that Bill would not return to group. We then planned a final session for Bill at his home. We met at my office and Alan arrived with a white stretch limousine to take us to Bill. The session included fond and humorous recollections of times when Bill had been well and David and Ted were alive. We also expressed love and respect for each other. Bill was excited and pleased that we had traveled to Brooklyn to be with him, especially in a white stretch limo. He had a sparkle in his eyes and a warm, caressing smile. The group and Bill shared a sense of completion and closure, one that included love, acceptance, and readiness for whatever would be. Bill said, "Thank you for being here for me. I love you." Bill had, I believe, as much as anyone can have, a healed life and death. He died the first week in December, in his mother's arms saying, "Momma, I love you."

Throughout December the members talked about Bill's death and their fears for themselves. Bruce decided not to rejoin the group after completion of his writing course, saying Bill's death was "too sad." Dan felt that with Bill's passing he would be viewed by others in the group as the next to die. He worked on this and owned his projection that he was seeing himself this way. He thought a group where others were as ill as he would be more helpful and less painful for him. Alan was taking vacation away from New York, which was one of his goals. By early January the group decided to end after four more sessions. Richard was sad, but felt finished with the group. Alan wanted to continue but accepted the others' decision and reported a conversation with his wife. "The group has been terrific. I have made important changes, a lot of progress and it is time to graduate, to move on." These words spoke for us all. I felt this decision was appropriate. The group had fulfilled its purpose with regard to HIV/AIDS and members' needs. In addition, I felt sad about ending an experience that, with all its pain, included so much human courage, love and esprit de vie ...

CONCLUSION

This group experience was beneficial for most of the participants. They worked on an array of personal and HIV/AIDS — related issues that touched every facet of their lives and made dramatic changes in the way they dealt with HIV/AIDS and in facing illness, dying and death. I, too, was enriched.

The group format importantly contributed to members' ability to gather information on alternative approaches toward dealing with HIV/

AIDS and to develop referral resources for social, medical, financial and emotional support. The group norm of respect for individual differences supported members expressing their needs, gaining trust and insight, and developing self-confidence and self-worth.

The group as a social setting provided an opportunity to satisfy important human needs for social expression and recognition. In the group, living, being ill and in pain, dying and death occur in a social context and can be recognized as social events. This fulfills an essential need in our social nature as human beings and contrasts with the Western cultural bias that fears, denies, conceals, isolates, sanitizes and devalues illness, dying and death. In the context of HIV/AIDS, the group provided a forum for members to witness and be witnessed in their struggle.

Gestalt Therapy by emphasizing contact, here-and-now experience and an experimental methodology supported members' developing their self function — their capacity to have clear, strong experiences and hence to more accurately know themselves and their world. Out of this process emerge greater security, self-confidence, self-esteem, and personal integrity, empowering members to change their lives beneficially.

This group experience held many surprises. Two stand out for me. The first was the myriad ways in which HIV/AIDS impacted members' lives. They were unpredictable, challenging and required continuous alertness and responsiveness. Each session held different possibilities and opportunities for self-examination, discovery and actualization. The second surprise was the nature and difficulty of dealing with HIV/AIDS dying and death. Repeatedly, illness and dying seemed to sneak up, overtake and overwhelm members and myself, taxing our capacity to bear the pain and suffering of the grieving that these losses demanded. AIDS-death was not a friendly visitor who gently announced himself. It demonstrated how an intelligent, sensitive person could breathe, smile, and speak one evening and be gone the next. This fragility of life was powerfully and painfully demonstrated. While grieving is normally deeply painful, in the context of this HIV/AIDS group where young people were dying and there were multiple physical and emotional losses and deaths, grieving was inadequate and incomplete. Members and myself often felt impotent, helpless and hopeless. This became an important challenge and learning opportunity, the challenge of defining success, as Gestalt Therapy does, not by outcome but by the process and effort of living — the quality of moment-to-moment experience, not the quantity — and learning to accept what "is." Success with respect to HIV/AIDS is not measured by survival, it is the living and loving and sometimes laughing that must be valued; it is the effort and "response-ability" in that process without blame or judgment.

The final year of the group was one in which members and myself were periodically overwhelmed by the multiple and concurrent emergencies, illnesses and losses that HIV/AIDS imposed. Under the inexorable pressure of illness and death, the group was unable to maintain a positive attitude, to assimilate losses and to rest and recuperate. Unable to reconstitute itself with new members, the group recognized it needed to adapt to a new reality. By ending, the group members exercised their capacity to orient themselves to change and to initiate action. This was another instance of creative adjustment, a product of their work in group. Although highly vulnerable, they were not paralyzed. They could feel, think, act and go on.

REFERENCES

Kitzler, R. (1980) In Feder B. & Ronall, R. (Eds.) *Beyond the hot seat.* New York: Brunner/Mazel.

Perls, F. S., Hefferline, R. & Goodman, P. (1951) *Gestalt therapy.* New York: Julien Press

◊

15

POLITICS AND PERSONALITIES IN GESTALT AND OTHER FIELDS

Gaie Houston

❖❖❖

FOREWORD

I shall discuss as foreground two European Gestalt training organizations I have seen growing over the last decade and longer. It is unusual in my life to have as much knowledge as I do here of some of the composted experiences in which an enterprise is both nourished and constrained. Images of larger systems come to my mind as I write, and from time to time I let this background emerge into this short study.

I joined the first organization, a British one I shall refer to as Beta, as a visiting staff member, in 1982. My role has expanded since, but I have never been a consultant to the organization in the way I am used to in many other settings, usually of larger and more formally structured enterprises. The other case I cite is in another European country. Here I have been both an advisor to the design of the training, and supervisor and lecturer. In both places I have a sense of being something like a visiting aunt, which is to say, one of the family, though not very often present.

PRE-CONTACT

I want to start with that ungraspable haze I will only falsify by naming it a beginning. For that beginning came from other pasts and other beginnings. This is the heart of what is fascinating me: the dynamism of old experience and new events and perceptions. This ever-modifying compost of old experience both informs and constrains the now. It is that part of what Perls called the middle zone (Perls, 1969) which add up to acculturation. This acculturation, the making of the two cultures in the organizations I shall describe, seems in part the result of processes that were not consistently aware and intentional. I hope I can present a clearer Gestalt of some of them now than I consistently did in the times I recount.

I start before Beta, even before the before of Beta, at the beginning of the seventies. A small group of radical thinkers set up, in what is now the University of North London, a diploma course in the behavioral sciences. What was radical was their handing over of a great deal of the academic decision-making about the program, to the students themselves. Both the woman who later founded Beta, and I, were students on that program. Both of us were exposed to the paradoxes and discoveries of this educational method. We found, separately, for we did not know each other closely, that students will set themselves a harder course than academic staff might wish on them. We exposed ourselves to the sort of experiment Carl Rogers was introducing in the States, in student-centered learning, warts and all. Anarchy was the style of the program, limited by an overt search for synergy. In the spirit of the times, there was also a good deal of left-wing ideological garnish expressed more in words than deeds.

The warts included a kind of deification of self-responsibility, narrowly interpreted to mean, going it alone. Getting help from the staff was very much a last resort. So we floundered and bludgeoned our way through the dynamics of organizational behavior, maintaining skepticism about much theory until we had bruised our shins pretty thoroughly. As an example, we organized ourselves into small learning groups, which met on the same floor of the same building on the same evening. What sometimes resulted was a florid intergroup event, characterized by that occasion when one group screwdrivered off the doors of all the meeting rooms. The stated rationale was to do with shared learning. The sensation was of deadly warfare on a petty feudal scale.

Decision-making was an excruciating affair, involving meetings of the whole faculty and student body, about thirty-five of us as I remember. Our anti-authoritarian leanings forbad any formal structures or roles, so we all learned, among more worthy material, our idiosyncratic responses to intense frustration and boredom.

There was a bright side. Truths learned so excruciatingly certainly stayed. Besides that benefit was another great one, that we taught each other most of what we knew. The rich mix of professions and theoretical grounds among the students was shared and then built on. We experimented outrageously, which is to say, with a fierceness of method quite inappropriate for the paying public, but immensely profitable to our own insight and change, with every therapy in the book and more that never got into the book.

Blake's maxim that the path of excess leads to the palace of wisdom seems with hindsight to have been a major tenet of our belief system, as we led our stoic counter-dependent student existence. In Tony Key's words, we risked being alive, sometimes to startling effect. By way of example, one sub-group of students, previously academics and social workers, during the program became a rock-group and lived for some years by this grisly trade.

At that time and later, Ischa Bloomberg was teaching Gestalt in the United Kingdom. I attended a few of his events and courses. The founder of Beta took a complete training with him. The foreground memory I have of him in this context is his clear view that he was a consultant hired by the student body he was teaching.

This aspect of reality often sinks deep into unawareness on other courses. The director not only takes the money, but calls all the shots. As I remember him then, Ischa was likewise fond of calling the shots. But he insisted on this organizational clarity: the student body set up public events, negotiated working hours and fees with him, and took responsibility for their training in far more than ink-monitor capacity.

From that time for several years I taught counselling on a training program, where I think I was formative in bringing in some of the student-centered methods which evolved from the experiences I have described here. With the active help of the whole learning community, we invented ways of running planning weekends in which the students could effectively design their own learning for the succeeding year. The director was enormously excited, I remember, to see how the enthusiasm which usually belongs to faculty alone during the planning stages of a program, was now shared around, along with angst, frustration and resulting creativity, among the students too. Faculty had to present a case for teaching anything they wanted taught or wanted to teach. Students had to present a case for what they wanted to learn. The budget had to be balanced if outside lecturers were called for. Evaluation methods had to be thought out and implemented. The course became one which had as much to do with academic innovation and organizational awareness as with counselling. We experimented, at a time when such things were considerable academic novelties, with methods of self-assessment and peer-assessment, and kept to them for the award of diplomas.

Here then were two notable academic experiments in London in the seventies. Two of the present directors of Beta earned their diplomas on the counselling course of which I have just spoken, and one of them also went to Ischa's training.

The Tavistock Institute of Human Relations in London has been responsible for major insights, and most daring experiential training, in the whole area of group dynamics. They and the Institute of Group Analysis are another part of the background of Beta, through me and one of the present directors.

In my experience, some of their training has raised the anxiety levels of participants to a considerable height. The advantage of this is that they offer the possibility of traumatic learning that will enter the bones and sinews of participants in a way that a trawl through even the best of theory books is unlikely to reproduce.

The disadvantage is that sometimes participants defend themselves against the terror of the learning in baby and bathwater mode. They close their boundaries to the training, and to any further study of their own behavior in groups. To my mind this is a catastrophic waste of opportunity.

I have been fascinated to find ways of achieving the profundity of learning that I feel I have been lucky enough to have on their programs, and the University of North London one, with enough sense of safety to make it likely that the baby-and-bathwater response is not called up.

Kurt Lewin had vast insight into the indivisibility of figure and ground. Put another way, my need or response in this moment is not just to do with a private urge nor yet just an interaction between me and the immediate environment. I perceive and act from a place in history and in geography. Life after life of apparently inconsiderable moments have shaped to this one where I do what I suppose I have lightly, casually, decided. I am a nodal point in a network that is tangled through time as well as through space.

So, just from the limited field of awareness I have as one individual nodal point, I can see these powerful antecedents to Beta itself.

BETA

The first director set up Beta in her own house, I think after Ischa had left and gone to continental Europe. When she added to it a supervision group for professional psychotherapists and counsellors, she asked me in to run it. Before that I had been invited to occasional weekend workshops with student groups. Early in the eighties she handed the whole concern to three former students, and the training moved to its own premises. What I have called my aunt role to the organization continued with cordiality on all sides.

Imagining the program itself as a child, it looks as if there was enough stability for it to continue to flourish when the mother handed over to three of the eldest children, with whom everyone set up a new home away from the first parental one. In terms of Daniel Stem's descriptions of beginnings, the program seems to have been, in those days, busy forming a core self. More accurately, the various groups of students who made up the phases of the training each tended to form a self, a sense of identity and of ownership of the staff. Since they met on different nights, this is unsurprising.

Weekly meetings gave regular exposure to the dynamics of small groups, the setting in which so much Gestalt work is done. To my mind, the education in this setting has been very fine on this program. Residential events, and keen staff interest in large group behavior, have helped to bring all the phases into contact and awareness of each other. In two succeeding years I was asked to lead summer school residential weeks. I was allowed the provocative title of Gestalt and the Unconscious for the first one, which was a synthesis of Gestalt and psychodynamics. The second was on The Large Group, and attempted to express the phenomena of the event in Gestalt rather than analytical terms.

Without such specific education, I imagine the program being no more than a microcosm of one aspect of current human society, which is to say, an interminable unresolved intergroup event. The evidence is all around us that when two groups of people are doing approximately the same task, in roughly the same area and without extensive communication, the tendency is for them to harden their contact boundaries towards each other to turtle shell or porcupine level. If they are also competing for resources, or even imagine this to be the case, then the building of fortresses and provisioning with boiling tar really sets in in earnest.

The faculty interest in large and median groups helped everyone address the contact boundary issues between the phases. Students slowly invented their own ways of acknowledging their membership of the larger community of the whole program, rather than just their comfortable weekly small family group.

Over a series of residential events, I recall ways in which we actively worked at this vital and often neglected aspect of Gestalt, and configured the system and sub-systems rather than only the therapeutic dyad.

Using the whole community, the faculty and phase groups, as a consultative committee about the nature of the education itself, immediately gave elder, rather than infant status, to everyone present. Learning structures which brought students together in small configurations across the phase boundaries was another device which led to relaxation of people's contact boundaries. They got safe with strangers one by one, rather than being faced with a mass of them.

Where the cross-boundary contacts flourished well, a polarity inevitably appeared. Some students would fear the loss of their phase group, or rather, of loyalty to it. In disastrous slow-motion, I imagine the same swing to have been experienced in those countries such as the USSR and Yugoslavia, which have operated for a period as apparent unities or single entities.

The re-establishment of the identity of the small groups which composed those nations has been panicky, bitter, ruthless and primitive. The puzzle appears to be, how to allow people to keep in awareness all at one time their sense of membership of secure small groups and of large container groups, ecosystems and yet more beyond.

In our residential, we respected students' calls for time in their phase groups, as well as in the whole community and in ad hoc task groups. My model was an interstate microcosm. The United States is one of exceedingly few examples in the world of a great nation which has allowed the sense of identity of its small groups, its various states, to be fostered alongside the sense of membership of the whole. I speak always of sense of membership. The membership is a fact. The sense, or lack of sense, of it is what people react to.

In Europe we are working towards becoming one entity, politically and economically. It is possible that the sense of small group is too long established for people to let in the idea of larger membership at more than fanciful, of-course-we-are-all-world-citizens, level.

Paul Goodman set a clear precedent for thinking at social and political level. I use his authority to make this pause and look at some more of the submerged past and present that affects both international relations and such small systems as a couple of education programs.

There are several forces in the field which I see tending to promote sense of large group membership. One is the bright flag. In ancient battles this was literally the rallying point for what was often a ragged and largely disaffected ad hoc army. The bright flag now is perhaps the trusted brand name, or the charismatic leader. When this awareness is uppermost, I guess the sense of belonging is a kind of individual bond between flag or leader and member. The sense of solidarity with other members is there, but is secondary.

Another force which often strengthens sense of group is a threat from the environment, or from an outgroup. Such threats may exist, but seem not to be used in boundary reinforcements in Beta. Nor is there the bright flag of charismatic leadership. What is clearly there is the core self (Stern, 1983), the internal coherence of having forms and structures which are owned by most people, and are seen to work, or are at least accepted as being Us.

On a residential weekend some years ago I introduced to the whole group on this training a dream-sharing exercise, in which the dreams were allowed a social as well as an individual meaning. The social meaning was there at process level, as well as in content: people might use the dream telling to hog group-time, or to license their need to show, or to comment at poetic level what they were not letting themselves take issue about more overtly. People found some talent in themselves for picking up or guessing at several levels of dreams. Then they added a social writing device to the original. This seemed to me the ownership ritual. Now it is commonplace for residential groups to start the day with dream-sharing, and in this way set a tone of attending to themselves and each other with some profundity. Other programs have other methods. The point, I believe, is the invention and ownership of a cohesive ritual which is more than symbolically useful to the life of the group.

I need to add a little more description of the field. Alongside the boom and then recession of the late eighties and the beginning of the nineties, the field of psychotherapy has changed in a different respect in Europe. The Treaty of Rome set up many conditions for partial unification by 1992. One of these was a requirement that every European Community country should have in place a national standard of accreditation for the profession of psychotherapy. Thereafter, anyone accredited in one country would be recognized and free to practice in any other participating country. The response from place to place to this edict has been varied. Some countries have taken precious little notice. In others, psychiatrists or psychoanalysts or some other particular interested parties have taken over the standard setting procedure.

In Britain, what was for some years called the Rugby Standing Conference did a remarkable job of keeping most of the interested professions talking together, and finally agreeing some common standards. From the Rugby Conference has emerged the United Kingdom Council for Psychotherapy, which holds a register of psychotherapists, and is agreeing training standards that combine rigor and enough commonality to apply to psychoanalysts, body therapists, and many other orientations that on the face of it are disparate.

Beta has been active in the Standing Conference, and is now registered with the Council. So, its training requirements have gone up year by year. What was a largely experiential training with many of the features I have listed for those courses I see as influential on it, is becoming more academic. Indeed, both the Council's existence, and the threatening economic climate, seems to have changed the ethos of the times towards more formalism.

This change is going on in Gestalt throughout the European Community countries, more markedly in some others than here. The last European Gestalt Conference was heavy with academic papers, and very light on experiential workshops. Leave your sense and come to your heads. Academic respectability has become a survival necessity, in a way it seemed not to be in the times of Goodman and Perls.

A year ago I made my own primitive response to all this, when I was lecturer for a three-day residential to the three top level phases of Beta: those devoted to producing psychotherapists. With a sense of violating norms, I began the first morning by announcing clearly that this was to be a teaching event. I said that everyone here, in my judgement, was skilled at diagnosing and operating in process groups. I was interested in using as many experiential structures as we could usefully invent; but this was a task group, not a process one. This is a little like saying we were a group of fish, but would do without water for a while.

The need for water showed up in a sub-group of students, some of whom, significantly, had arrived late and not taken on board my task group remarks. As I remember, I had suggested that, as in most organizations, they took care of their emotionality in the informal parts of the time we had together. The way they did this was well in line with Wilfred Bion's (Bion, 1961) observations about the flight to the basic assumption group.

The task was very well attended to. It was an extended seminar and teach-in on infant observation, with a twelve-week baby and his mother in the group. I had said at the beginning that babies are emotionally very provocative in a stack of ways, and that the first priority I had in the weekend was respect for this youngest member of the group. The disaffected could see this as a gagging, and blame me for it. As the baby turned out to take the liveliest pleasure in hearing noise and seeing people jumping about, the gag was hardly a tight one. By the penultimate evening, I had the battened-down feeling and sense of dread I have learned in psychoanalytic events to associate with bad vibes, mostly directed at me.

The large group splintered in informal time, to make an interesting readout of some of the vectors around. One sub-group ended the evening with mugs of cocoa, wrapped in dressing-gowns, and having one of their members read a child's story book, of some banality as I remember, aloud to them. An almost polar sub-group joined some other people in the building for a dance that they later described as threatening to be Bacchanalian. Their only justification for this somewhat hysterical, (or hopeful?) conclusion was that one of the outsiders removed her shirt. The students I describe are sophisticated and intelligent, not ordinarily given either to demanding in querulous infant tones to see the pictures in a story book, nor yet, as happened on this occasion, to making pacts that the men would not walk upstairs without another male for company, presumably out of fear of the Shirtless Woman and all she represented.

As the only faculty member present, I felt lonely, uneasy and not in good state to gestalt all this material into the meanings that now seem obvious. Next morning a student said she wanted to start by telling a dream. Privately, I thought this might be another way of regressing, and avoiding the task of the group. Dream after dream was told, heard, commented, noted. The group moved in this way through the learning so far accomplished, and into all the sexual material that can be avoided in the more kootchykoo atmosphere of the nursery. Our topic was gestalted every which way: in terms of students' own lives, in terms of the present political climate in European Gestalt, in terms of the ousting of the male that is often implicit around babies; in terms of their own training and what they called their resistances to the new.

What I call the core self of this training had re-emerged. The mildly mad behavior of the evening before had not merely re-stimulated what Perls calls the schizophrenic levels. The rattling had happened to a solid enough collective self that it could be integrated creatively in such a short time.

GAMMA

Through Beta, I was introduced to a lively woman who had set up a program of her own in another European Community country. She asked if I would be what she called the consultant to the course, which I shall call Gamma, as well as an occasional lecturer on it. I agreed, and for a time she used to come to London and spend time talking through the design of her training, and the problems she was encountering. She admired some of the ethos of Beta, though not all. In the early days of this arrangement, we discussed the whole design of Gamma. At that stage she was coming to the end of her first year, and with me decided to have an annual intake of students, on the British model, so there was a rolling program or school.

I remember speaking with enthusiasm of the need for an initial planning weekend at the beginning of the new year, in which new and old students could meet each other, and work out a learning program which resulted in the sharing of resources such as lectures and particular seminars, while also devising their own year's work. She seemed a little hesitant, and said that the first year of training was really for saying hello. I opposed this view, forecasting that the time would be more productively spent in finding out, Berne-style, what to say after that initial greeting. One of the training devices in Beta was apprenticeship. Senior students took turns accompanying faculty members on teaching or process consultancy assignments. She extended this device in Gamma into a monitorial system: two senior students would be assigned to each small family sub-group of new trainees, who would meet fortnightly in their own time.

With twenty-twenty hindsight, I now notice that I let myself suppose that she was only asking my advice about details of methodology, as we talked over such matters. I managed to be much less aware of how profoundly novel she found the whole training ethos that I and Beta represented, and how low her sensitivity was to the vectors and valences, the forces in the field.

The discovery came soon enough, at the first weekend I ever spent with her students, at the beginning of the senior group's second year. As a learning occasion, this was highly satisfactory. The students had all, over the preceding fortnight, made their first visit to the junior students' family groups. These family groups had had one meeting alone before that. From the reports, it seemed that they had in almost every case formed a group contact boundary of porcupine quality in this brief time. Like Noah's animals, the seniors had gone two by two, not into an ark, but into a series of lions' dens. One family group to be visited had changed their meeting place, so the contact boundary between senior and junior year was only excited in fantasy. Another group had mysteriously run out of coffee, so none was available for the visitors, though all the juniors were drinking from large mugs. And so on. Creative hostility had evidently been the challenge, and one the juniors rose to magnificently. The students before me were bewildered as well as furious. They had travelled considerable distances at their own expense, full of goodwill and wisdom and humility, only to be met by contemptuous questioning of their task, role, and general fitness to belong to the human race.

That there would be up-down responses, and a sense of invasion, was something I had talked through in London when the idea was put forward. Apparently, the director had not fully recognized the depth of emotionality likely in such scenes. Until the day before this first visit the junior year had apparently not been told, let alone consulted about their willingness to accept, that they would be given quasi-leaders. In the group and intergroup-aware training that had become second nature to me, this process the students were describing was in my mind sure to lead to negative feeling.

And, as I hinted, the good news was that there was clear experiential learning. The seniors gained a strong understanding of Lorenz's dictum on Chaos Theory, that there is sensitive dependence on initial conditions in non-linear systems. And they appeared to incorporate a respect for the rivalrous feelings so easily provoked between groups.

By the next time I arrived at Gamma, this time with both years and the director, she had come to be called The Empress. In her language the word sounded even more imperious than it does in English. She did work at raising her own awareness of what she called her monarchic tendency, and saw it was at variance with her democratic ambitions for her program. But her acculturation was against her. She had been trained by some of the more florid emoters of the old school of Gestalt. I remember her strict rule about people taking their shoes off inside the Centre where we worked. I saw one morning of Wagnerian passion when an unfortunate student overlooked this rule. The whole group joined in with a will, taking sides, calling for meetings, and playing out victim and oppressor roles with the verve and inventiveness that can usually be evoked on such occasions. It took time for her to configure the program with the, albeit fitful, awareness that the students too had an interest in the cleanliness of building, as in every aspect of their training.

Another time I arrived for a week's work to find her gloomy at the scene she could imagine when she told two students that they were not yet ready to take on clients. It appeared that she had not consulted them about their readiness, and when I suggested we do so, she was skeptical of their response. In the event they both had perfect clarity that they did not yet feel competent. She considered this outcome a fluke; it did not match her fixed Gestalt of people as untrustworthy.

I could write another piece showing the enormous creativity of design on her program, and the many successful aspects of it. Here I am interested in what in my view led to the present state of the two training schools under discussion.

An event from the end of the senior group's training, when I had known them for two years, comes to the foreground. By this time we had three year-groups together on one residential. The director had just invented a very productive training technique which involved them all, and our week seemed highly satisfactory. It was to end with a certificate-awarding ceremony on the last evening. She reported to me that the senior group, the recipients of the certificates, were going to be given a party by the other students. I was impressed at this display of generosity. Then rumors and grumpy talk began to be heard here and there.

Alone with the seniors, I asked about this party, and they laughed with suspicious -glee. Their version of events was that the director had suggested to them that they tell the junior students to make a party, and that they backup this order by saying that it was a tradition. Freud's observations about the hostility of jokes had a place here. I reminded them of the antipathy between them and the phase below, two years before. They retreated, fogging the contact-boundary towards me, and preserving their glee behind it. By the day of the party they were more anxious. Nobody had been round to collect money for drinks. No plans had leaked. Perhaps it was to be a super surprise, a well-kept secret until the last minute? They did not sound as if they were convincing themselves, as they speculated.

The kitchen staff had added some festive elements to our last meal, and all the senior students dressed up for the occasion. So there was some sense of occasion. However, among the rest, there was a certain sweet disorder in the dress, and a strong tendency to leave the seniors to themselves. After dinner a good deal of nothing happened. Then late in the evening aggressively loud dance-tapes were put on, and there was drinking and dancing, again with a leaving of the seniors to themselves.

The memory of that attempt at inflicting tradition has lasted at Gamma for eight years, until the present. Year on year it has been a contentious issue, though several times ending with a warm event. Like the other incidents I report, this was a visiting of the style of the leader on the group itself, to their detriment.

As a consultant to the course, I raised the topic of accreditation, as crucial to this program as to Beta. I urged the director, who is politically well placed in her profession through her own background training, to start up something analogous to The Rugby Conference in her own country. Such processes are power-struggles between roughly similar groups. Thus they are dynamite, which can result in an explosion of creative, or destructive energy. She was not enthusiastic. I urged her at least to make an alliance with all the other Gestalt training in her country. She made links to one, and for a time until there was a quarrel, they exchanged students and had faculty visits. A larger Gestalt than this seemed not to excite her. Now the accreditation procedure in her country has been taken over by the psychiatrists, who form what is arguably not the most appropriate body to decree who is and who is not a psychotherapist.

Over the last two years she has stopped doing the work in London that made it convenient to come and see me there to talk through her program. When I am in her country to work with her students, she has me do some consultancy with her and the management board she realized, late in the day, that the law of her country required her to have. To this board she has told, in my presence, some considerable inexactitudes about what goes on in the training. Asked about this in private, she shrugs and says that is the way of the world. Certainly there has been a great deal of political scandal in her government over the last year or two, so it probably is the way of her world. I confine myself to awareness raising, asking her about the possible outcomes of having her inexactitudes revealed, and so forth.

Very recently there has been a huge rift within the student body. About a third of them, including most of the present senior year, have broken away and set up a do-it-yourself core, employing a recent graduate from another school, known to them through the exchange scheme. Both fragments of this new configuration have written to me asking me to work with them. The director, judging that this might happen, notified all concerned that any staff working with the defectors would not be allowed to work with her. I phoned to ask if I counted in this arrangement, and she said no, although she would be extremely hurt if I did anything to encourage such outrageous disloyalty, pilfering of her excellent ideas, and so on, as the defectors were guilty of. In other words, she still talks of subjects and possessions. She still talks like an Empress.

The convention is that revolutions manage to overthrow the old regime entirely, or else get quashed. Quashing is obviously the lively figure for her just now. I, perhaps like you, am interested in allowing in the learning of the now, so that new awareness leads to a new solution. What a magnificent program might result if the revolutionaries can bargain their way back into the old kingdom, reconstituted on some other political model. To do that I guess they would need to attend not only to their own neurotic needs for what Fritz Perls calls petty victory, but also to show patience and generosity and firmness to a fallen leader. It may be too much to ask that all that can happen in this present configuration, whose now is already coated and infused with indignation over recent history.

The outcome I look for is that, at least, most of the students gain insight, and so equip themselves to be more organizationally sensitive and astute in future. The next hope is to work with the director towards her willing rejection of all her directorial privileges or else her acceptance that keeping them will continue to entail penalties.

CONCLUSION

There the narrative ends for now. I have described two trainings in which the leaders thought that they espoused the same values. One training has by a slow discernible acculturation, by the build-up of countless small Gestalts, achieved what I call a stable core self. The word community is often used by them about themselves. The other is, at least for now, polarized, and fragmented. The acculturation the director influenced could only include the attitudes gestalted into her in a far longer process than the occasional consultations with me represented.

One of the thousand pieces of learning I take from all that I have told is about the organizational illiteracy that is common enough to keep hordes of consultants in work. Rogers, Goodman, Perls, Lewin, Goldstein: the line of visionaries stretches back, still influencing our visions. Their ideas seem attractive is small doses, but unpalatable to many people when carried through to realization. Even Beta, which I see as successful, bumps and jostles between democracy and expedient bits of autocracy with its consequences of unrest and grump. Anarchy is maybe too evolved a political system for us to achieve yet.

The director of Gamma, with her vitality, creativity, charisma, represented some of the values shown in Fritz Perls himself, as far as I can understand. I see other breakaway, innovative doctors and therapists turn to Gestalt and to some extent use it as a weapon, a symbol of their iconoclasm, as well as for its intrinsic worth.

More education, from earlier in life, seems needed. I would like to see our children taught in school about how they function as organisms, how they deal with each other and with authorities and the rest of the environment, and how they are indivisible from systems, right from their own family and class, through to the stem of system that is the whole planet and everything on it.

The cases I have talked of illustrate just a little of how much awareness-raising needs to be put in to creating well-functioning systems, in far more fields than Gestalt training. Specially in Gestalt, however, the contradictions between a philosophy of anarchy, and a history of rebellion leading to autocracy and feudalism, is an urgent puzzle.

REFERENCES

Berne, E. (1972) *What do you say after you say hello?* New York: Grove Press.

Bion, W. (1961) *Experiences in groups.* London: Tavistock.

Foulkes, S. and Anthony E. (1957) *Group psychotherapy.* London: Penguin.

Gleick, J. (1987) *Chaos: Making a new science.* London: Penguin.

Goldstein, K. (1939) *The organism.* Boston: American Book Co.

Goodman, P. (1952) *Utopian dssays and practical proposals.* New York: Random House.

Keys, T., Oldham, J. and Starak, L. (1978) *Risking being alive.* Victoria: P.L.T. Press.

Lewin, K. (1951) *Field theory in social science.* New York: Harper and Bros.

Perls, F., Hefferline, R., and Goodman, P. (1951) *Gestalt therapy.* New York: Julian Press.

Perls, P. (1969) *Gestalt therapy verbatim.* Moab, UT: Real People Press.

Rogers, C. (1957) Personal thoughts on teaching and learning. *Merrill-Palmer quarterly, 3*, pp. 241–253.

Stem, D. (1985) *The interpersonal world of the infant.* New York: Basic Books.

◇

ABOUT THE CONTRIBUTORS

JACK AYLWARD, Ed.D. is in the active practice of Gestalt Therapy and has been the director of the Plainfield Consultation Center in Plainfield, New Jersey, since 1978. He has had several years of training and experience in group and marathon therapy and currently co-leads a year long training group. He is a member of the Association for the Advancement of Gestalt Therapy and serves on the editorial board for the Gestalt Review.

ELAINE BRESHGOLD, Psy.D. is a clinical psychologist in private practice in Portland, Oregon and Vancouver, Washington. She began studying and practicing Gestalt therapy in 1978. Her practice includes work with individuals and couples, as well as supervision and training. She has written several articles on the theory and practice of Gestalt therapy and has a special interest in how current psychoanalytic theory articulates aspects of the patient-therapist relationship, and the benefits of integrating these concepts into the practice of Gestalt therapy. She is co-director of Gestalt Therapy Center-Northwest.

FELICIA CARROLL, M.Ed. in Educational Psychology and M.A. in Child Development and Counseling Psychology, is a licensed Marriage and Family Counselor in Santa Barbara, CA. She has studied and been a training co-leader with Dr. Violet Oaklander for ten years. She is in private practice and is Program Coordinator for the Violet Oaklander Institute in Santa Barbara. She has recently led trainings in Gestalt Psychotherapy with Children and Adolescents in Germany and throughout the U.S.A.

JAY EARLEY, Ph.D. is a psychotherapist in private practice who has been developing his method of leading Interactive Gestalt Groups since 1978. He is Director of the Group Therapy Center of Long Island and is on the adjunct faculty of the Gestalt Center of Long Island. He is author of Inner Journeys.

RAY EDWARDS, BSc, MA, Ph.D., Fellow of the Royal Society of Medicine, now retired, was a free-lance Gestalt counsellor who was trained mainly at the Metanioia Psychotherapy Training Institute with Petruska Clarkson. He has the Masters Degree in the Psychology of Therapy and Counseling from Antioch University. When in London, he was student counsellor in the Institute of Child Health and the Postgraduate Medical Federation, University of London and his Gestalt group work in Hampstead occurred within 100 meters of Freud's house. He taught counselling skills in the Westminister and Camden Adult Education Institutes.

BUD FEDER has been a Gestalt therapist for twenty-five years and quite active in the N.Y. Institute for Gestalt Therapy, for which he with Ruth Ronall organized two conferences on Gestalt groups. In 1980 he and Ruth Ronall co-edited *Beyond the Hot Seat: Gestalt Approaches to Group*, so this is their second book together. They have also co-led many workshops and training groups. He often offers training experiences in Europe and Canada.

JON FREW, Ph.D. is on the faculty of the School of Professional Psychology at Pacific University in Forest Grove, Oregon, where he teaches courses in Gestalt Therapy and Organizational Consultation. He also teaches in both the Psychology and Management Departments of Washington State University in Vancouver, Washington, where he has a private practice. He is co-director of the Gestalt Therapy Training Center Northwest and has been practicing and training others in Gestalt therapy since 1981. He is the author of several articles in the area of group work and Gestalt therapy theory and practice and is a member of the editorial board of the Gestalt Review.

GAIE HOUSTON, M.A. (Oxon), Dip. App. B.Sc. first came on Gestalt when on group training with National Training Laboratories. John Weir was her chief mentor in The States. She works now as a writer, Gestalt practitioner, supervisor, trainer and organization consultant. She is a faculty member of The Gestalt Centre in London, and two Gestalt Institutes on the continent.

PERRY KLEPNER, CSW is a Gestalt therapist in private in New York City and Kingston, New York, since 1977. A member and past president of the New York Institute for Gestalt Therapy, he studied with Laura Perls, Isadore From and Richard Kitzler. He has been on the faculty of several institutes and in his private practice provides training, supervision and individual, couples and group therapy. Intimacy is a particular area of interest in which he conducts workshops for individuals and couples. He has been working with people with AIDS since 1983, and authored "AIDS! HIV and Gestalt Therapy," The Gestalt Journal, Fall 1992.

RUTH LAMPERT is a Los Angeles psychotherapist and free-lance writer. She has taught and presented workshops in the United States and Europe, and has published widely in the professional general press. A Certified Member of the Gestalt Therapy Institute and a California licensed Marriage Family and Child Counselor, her book in progress is called "A Child's Eye View of Gestalt Therapy."

GINNY McFARLANE is a family physician practicing Psychiatry and Gestalt Therapy in Toronto, Ontario. Ginny studied Psychology, majoring in abnormal and physiological psychology, at The University of Toronto. She completed her medical degree and residency in Family Medicine at McMaster University in Hamilton, Ontario. In 1995, she completed the three year training program in Gestalt Therapy Theory and Methodology at The Gestalt Institute of Toronto. She is a-single mother of a six year old daughter, Robin. Ginny wrote this chapter in memory of her teacher, Jorge Rosner, who said when she first met him, "For a school of psychotherapy to survive, there must be writing."

JOHN MITCHELL is a Gestalt therapist working with individuals, couples and groups in and around Bath, U.K., and also involved in the supervision and training of counsellors and therapists. He enjoys playing the comet, listening to music (in particular old jazz records), tending his garden, cooking, walking, sailing, pottering about with no particular purpose in mind, and the company of friends.

MALCOLM PARLETT has an academic background in psychology and research. He trained in Gestalt at the Gestalt Institute of Cleveland in 1977-78. He co-founded the Gestalt Psychotherapy Training Institute in the United Kingdom, is Editor of the British Gestalt Journal, and has a therapy, supervision, training and consulting practice based in Bristol, England.

RUTH RONALL, M.S., C.S.W. (Deceased) is a psychotherapist in New York City, working with individual, couples, families and groups. She was educated at the Universities of Vienna and London, and received her master's degree in social work from Columbia University in New York. Since 1970, in addition to maintaining a private practice in New York, she traveled extensively to Europe, Canada, and various places in the United States leading training and personal growth workshops in Gestalt therapy. She was on the faculties of New York Institute for Living-Learning. She recently co-chaired, with Bud Feder, two conferences on Gestalt Group Process for the New York Institute for Gestalt Therapy.

ANNE TEACHWORTH is founder and director of the Gestalt Institute of New Orleans (1976). She received her Fellowship in 1977 from the Gestalt Institute of Houston and then trained with Laura Perls in New York City. She also trained with Richard Bandler, co-developer of NLP. Anne has taught mental health professionals worldwide for the last 30 years. She is a Fellow in the American Psychotherapy Association and an Associate member of the New York Institute of Gestalt Therapy. She is author of *Why We Pick The Mates We Do* (1997), The Psychogenetic System of couple and parenting therapy which she developed in 1991. She has written numerous articles and chapters on the subject, and her second book *History*

Repeats Itself is being published now. She maintains a private practice in New Orleans specializing in couple therapy and runs a publishing company entitled Gestalt Institute Press.

RUTH WOLFERT (Deceased) has was on the faculty of the New York Institute for Gestalt Therapy for almost twenty years and served as Vice President, Conference Co-Chair and Workshops Chair as well as participating in many committees. Her training was with Laura Perls, Richard Kitzler and Patrick Kelley of the Institute. She was also on the board of the Association for the Advancement of Gestalt Therapy, a member of the visiting faculty of the Gestalt Institute of Atlanta and the past president of the Association for Humanistic Psychology Eastern Regional Network. She had a private, group and training practice in New York City and offers many training workshops.

STEPHEN G. ZAHM, Ph.D. is a licensed psychologist in private practice in Vancouver, Washington and Portland, Oregon. A graduate of the Gestalt Training Center-San Diego, he has been practicing Gestalt therapy since 1971 and has been training therapists and leading workshops in Gestalt therapy since 1976. He has written and presented on the topic of integrating self psychology developmental theory into the practice of Gestalt therapy. He has a special interest in bringing Gestalt therapy into academic settings. He is a Professor at Pacific University School of Professional Psychology in Forest Grove, Oregon, where he teaches Gestalt therapy, group therapy and supervises the psychology interns. He is a founding member of the Gestalt Therapy Training Center-Northwest.

◊

Books from Gestalt Institute Press

Gestalt Therapy, The Second Generation: $20
A Living Legacy to Fritz and Laura Perls
Edited by Bud Feder and Ruth Ronall

A Funny Thing Happened On The Way To Enlightenment $20
Lenny Ravich

Beyond The Hot Seat Revisited: Gestalt Approaches To Group $30
Edited by Bud Feder and Jon Frew

Eccentric Genius: An Anthology Of The Writings $40
Of Master Gestalt Therapist, Richard Kitzler
Richard Kitzler, edited by Anne Teachworth

Gestalt at Work: Integrating Life, Theory & Practice, Vol. I $30
Seán Gaffney

Gestalt at Work: Integrating Life, Theory & Practice, Vol. II $30
Seán Gaffney

Gestalt Group Therapy $20
Bud Feder

Run Ruby Run $20
Ruby Reed Lyons with Sean David Hobbs, edited by Anne Teachworth

Suffering In Silence: The Legacy of Unresolved Sexual Abuse $20
Anne Schutzenberger and Ghislain Devroede

The Bridge: Dialogues Across Cultures $40
Edited by Talia Levine Bar-Yoseph

Those Who Come After $20
Renate Perls with Eileen Ain

T'was the Night Before the Storm: A Katrina Story for Kids $15
Michelle O'Brien, edited by Anne Teachworth

Why We Pick The Mates We Do $20
Anne Teachworth

To order additional copies of this book, contact:

THE GESTALT INSTITUTE PRESS
433 METAIRIE ROAD
SUITE 113
METAIRIE / NEW ORLEANS, LOUISIANA 70005 USA

Phones: 1.800.786.1065 or 504.828.2267

Website: www.gestaltinstitutepress.com / www.teachworth.com

Email: ateachw@aol.com